THE DOCTRINE AND COVENANTS

THE DOCTRINE AND COVENANTS
REVELATIONS IN CONTEXT

edited by
Andrew H. Hedges, J. Spencer Fluhman,
and Alonzo L. Gaskill

THE 37TH ANNUAL
BRIGHAM YOUNG UNIVERSITY
SIDNEY B. SPERRY SYMPOSIUM

RSC
BYU

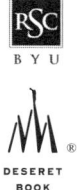

DESERET
BOOK

The Sperry Symposium is sponsored annually by Brigham Young University and the Church Educational System in honor of Sidney B. Sperry. In the course of his forty-five-year career as a religious educator, Dr. Sperry earned a reputation for outstanding teaching and scholarship. The symposium seeks to perpetuate his memory by fostering continuing research on gospel topics.

Copublished by the Religious Studies Center, Brigham Young University, Provo, Utah, and Deseret Book Company, Salt Lake City, Utah.

http://religion.byu.edu/rsc_pub.php

© 2008 Brigham Young University

All rights reserved.

Any uses of this material beyond those allowed by the exemptions in U.S. copyright law, such as section 107, "Fair Use," and section 108, "Library Copying," require the written permission of the publisher, Religious Studies Center, 167 HGB, Brigham Young University, Provo, Utah 84602. The views expressed herein are the responsibility of the authors and do not necessarily represent the position of Brigham Young University or the Religious Studies Center.

DESERET BOOK is a registered trademark of Deseret Book Company.

Visit us at DeseretBook.com

Library of Congress Cataloging-in-Publication Data

Sperry Symposium (37th : 2008 : Brigham Young University)
    The Doctrine and Covenants : revelations in context : the 37th annual Brigham Young University Sidney B. Sperry Symposium / edited by Andrew H. Hedges, J. Spencer Fluhman, and Alonzo L. Gaskill.
        p.   cm.
    Includes bibliographical references and index.
    ISBN 978-1-60641-015-8 (hardcover : alk. paper)
      1. Doctrine and Covenants—Criticism, interpretation, etc.—Congresses.
2. Smith, Joseph, 1805–1844—Congresses.   3. Private revelations—Congresses.
4. Church of Jesus Christ of Latter-day Saints—Doctrines—Congresses.
5. Mormon Church—Doctrines—Congresses.
I. Hedges, Andrew H., 1966–   II. Fluhman, J. Spencer.   III. Gaskill, Alonzo L.
IV. Title.
    BX8628.S73 2008
    289.3'2—dc22
                                                                                                      2008018747

Printed in the United States of America
Sheridan Books, Chelsea, MI

10   9   8   7   6   5   4   3   2   1

CONTENTS

Preface vii

1. Acceptance of the Lord
   Elder C. Max Caldwell 1

2. Discoveries from the Joseph Smith Papers Project: The Early Manuscripts
   Robert J. Woodford 23

3. One Continuous Flow: Revelations Surrounding the "New Translation"
   Kerry Muhlestein 40

4. The Joseph Smith Revelations and the Crisis of Early American Spirituality
   J. Spencer Fluhman 66

5. John the Beloved in Latter-day Scripture (D&C 7)
   Frank F. Judd Jr. and Terry L. Szink 90

6. "The Laws of the Church of Christ" (D&C 42): A Textual and Historical Analysis
   Grant Underwood 108

7. Joseph Smith, Emanuel Swedenborg, and Section 76: Importance of the Bible in Latter-day Revelation
   J. B. Haws 142

8. Universalism and the Revelations of Joseph Smith
   Casey Paul Griffiths 168
9. Redemption's Grand Design for Both
   the Living and the Dead
   Jennifer C. Lane 188
10. "All Things Are the Lord's": The Law of Consecration
    in the Doctrine and Covenants
    Steven C. Harper 212
11. Index 229

PREFACE

As the capstone of our religion, the Doctrine and Covenants provides insights to the restored gospel of Jesus Christ not found in any other of the standard works. Here we can find detailed information about priesthood offices, Church organization, the Millennium, consecration, and a host of other topics only hinted at elsewhere, and we would be hard-pressed to quibble with the idea that the Doctrine and Covenants is "a book of answers" to modern questions. It is easy to forget that the revelations that make up this book of scripture, like all revelations, were received in response to specific questions asked by real people at specific points in time, placing it in the larger historical and cultural backdrop of nineteenth-century America. It is easy to forget, too, that just like the New Testament or Book of Mormon, the Doctrine and Covenants has a rich textual history, and the form in which we find the revelations today is the product of a complex process of revelation, recording, editing, publication, and prophetic revision that continues today.

While we need not be aware of the revelations' settings and textual development to learn important truths from the Doctrine and Covenants, such awareness enhances our appreciation for the revelations and for the prophets through whom they came. It also draws our attention to important truths we might otherwise miss and helps us better understand and more appropriately apply the revelations in our personal lives. Furthermore, an awareness of the background of Joseph Smith's revelations allows us to better understand their significance.

This collection of essays is designed to help members of the Church begin to do precisely that. The articles, written by scholars trained in a variety of fields, provide insight to the historical, cultural, religious, and textual backgrounds of select revelations. They are intended to help Latter-day Saints better appreciate the setting in which Joseph received his revelations and to make them aware of the types of things that can be learned through a careful study of each revelation's background. It must be emphasized that no attempt has been made to provide a comprehensive overview of the background and development of each revelation or of the Doctrine and Covenants as a whole; our overall approach has been to look in depth at a few sections rather than to provide a broader, less-detailed overview. Each essay, correspondingly, stands largely on its own, and should not be considered a chapter in a larger and developing theme or argument of the entire volume.

The variety of approaches the authors have taken testifies of the richness of the revelations' texts and contexts, and to the number and types of questions that might be asked of them. One also sees in these essays the influence of various Church- and BYU-sponsored research projects, such as the Joseph Smith Papers Project and Scott H. Faulring, Kent P. Jackson, and Robert J. Matthews's critical text of *Joseph Smith's New Translation of the Bible*. The increasing attention Joseph has received at the hands of non-LDS scholars in recent years is also evident. One sees in these essays the fruit of an unprecedented level of scholarly inquiry into the life and times of Joseph Smith and scholars' belated recognition of his importance in the history of American culture, society, and religion. Our hope as editors is that this collection of essays, written from the combined perspectives of faith and scholarship, will prove an important addition to this growing body of research into the life and thought of the Prophet of the Restoration and will help readers better understand and appreciate the significant roles Joseph Smith's revelations have played, and continue to play, in the dispensation of the fulness of times.

1

ACCEPTANCE OF THE LORD

Elder C. Max Caldwell

Motivation for this presentation has come from observing fellow beings who either struggle to find and feel peace in their lives or are frustrated with a lack of contentment and instead struggle with feelings of failure. In the attempts we all make to obtain the former and avoid the latter, we sometimes neglect to gain a true perspective of either. In other words, our own lack of understanding and application of certain principles may be a self-inflicted cause for dissatisfaction with ourselves. On the other hand, those who feel comfortable with their current circumstances are commonly heard to describe the results of their efforts as success.

I recall overhearing one side of a telephone conversation in an airport terminal. The speaker declared rather triumphantly, "I finally succeeded today." Since I heard nothing else, I was left to wonder about the nature of his success. Might he be a skillful salesman who had concluded negotiations on a contract? Or perhaps he was a persistent

---

Elder C. Max Caldwell served from 1992 to 1997 as a member of the Second Quorum of the Seventy of The Church of Jesus Christ of Latter-day Saints.

medical patient recovering from limitations imposed through surgical procedures and was emerging from rehabilitative processes. Possibly he was a determined diplomat who had been laboring in persuasive negotiations. Or he may have been a troubled teacher trying to train students in some difficult skill or concept previously foreign to them.

I did not know which, if any, of these assumptions might be true. But I did know he was rejoicing in feelings of success. I wished then, and often have since, that all people could enjoy such feelings frequently. But this raises an important question: should the determination of success be based on pleasing self or other people?

Perhaps an equally common experience is feeling failure. This is not a happy emotion. Each of us has been part of a competitive group wherein someone is selected or designated as a winner. Might others have simultaneously sensed they were being designated losers? When participating in graded exercises, should those receiving lesser grades consider themselves less successful and therefore categorized as either partial or total failures? When we praise or honor people based on statistically measurable performances, might we also be creating an assumption that others not praised did not do well? Do well-intentioned motivators set up desirable, though perhaps for many, unattainable, goals that can create frustration for the underachievers?

When people despair or become despondent, is it commonly because they have failed to reach some self-determined goal or condition or maybe did not do so within a personally set time frame? A very depressed friend told me he had spent a couple of miserable weeks pondering over his failings and weaknesses. He was concerned that over the years, he may have failed to make good use of time, be responsive to family needs, or be considerate in treating people as he should. I suppose most of us have had similar thoughts. Elder Neal A. Maxwell observed: "Some of us who would not chastise a neighbor for his frailties have a field day with our own. Some of us stand before no more harsh a judge than ourselves, a judge who stubbornly refuses to admit much happy evidence and who cares nothing for due process."[1]

I am constrained to ask a second important question: should a feeling of failure be based on being unable to please self or other people?

Sometimes the Church is criticized for encouraging members to reach for goals that seem to be unattainable, such as being a model mother, a record-setting missionary, a superman bishop, and especially the attainment of perfection. It is not uncommon for bishops to hear Church members say, "Well, I'm not perfect," or declare, "Nobody is perfect." This philosophy is sometimes used as a justification for mediocre effort or even sin. It may also deepen discouragement because of failure to reach self-determined goals or even the Lord's mandated objective of perfection. Critics say our people will always be a group of frustrated failures who never experience success and thus will never feel fulfilled. Certainly we do not apologize for any celestial goal set for us by a celestial being. But, as Elder Maxwell observed, "Following celestial road signs while in telestial traffic jams is not easy."[2]

Today, we will discuss the following three concepts from the Doctrine and Covenants. First, what is true success or failure? We will spend most of our time with this one. Second, how do we obtain acceptance of the Lord? Third, where do we see this acceptance in the life of Joseph Smith?

Concept 1: What Is True Success or Failure?

Obtaining insights to these concerns seems to justify a discussion of a doctrine that, when understood and applied, will provide a positive impact in the life of every Latter-day Saint. From the sacred truths contained in the Lord's book of revelations in this dispensation, the Doctrine and Covenants, we learn something of how we should determine what is real success or failure.

Instead of feeling satisfaction with temporal or temporary achievements that please ourselves or others, might we be wiser to strive toward a more meaningful level of internal and eternal contentment? Scriptural declarations justify the conclusion that true success or failure is equated with either an acceptance or a condemnation of the Lord. It seems fitting that one of our greatly loved patriotic songs contains a plea to God for his refinement, "Till all success be nobleness, and every gain divine."[3] No work or success can be more noble than that which merits the divine favor and approval of God.

Permit me now to call attention to some of the sections in the Doctrine and Covenants where we find this concept. It is one of the predominant themes of this latter-day scripture that provides a meaningful standard by which we should determine our success or failure.

Section 23. In this section we have an illustration of the opposing levels of a relationship with the Savior which are identified as acceptance or condemnation. The very month the Church was organized in 1830, the Lord addressed five men and gave them specific direction in their personal lives as well as their respective duties concerning the work of the kingdom. Four of the five were told they were "under no condemnation," but the fifth was not given such an assurance. All of these brethren, except Joseph Knight Sr., had been baptized and were established in a covenant relationship with the Savior. These four had successfully pleased the Lord and were certainly expected to continue in a level of acceptance before Him. They had apparently done what the Lord required of them up to that time.

The fifth man, Joseph Knight, had not been baptized, though he knew he should. Previously he had manifested a belief in Joseph Smith's work with the Book of Mormon plates and asked for a revelation to instruct him as to his part in the work of the Restoration. The Lord had responded and exhorted him to "seek to bring forth and establish the cause of Zion" (D&C 12:6). Obviously he would need to be baptized in order to do so. Once when he attended a baptism of others, he ignored a distinct impression at that time that he should also be baptized and waited instead until June 1830. Thus, the Lord considered him to be under condemnation and stated it was his "duty to unite with the true church, . . . that [he] may receive the reward of the laborer" (D&C 23:7).

When the Lord reveals a truth to a person, He expects compliance; otherwise the person is under condemnation before the Lord. When we know eternal principles such as tithing, fasting, or Sabbath observance and do not comply, we will surely feel failure. The Lord declared, "For of him unto whom much is given much is required; and he who sins against the greater light shall receive the greater condemnation" (D&C 82:3).

Sections 39 and 40. A Reverend James Covill had served for forty years as a Baptist minister before he heard the message of the Restoration through the Prophet Joseph Smith. He thereupon covenanted he would do anything the Lord would require of him. Previously in his ministry, Reverend Covill would have, as present Protestant ministers do, invited his listeners to accept Jesus Christ as their personal Savior as a condition of their hope for salvation. However, he could not also provide them with information as to *how* they could attain unto their hoped-for heavenly heritage. He could not have offered them an authorized baptism with its attendant covenants.

Building upon Covill's limited understanding and background, the Savior revealed that to receive Christ is to receive His gospel, which includes repentance and baptism. The Lord challenged him to be baptized and enter into eternal covenants that he might receive the Lord's Spirit (see vv. 5–6, 10).

It is interesting that the Lord did not use traditional Protestant verbiage. He did not suggest any such process of "accepting Christ." Rather, the revealed wording dealt with "receiving" the Savior. Indeed, if mortals are challenged to determine whether to accept Christ, there is an implied message that man must judge if Jesus is acceptable to mortal man. Jesus is not on trial; He is the judge. Man is on trial; he must be acceptable unto Christ by receiving the Savior's atoning gifts and placing his life in harmony with revealed gospel principles.

A search through scriptural texts discloses that terms like *accept, accepted, acceptance,* and *acceptable* are always used in a context in which man and his works are being judged as to their acceptability unto the Lord. Such terms are not used with reference to God being accepted by man. Our conclusion must be that we attain an acceptance of the Lord when we worthily receive and partake of His doctrines and ordinances.

Interesting to us are some of the meaningful uses of the root *cept* of Latin origin. Ac-*cept*-ance is of Christ. Re-*cept*-ion is our choice, and being re-*cept*-ive is our opportunity. Per-*cept*-ion is a spiritual gift, whereas de-*cept*-ion is of Lucifer. Each has distinctive meaning. We ought not to be confused.

Unfortunately, James Covill rejected the word of the Lord and failed to keep his covenant. He failed to receive the Lord's gospel, which is tantamount to failure to receive the Lord. Though Covill did not formally enter into a covenant through baptism, the Lord referred to his verbal promise to be obedient as a binding covenant. The Savior declared, "Wherefore he broke my covenant, and it remaineth with me to do with him as seemeth me good" (D&C 40:3). Covenant breakers are failures who are not acceptable to our God.

Section 41. In the first revelation recorded after Joseph Smith moved to Ohio, the Lord provided His definition of discipleship as follows: "He that receiveth my law and doeth it, the same is my disciple; and he that saith he receiveth it and doeth it not, the same is not my disciple, and shall be cast out from among you" (v. 5).

To be a true disciple of Christ and thus be accepted of Him requires more than verbal commitment to Him. One must be both a receiver and doer of the Lord's law. Those who receive rewards for discipleship fulfill both of these two expectations. In this same revelation is an example of such a person. The Lord called Edward Partridge to be the first bishop of the Church and described him as a man whose heart was pure and in whom there was no guile (see v. 11). He was a disciple of the Lord and was acceptable to Him.

Conversely, to represent oneself as having received the Lord's law yet unwilling to comply with the responsibilities of sacred covenants is to misrepresent the author of the law. This is hypocrisy, a condition oft condemned by the Lord. Such a person has an impure heart, is guilty of guile, and is unacceptable to the Lord.

Section 38. In the meridian of time, the Savior prayed for unity among His disciples (see John 17:20–21). Eighteen centuries later, the Lord mandated that the members of the Church should have unity. He said, "Be one; and if ye are not one ye are not mine" (D&C 38:27). We note that failure to achieve oneness with the Lord would be evidence of, and reason for, our unacceptability to Him. To the Nephites, the Savior proclaimed, "He that hath the spirit of contention is not of me" (3 Nephi 11:29). Those who are in harmony with the Lord and His teachings have a oneness with Him. They are also those who live in harmony with each other. They have obtained the approval and acceptance of the Master.

Section 46. In this revelation, the Lord identified many of the gifts of the Holy Spirit and counseled Church members to seek for the best gifts as suited to their specific needs. He explained the value of these gifts and proclaimed that "they are given for the benefit of those who love me and keep all my commandments, and him that seeketh so to do" (D&C 46:9).

We learn that eligible recipients of these spiritual gifts include those who keep all the commandments. At first thought, one might conclude no one fits that category. But if no one does, why would such a situation even be mentioned? Further thought suggests that we must not infer something the Lord didn't say. He did not say the gifts are for those who keep all the commandments *all the time.* No one does. But many do keep all the commandments *most of the time.* A second category of acceptable people describes those who are genuinely and sincerely *seeking* to keep all the commandments. Though they may not always reach their intended spiritual goals, they are striving to do so. Though they may sometimes fail or fall, they arise, repent if necessary, and continue striving to live righteous and acceptable lives.

Thus, many Latter-day Saints are eligible to obtain gifts of the Spirit, participate in privileges extended to faithful Church members, and have claim on promises made by the Lord to His covenant-keeping people and are, most important, acceptable unto the Lord. They are worthy, though imperfect, Saints. When their bishop asks if they are worthy to participate in the various experiences and privileges of the Church, they can answer with a resounding yes. These are they who partake of sacramental emblems in peace, who participate in temple ordinances and covenants in comfort, who perform and receive priesthood ordinances with confidence, who seek for and expect the gifts of the Spirit with the assurance that the Lord's promises will be fulfilled. These are they who are accepted of the Lord and who enjoy the accompanying peaceful feelings of lives well lived.

Concept 2: How Do We Obtain Acceptance of the Lord?

Section 52. This revelation contains a welcome "pattern in all things" (v. 14) wherein the Lord describes a person whose actions and attributes are acceptable to Him. Anyone whose nature and behavior is in conformity with the Lord's pattern has the revealed assurance he is complying with the Savior's expectations for the present time. The Master declared:

Wherefore he that prayeth, whose spirit is contrite, the same is accepted of me if he obey mine ordinances.

He that speaketh, whose spirit is contrite, whose language is meek and edifieth, the same *is of God* if he obey mine ordinances.

And again, he that trembleth under my power shall be made strong, and shall bring forth fruits of praise and wisdom, according to the revelations and truths which I have given you. (vv. 15–17; emphasis added)

The Lord identifies at least five definitive qualities or traits that are inherent in the person who is accepted of Him:

One who prays. This is a person who relies on the Lord rather than his own understanding, reasoning, power, and judgment. Obviously such a person has faith in God, a prime prerequisite to be accepted of Him. Elder John A. Widtsoe of the Quorum of the Twelve Apostles has said: "Man is just as great as his private prayers. The individual is no bigger than his private prayers. If he is a prayerful man he grows to a high stature. If he is not he shrinks to smaller stature."[4]

One whose spirit is contrite. This is a person of humility who has sorrowed for sins and knows the power of the redemption of Christ. He is both teachable and responsive to correct teachings. He has heard and responded to the Savior's invitation to come unto Him. A repentant spirit pervades his soul, wherein a changed heart has resulted in acceptable attitudes and behavior. President Ezra Taft Benson observed, "The miracle of forgiveness is real, and true repentance is accepted of the Lord."[5]

One who obeys the Lord's ordinances. Certainly one cannot obey ordinances unless one receives the ordinances. A person is not acceptable to the Savior until he comes to the Savior through the ordinances and covenants of the priesthood. A son or daughter of God who elects to remain outside God's kingdom or a Church member who chooses not to receive all priesthood ordinances is certainly loved by Him but is not acceptable to Him. To comply with the Lord's will is to make and keep covenants received of Him.

One whose language is meek and edifying. Speech generally portrays thoughts and nature. Language can portray an ostentatious nature or betray an unclean mind and an impure soul. A person who spews out profanity, vulgarity, or obscenities is denying the edifying powers of the Holy Spirit and is neither desirable nor acceptable. On one occasion, I had to tell a close associate that unless he cleaned up his language, I could no longer afford his friendship. He did cease to speak crudely, at least in my presence, and I was grateful.

Criticism and gossip can also offend and deny the Spirit. President Gordon B. Hinckley has counseled as follows:

> Criticism is the forerunner of divorce, the cultivator of rebellion, a catalyst that leads to failure. I am asking that we turn from the negative that so permeates our society and look for the remarkable good among those with whom we associate, that we speak of one another's virtues more than we speak of one another's faults, that optimism replace pessimism, that our faith exceed our fears. When I was a young man and was prone to speak critically, my father would say: "Cynics do not contribute, skeptics do not create, doubters do not achieve."[6]

Conversely, verbal expressions may represent purity of heart and mind and may convey insights of eternal value. Who has not been lifted to spiritual heights while listening to testimonies and divine declarations of revealed truths?

One whose works and teachings reflect truths given by the Lord. The Lord is the source of all truth. The means by which we access that truth include living prophets, standard works of scripture, and inspiration from the Holy Ghost (see vv. 9, 36). The Lord looks with disfavor upon the teaching of untruth, whether those falsehoods are deliberate or inadvertent misrepresentations of His mind and will. Such teaching might be the means of leading souls away from God. President Joseph F. Smith warned the Church:

> Among the Latter-day Saints, the preaching of false doctrines disguised as truths of the gospel, may be expected from people of two classes . . . :
>
> First—the hopelessly ignorant, whose lack of intelligence is due to their indolence and sloth, who make but feeble effort . . . to better themselves by reading and study; those who are afflicted with a dread disease that may develop into an incurable malady—laziness.
>
> Second—The proud and self-vaunting ones, who read by the lamp of their own conceit; who interpret by rules of their own contriving; who have become a law unto themselves and so pose as the sole judges of their own doings. More dangerously ignorant than the first.
>
> Beware of the lazy and the proud; their infection in each case is contagious; better for them and for all when they are compelled to display the yellow flag of warning, that the clean and uninfected may be protected.[7]

Each of us can do a personal introspection and determine if we fit the Lord's pattern of acceptability. Any variations on our part should result in appropriate modifications to our thinking, feelings, or behavior. Additionally, all of us can evaluate what we see or hear in others and know whether we should be receptive of their ways. Tolerance and acceptance are not the same. Though we should love and be tolerant of people who deviate from the Lord's standard, we are not also expected to embrace and accept diversions and exceptions to the Lord's acceptable pattern.

Section 75. In this revelation we see that to be acceptable to the Lord is to do what is pleasing to Him and determine that our will becomes His.

While traveling with some elders to a church conference, the Prophet Joseph Smith noted, "The Elders seemed anxious for me to inquire of the Lord that they might know His will, or learn what would be most pleasing to Him for them to do."[8] The revelation that followed Joseph's inquiry identified several ways missionaries could please the Lord:

Behold, I say unto you that it is my will that you should go forth and not tarry, neither be idle but labor with your might—

Lifting up your voices as with the sound of a trump, proclaiming the truth according to the revelations and commandments which I have given you.

And thus, if ye are faithful ye shall be laden with many sheaves, and crowned with honor, and glory, and immortality, and eternal life. (vv. 3–5)

A review of the Lord's expectations and counsel from this and other revelations provides the missionary with a plan for effective missionary work. He has the means by which he can evaluate his service in the ministry and know when the Lord is pleased. He is not to be compared with other missionaries, nor is his work to be judged by the results accomplished by others or by other missions. If he has subjugated his will to be harmonious with the will of the Lord, he knows he has presented an acceptable offering and enjoys the quiet confidence that accompanies the fulfillment of a successful mission.

While I served as a mission president, a missionary said to me as he was being released, "I am going home without any regrets. I kept all the mission rules, I worked hard and did my best to do everything I knew the Lord expected of me. I am happy to say I served a successful mission."

Section 97. As a bit of background for a gospel principle contained in this section, it is good for us to recall a pinnacle moment in the mortal history of the Lord's people. It happened just after the cataclysmic destruction took place on this continent in connection with the Lord's Crucifixion. The Lord spoke from the heavens and announced a change in the law of sacrifice. The Lord's people had faithfully obeyed that law by offering blood sacrifice since the days of Adam some four thousand years earlier. In His announcement, the Lord abolished the practice of blood sacrifice. Though the law was not discontinued, the way by which it was to be kept was changed. The Lord commanded them to "offer for a sacrifice . . . a broken heart and a contrite spirit" (3 Nephi 9:20).

In this dispensation, the Lord reaffirmed that commandment in

1831 (see D&C 59:8) and then two years later added a very meaningful and most significant word to the commandment: "Verily I say unto you, all among them who know their hearts are honest, and are broken, and their spirits contrite, and are *willing* to observe their covenants by sacrifice—yea, every sacrifice which I, the Lord, shall command—they are *accepted* of me" (D&C 97:8; emphasis added).

Whatever sacrifice we may be asked to make, the Lord has emphasized that we are to make it with a *willingness* to do so. A sacrifice made unwillingly is not a fulfillment of the Lord's expectation, and the individual should expect to have feelings of failure in his effort to please the Lord. The prophet Mormon explained that process when he said:

> For behold, God hath said a man being evil cannot do that which is good; for if he offereth a gift, or prayeth unto God, except he shall do it with real intent it profiteth him nothing.
>
> For behold, it is not counted unto him for righteousness.
>
> For behold, if a man being evil giveth a gift, he doeth it grudgingly; wherefore it is counted unto him the same as if he had retained the gift; wherefore he is counted evil before God. (Moroni 7:6–8)

Conversely, the person who complies with the Lord's request with a willing heart is accepted of Him. There is yet an additional dimension of this matter. A person may not be requested to make a specific sacrifice, but if his heart is willing to do so, he is accepted of the Lord. The condition of willingness is the crucial issue.

We all know we are to be judged according to our works, but sometimes our works become our only focal point. What if a person is physically unable to perform certain works? Or what if some of us never have opportunity to contribute in the same meaningful ways as others? We have all noticed that some people have strengths and talents that permit them to do some things easier, faster, or better than others. Is one who outwardly performs less productively to be judged with a lesser reward for his efforts?

Pertaining to these questions, the Lord affirmed an eternal

principle in a revealed statement given to Joseph Smith during his vision of the celestial kingdom, recorded in section 137 verse 9 of the Doctrine and Covenants: "For I, the Lord, will judge all men according to their works, according to the desire of their hearts." Truly our acceptance before the Lord is predicated upon not only our actions but also our attitudes.

I vividly recall a statement made to me by a senior missionary couple when they returned from an eighteen-month mission to a European country. I asked them how they felt about their mission. The brother said, "I guess we wasted our time and money. We didn't baptize a single person." I was disturbed to hear such a comment and asked them to tell me more about their mission. They indicated they had worked hard to find people to teach, but no one would listen to their message. I was not surprised at that report because I knew the mission where they served to be an extremely difficult place for missionaries to teach and baptize. I asked if they had any other responsibilities or experiences. They said they were involved in activation efforts in a small branch. I inquired about those efforts. They expressed their great love for the members they worked with and described many positive results of increased faith and strength in the spiritual lives of more than twenty people.

Let me digress and propose a few questions for our consideration. Did these missionaries not work diligently? Were they not willing to serve and sacrifice time and means to assist in the Lord's work? Did their hearts not have a desire to accomplish His will? Do we not think their missionary service was acceptable to the Lord? Is not His acceptance a greater measurement of success than to presume failure due to their notion of what constituted a valid evaluation of their missionary efforts? After asking similar questions of them, I sensed the presence of peace as they considered the criteria the Lord uses for His judgment and acceptance.

This concept is reinforced again by the Lord in section 124. The Lord had previously directed the Saints in Missouri to build a temple. Though they began the work, they were unfortunately prevented from completing it due to subsequent actions taken against them by Missouri mobs. After being driven from Missouri and later settling in Nauvoo, they were comforted, though they failed to accomplish their task; the Lord revealed their status with Him in the following verse: "Verily, verily, I say unto you, that when I give a commandment to any of the sons of men to do a work unto my name, and those sons of men go with all their might and with all they have to perform that work, and cease not their diligence, and their enemies come upon them and hinder them from performing that work, behold, it behooveth me to require that work no more at the hands of those sons of men, but to *accept of their offerings*" (D&C 124:49; emphasis added).

President Joseph F. Smith emphasized the need for all of us to keep trying when he taught:

> There should be no such thing as quitting when we put our hands to the plow.... There must be no such thing as being discouraged. We may fail over and over again; ... we may fail to accomplish the object we have in view.... If you fail, never mind. Go right on; try it again; try it somewhere else. Never say quit. Do not say it cannot be done. Failure is a word that should be unknown.... The word "fail" ought to be expunged from our language and our thoughts.... We will get the reward for all the good we do. We will get the reward for all the good we desire to do, and labor to do, though we fail to accomplish it, for we will be judged according to our works and our intent and purposes; ... we who try ... will not fail, if we do not quit.[9]

I treasure the memory of one of my missionary elders. He had difficulty learning Spanish and had not received favorable evaluations of his progress in the Missionary Training Center. Though he was diligent in his efforts, others in his district made much greater progress in their language studies.

After his arrival in the mission, he still struggled to communicate with Spanish-speaking people; he labored under many limitations when he attempted to speak to them. Nonetheless, he did not give up; he refused to be discouraged. He carried a marvelous spirit, so when he introduced the Book of Mormon to people and bore his testimony they knew he knew the book was true. Many responded favorably to his invitation to read it and later permitted him and his companion to come into their home and teach them. He still struggled to converse and teach, but he prayed and studied diligently. A considerable number of his investigators were brought into the Church. I knew the Lord accepted his efforts because of his willingness to do all he could to fulfill the Lord's expectations.

Over time, his language skills increased. Eventually, he was called to be a zone leader in the Spanish zone, and when I spoke to the Spanish branch he translated for me. His mission was his opportunity to gain the Lord's acceptance and have that status confirmed to him.

Though the Lord expects us to put forth our best effort to achieve a level of perfect performance, it is comforting to know that for us here and now, He has established a lesser level of acceptance. Our efforts might be described as "Persistence towards Perfect Performance." We have learned from the Lord's revelations of His expectations relative to our responsibilities while working to achieve certain established goals. We are expected to *seek* to reach His described levels of performance. We are taught to sincerely *strive* to attain unto His characteristics of character and make genuine efforts to *follow* His example of behavior in all situations. If our hearts are right and we are willing to do His will, we can and will be acceptable servants unto the Most High.

Being accepted of the Lord is really the result of living by the first principles and ordinances described in article of faith 4, namely faith in Christ, repentance, baptism, and the gift of the Holy Ghost. There is one more principle we need to mention. After embarking on our journey along the strait and narrow path as acceptable children of God, we must continue our efforts and endure to the end (see 2 Nephi 31:15–21). The Lord used a word forty-six times in the Doctrine and Covenants, which basically means the same as "endure" but carries a slightly different connotation. The word is "continue." I like to hear the Lord use that word because it implies His current acceptance and also validates a person's current direction on the path toward eternal life. As an example of this concept, we can read a statement made by the Lord to John C. Bennett: "I have seen the work which he hath done, which *I accept if he continue,* and will crown him with blessings and great glory"

(D&C 124:17; emphasis added). Unfortunately, John Bennett did not continue but instead broke away from the Lord and His Church and lost the glorious promised blessings. For a positive example, we refer to the Lord's assurance to Lyman Sherman of his acceptable standing before the Lord and promises of marvelous future blessings if he would *continue* faithful (see D&C 108:2–5). He did so until his death.

Concept 3: Where Do We See the Lord's Acceptance of Joseph Smith?

We will look at one more example of our subject in the Doctrine and Covenants. We see a pattern from the life and ministry of the Prophet Joseph Smith wherein he sought for and obtained the acceptance of the Savior. We will select a few significant passages of scripture in this portrayal. We should notice there are some parallels to us and our destiny.

We are all aware that Joseph was a very young man when the Lord entrusted him with a most overwhelming responsibility to lay the foundation of and build up the kingdom of God on earth. But the whole load was not placed upon him at once. He grew through his assignments and experiences one step at a time. For instance, because of the loss of 116 pages of Book of Mormon manuscript, Joseph was chastised and reminded that he had the gift of translation but was not to seek for or pretend to have any other gift until he finished translating the plates (see D&C 5:4). He was to focus all his efforts on that one assignment. By so doing, he learned how to receive revelation and became more acquainted with the mind and will of the Lord while learning principles of truth and doctrine.

A year later the translation was completed, Joseph was sustained as the Lord's prophet, and the Church membership was commanded to "give heed unto all his words and commandments which he shall give unto you. . . . For his word ye shall receive, as if from mine own mouth" (D&C 21:4–5). What a weight of responsibility to be carried by a twenty-four-year-old young man with no Church leadership experience! But he could be sustained by the assurance he was accepted of the Lord who manifested a marvelous level of trust in him. He also knew he would not work alone; the Lord intended to direct him in his calling.

However, it is also apparent that, though the Lord was accepting of Joseph at that time, still the young prophet was serving in a conditional or probationary status. He still needed to prove himself worthy of a *continuing acceptance*. During the first few years of his service, some of the revelations he received reminded him of the need to be diligent and faithful to his sacred trust. We will read from a few of those scriptural passages.

In June 1829, almost a year before the Church was organized, the Lord made the following conditional statement: "And now, marvel not that I have called him unto mine own purpose, which purpose is known in me; wherefore, *if* he shall be diligent in keeping my commandments he shall be blessed unto eternal life; and his name is Joseph" (D&C 18:8; emphasis added).

A little over a year later, in September 1830, after Hiram Page professed to be receiving revelations, the Lord reminded the Saints that Joseph still served as his prophet and the only one authorized to receive revelation for the Church: "But, behold, verily, verily, I say unto thee, no one shall be appointed to receive commandments and revelations in this church excepting my servant Joseph Smith, Jun., for he receiveth them even as Moses" (D&C 28:2).

Three more months went by while Joseph worked on a Bible translation. Sidney Rigdon visited Joseph and was called by the Lord to assist Joseph as his scribe. Sidney was reminded of Joseph's high calling, though it was still a conditional one. The Lord said: "And I have given unto [Joseph] the keys of the mystery of those things which have been sealed, even things which were from the foundation of the world, and the things which shall come from this time until the time of my coming, *if* he abide in me, and if not, another will I plant in his stead" (D&C 35:18; emphasis added).

Only two more months went by before a woman by the name of Hubble came among the Saints making pretensions of revealing commandments and laws for the Church and professing to be a prophetess. We might refer to these problems as "Hubble Trouble!" Because some of the Saints were deceived into thinking she represented the Lord, Joseph Smith inquired of the Lord and received a revelation that included the following divine declaration to the Saints: "Ye have received a commandment for a law unto my church [section 42], through him whom I have appointed unto you to receive commandments and revelations from my hand [Joseph Smith]. And this ye shall know assuredly—that there is none other appointed unto you to receive commandments and revelations until he be taken, *if* he abide in me" (D&C 43:2–3; emphasis added).

Once again, in the fall of 1831, the Lord made still another conditional statement of the prophetic position Joseph occupied. He stated, "The keys of the mysteries of the kingdom shall not be taken from my servant Joseph Smith, Jun., through the means I have appointed, while he liveth, *inasmuch* as he obeyeth mine ordinances" (D&C 64:5; emphasis added).

In the earliest days of the Church, it was needful that the Lord frequently emphasize that Joseph Smith was the only mortal being authorized to speak for Him and receive revelations for His Church. But it is interesting that during a period of twenty-seven months, from June 1829 to September 1831, we read that the Lord cautioned Joseph five times that his calling was contingent upon keeping the commandments and obeying the ordinances. However, the next recording of the Lord speaking of Joseph's calling in the kingdom contained a most remarkable statement. In section 90, given March 8, 1833, the Lord told Joseph: "Verily I say unto you, the keys of this kingdom shall *never* be taken from you, while thou art in the world, neither in the world to come" (D&C 90:3; emphasis added).

After the many times the Lord emphasized the conditional status of Joseph, He now declares the sacred calling and role of Joseph to be eternal and unconditional. We wonder what happened? Why the change? When we read section 132, we find the answer. The Lord declared to Joseph: "For I am the Lord thy God, and will be with thee even unto the end of the world, and through all eternity; for verily I seal upon you your exaltation, and prepare a throne for you in the kingdom of my Father, with Abraham your father" (D&C 132:49).

Some will wonder how the Lord's declaration in section 132 could have any bearing upon a statement that was made back in section 90. The simple reason is that section 132 was received by Joseph Smith at least a year before section 90, as early as 1831, though not officially written until 1843. So when Joseph's calling and election was made sure by the Lord some time in the last three months of 1831, it preceded the 1833 revelation in section 90 wherein the Lord unconditionally affirmed Joseph Smith's prophetic position in this world and in the world to come.

We pause for a brief explanation of "calling and election:"

> To be called is to be a member of the Church and kingdom of God on earth; . . . it is to have a conditional promise of eternal life. . . . The call itself is to the gospel cause; it is not reserved for apostles and prophets or for the great and mighty in Israel; it is for all the members of the kingdom.
>
> To have one's calling and election made sure is to be sealed up unto eternal life; it is to have the unconditional guarantee of exaltation in the highest heaven of the celestial world; . . . it is, in effect, to have the day of judgment advanced.[10]

During the first phase of Joseph Smith's mortal life and ministry, the Lord repeatedly reminded him that he needed to keep his covenants and thus prove himself worthy to rise beyond his conditional status in the Lord's kingdom. After doing so, Joseph moved from an awareness of his conditional acceptability before the Lord to a level where he was given certain knowledge of his permanent and ultimate state of acceptance, even that of having his exaltation sealed upon him.

We commented earlier that when we examined Joseph Smith's experiences in connection with his acceptance of the Lord, we would notice several parallels to our own quest to receive the Lord's approval. Let me mention a few. Like Joseph, we too enter into covenants and promise that we will sincerely strive to keep them, knowing of the Lord's promise of eternal life for those who are faithful. We also need to be warned of the pitfalls and temptations of mortality and seek diligently to avoid any departures from the Lord's plan for our happiness.

We have observed that Joseph was chastised by the Lord when it was needed, but after genuine repentance he was reinstated to a favorable relationship with Deity. We will not always do the right thing either. But when we stumble or displease the Lord, we also repent and then strive to do better. By so doing, we can expect the same loving help from on high. Observing that we will not reach all levels of perfection in this life, President Lorenzo Snow provided some comforting insights and counsel:

> If we could read in detail the life of Abraham, or the lives of other great and holy men, we would doubtless find that their efforts to be righteous were not always crowned with success. Hence, we should not be discouraged if we should be overcome in a weak moment; but, on the contrary, straightway repent of the error or the wrong we may have committed, and as far as possible repair it, and then seek to God for renewed strength to go on and do better.
>
> We must not allow ourselves to be discouraged whenever we discover our weakness. We can scarcely find an instance in all the glorious examples set us by the prophets, ancient or modern, wherein they permitted the Evil One to discourage them; but on the other hand they constantly sought to overcome, to win the prize, and thus prepare themselves for a fulness of glory.[11]

As we examine the final destiny of Joseph Smith and consider that his calling and election was made sure, many may think we will not be able to follow his pattern. But the primary difference between us and Joseph is that the sealing of his exaltation took place during his mortal life; certainly some of us may also do the same and yet many may not. However, the time frame for the event makes no difference in the eternal scheme of things. Those who find acceptance of the Lord in this life and depart mortality having endured to the end in that relationship will also be sealed up to eternal life. Listen to the confirming teachings of an Apostle, Elder Bruce R. McConkie, as he spoke on this matter:

> All the faithful Saints, all of those who have endured to the end, depart this life with the absolute guarantee of eternal life.

There is no equivocation, no doubt, no uncertainty in our minds. Those who have been true and faithful in this life will not fall by the wayside in the life to come. If they keep their covenants here and now and depart this life firm and true in the testimony of our blessed Lord, they shall come forth with an inheritance of eternal life.

We do not mean to say that those who die in the Lord, and who are true and faithful in this life, must be perfect in all things when they go into the next sphere of existence. There was only one perfect man—the Lord Jesus whose Father was God. . . .

But what we are saying is that when the saints of God chart a course of righteousness, when they gain sure testimonies of the truth and divinity of the Lord's work, when they keep the commandments, when they overcome the world, when they put first in their lives the things of God's kingdom: when they do all these things, and then depart this life—though they have not yet become perfect—they shall nonetheless gain eternal life in our Father's kingdom; and eventually they shall be perfect as God their Father and Christ His Son are perfect.[12]

So we really can follow the same path as Joseph Smith. We have learned that true success in mortal life is the obtaining of our God's approval and to be accepted of Him. All who obtain that status can know it by the peaceful presence of the Holy Spirit. The Lord told Joseph Smith he would know when he was where the Lord wanted him to be by the "peace and power of my Spirit, that shall flow unto you" (D&C 111:8).

No one in this Church would question the success Joseph achieved in his life. But what did he do? He found acceptance of the Savior,[13] though for a time it was a conditional relationship. He had to prove himself like everyone else. But he endured faithfully and obtained the Lord's unconditional promise of eternal life. Little wonder that Joseph Smith has exclaimed to us: "Oh! I beseech you to go forward, go forward and make your calling and election sure."[14] In considering *how* we fulfill the Prophet's charge, we simply say to our fellow Saints, "Receive all available priesthood covenants, including those in the temple, and keep them." To simplify even further, we say, "Keep the baptismal covenant and endure to the end; the promise is eternal life" (see Mosiah 18:8–10). Eternal life, or exaltation, is the ultimate level of the Lord's acceptance. He provides no greater gift (see D&C 14:7); it is bestowed upon all those who are *accepted* of Him who then *continue* to maintain that status. There is no greater success. That we all may constantly seek to attain it is my desire and prayer.

NOTES

1. Neal A. Maxwell, in Conference Report, October 1976, 14.
2. Neal A. Maxwell, in Conference Report, October 1976, 14.
3. "America the Beautiful," *Hymns* (Salt Lake City: The Church of Jesus Christ of Latter-day Saints, 1985), no. 338.
4. John A. Widtsoe, *The Message of the Doctrine and Covenants* (Salt Lake City: Bookcraft, 1969), 38.
5. Ezra Taft Benson, *The Teachings of Ezra Taft Benson* (Salt Lake City: Bookcraft, 1988), 70.
6. Gordon B. Hinckley, *Stand a Little Taller* (Salt Lake City: Eagle Gate, 2001), 161.
7. Joseph F. Smith, *Gospel Doctrine* (Salt Lake City: Deseret Book, 1963), 373.
8. Joseph Smith, *History of the Church of Jesus Christ of Latter-day Saints*, ed. B. H. Roberts, 2nd ed. rev. (Salt Lake City: Deseret Book, 1980), 1:243.
9. Smith, *Gospel Doctrine,* 132–33.
10. Bruce R. McConkie, *Doctrinal New Testament Commentary* (Salt Lake City: Bookcraft, 1973), 3:326, 330–31.
11. Lorenzo Snow, "Blessings of the Gospel Only Obtained by Compliance to the Law," *Ensign*, October 1971, 19, 21.
12. Bruce R. McConkie, in Conference Report, October 1976, 158–59.
13. Smith, *History of the Church*, 1:316.
14. Joseph Smith, *Teachings of the Prophet Joseph Smith*, comp. Joseph Fielding Smith (Salt Lake City: Deseret Book, 1967), 366.

2

DISCOVERIES FROM THE JOSEPH SMITH PAPERS PROJECT: THE EARLY MANUSCRIPTS

Robert J. Woodford

The Joseph Smith Papers Project is a multivolume work that will make available to the public more than four thousand documents related to Joseph Smith, including journals, diaries, correspondence, discourses, revelations, written history, and legal papers. This is a work of monumental proportion made possible only through the generous cooperation of the Church History Library, various universities, libraries, historical societies, and church groups who have these papers in their possession. The finished work will allow interested persons to study the original documents without having to travel to the various locations where they are housed, helping preserve these documents from the deterioration that is a natural part of researchers handling them.

The first two volumes of the Documents Series of the Joseph Smith Papers series contain over one hundred revelations, most of which are in the Doctrine and Covenants. Two colleagues and I edited these

---

Robert J. Woodford is a retired Church Educational System instructor and an editor of the Joseph Smith Papers.

volumes, which contain revelations through 1833. Other editors are reviewing the material received after 1833. Greater access to the manuscripts and early writings has expanded our view concerning the writing, editing, and publication of the revelations. One purpose of this paper is to present a survey of some of those discoveries deemed important and interesting, with greater detail concerning them becoming available only when the volumes are published. Another purpose is to demonstrate techniques we developed that have greatly enhanced our ability to compare and date multiple documents related to single revelations.

So that all readers have a common background, the following well-documented facts are presented without any references or further discussion.

> Joseph Smith rarely wrote the revelations given him but dictated them to scribes.
>
> Joseph Smith and John Whitmer began in the summer of 1830 to arrange and copy the revelations he had already received; hence copies were made from the originals.
>
> Early on, the manuscript revelations were also copied by Church members and missionaries, thus multiplying the number of manuscript copies.
>
> Few original manuscript revelations can be positively identified.
>
> Joseph Smith altered revelations to correct errors and to conform to later revealed knowledge and growth of the Church.
>
> In November 1831, Joseph Smith and other elders of the Church decided to print the revelations in Missouri. The compilation was to be titled "A Book of Commandments for the Government of the Church of Christ" but is commonly known as the "Book of Commandments." Joseph Smith reviewed the revelations and made corrections as needed for publication.
>
> Publication of the Book of Commandments ended on July 20, 1833, when antagonists destroyed the press and scattered the pages of the book.

- Incomplete copies of the Book of Commandments were bound by various individuals for their own use.
- On September 24, 1834, the high council at Kirtland, Ohio, voted that Joseph Smith and others should assemble the revelations a second time for publication. Major editing of the revelations occurred at this time.
- On August 17, 1835, the Doctrine and Covenants was presented at a conference of the Church and accepted as the word of the Lord to His people.
- The 1835 edition of the Doctrine and Covenants contained seven "Lectures on Faith" and 103 revelations.
- Later editions (particularly 1844, 1876, and 1981) increased the number of revelations.
- The "Lectures on Faith" were deleted in the 1921 edition.

Research Method concerning the Revelations

In preparing the revelations for the Joseph Smith Papers Project, the earliest complete manuscript of each revelation was used as the featured text, with all others listed in appropriate source notes. Sometimes it was difficult to determine which was the earliest version. In those cases we looked at known historical facts, scribes, and the text itself to make a determination. Even then, there are a handful of revelations for which we were only able to make a "best guess" as to which manuscript was earliest.

With regard to variations in text of revelations, these are often of real concern, especially if the differences are of doctrinal import. Variations are a reality, but any suitable discussion of them is beyond the scope of this paper. The published volumes discuss those variations that are significant. It is important to note that these alterations have historic value only, and the current edition of the Doctrine and Covenants is the only authorized text of these revelations.

Setting a Standard Text

More than one Book of Mormon scholar has written about the textual variations that exist between different copies of the 1830 edition of the Book of Mormon. Royal Skousen helps to answer the question of how these variations occur. The printer of the 1830 edition of the Book of Mormon would typeset one section of sixteen pages at a time (each section is called a signature). Then he would print five thousand copies of that signature, then typeset the next signature and print it, and so on. While printing off copies of a given signature, the printer would look for typos by examining one of the sheets coming off the press. After going through that sixteen-page signature, he would stop the press, correct the errors in the type, then continue printing the sheets for that signature. The uncorrected sheets that had already been printed, however, were not discarded but were used later when copies of the Book of Mormon were bound, even though some of these sheets would have contained minor errors. For some signatures, the 1830 printer interrupted the printing more than once (in one case, five times) as he continued to find typos. On the other hand, for some of the signatures, the printing was never interrupted and those signatures were the same throughout the entire press run. Skousen, in his examination of about one hundred copies of the 1830 edition, has yet to find two bound copies that are identical with respect to all these in-press changes.[1]

An article can now be written concerning similar variations found in different copies of the Book of Commandments. We have always known there are at least three different title pages in the surviving copies, but now we know there are also variations in the text. Though the variations are minor, it is important to at least establish a standard by which all other texts may be compared. The editors of the Joseph Smith Papers have selected the copy of the Book of Commandments housed in the Church History Library that was donated by Wilford Woodruff.

Text Comparison

We developed an interesting method to compare various texts of a single revelation that became known as "lineups." We placed a line of text from the earliest document first on a page with the corresponding text from all the other documents in their proper order immediately below it, repeating the process to the end of the revelation. Example 1 is from the latter part of Doctrine and Covenants 4 and contains one manuscript and three published versions: the Book of Commandments and the 1835 and 1844 editions of the Doctrine and Covenants. The major variations occurred between the Book of Commandments and the 1835 edition of the Doctrine and Covenants. Joseph Smith headed the group working on the 1835 edition, and changes were made under his direction. Members of the Church then sustained the 1835 edition as the word of the Lord to them.

EXAMPLE 1

MS1133	layeth up his store that he perish not but bringeth salvation to his own	soul & faith
BC	layeth up in store that he perish not, but bringeth salvation to his	soul, and faith,
D&C35	layeth up in store that he perish not, but bringeth salvation to his	soul, and faith,
D&C44	layeth up in store that he perish not, but bringeth salvation to his	soul, and faith,

MS1133	hope charity & love with an eye single to the glory of God constitutes	him for the work
BC	hope, charity, and love, with an eye single to the glory of God, qualifies	him for the work.
D&C35	hope, charity, and love, with an eye single to the glory of God, qualifies	him for the work.
D&C44	hope, charity, and love, with an eye single to the glory of God, qualifies	him for the work.

MS1133	remember temperance patience
BC 2.	Remember temperance, patience,
D&C35	2. Remember faith, virtue, knowledge, temperance, patience, brotherly kindness,
D&C44	2. Remember faith, virtue, knowledge, temperance, patience, brotherly kindness,

MS1133	humility diligence & C.	Ask & ye shall receive knock & it shall be
BC	humility, diligence, &c.,	ask and ye shall receive, knock and it shall be
D&C35	godliness, charity, humility, diligence.	Ask and ye shall receive, knock and it shall be
D&C44	godliness, charity, humility, diligence.	Ask and ye shall receive, knock and it shall be

MS1133	opened unto you amen
BC	opened to you: Amen.
D&C35	opened unto you. Amen.
D&C44	opened unto you: Amen.

Example 2. In the following much more complex example from a line in Doctrine and Covenants 42, six manuscript copies are compared with five published ones: PT (*Painesville Telegraph,* September 1831), EMS (*Evening and Morning Star,* July 1832), BC (Book of Commandments, July 1833), and the Doctrine and Covenants 1835 and 1844 editions. The documents are arranged with the earliest identified listed first. (The abbreviations used to identify the manuscript versions are in-house and

will be given no further identification here. In the published volumes, they will be fully identified.)

The text in our current Doctrine and Covenants first appeared in the manuscript BkA, dated fall 1831. The ZC and JW manuscripts obviously copied one from the other or had a common source that may reflect an earlier, less refined text. The one noted as BCR, which was the manuscript from which EMS and BC were printed, shows later editing, which editing conforms to these printed versions. But interestingly, even though BCR is the earliest text identified, we used RWD as our featured text in this case because it includes a block of material not found in any of the others.

EXAMPLE 2

BCR	hath [has]	authority &	it is known to the Church that he hath has	authority & has
RWD	hath	authority &	it is known to the church that he hath	authority & have
PT	hath	authority, and	it is known to the church that he hath	authority, and have
BkB	hath	authority &	it be known to the Church that he hath	authority & has
BkA	has	authority &	it is known to the Church that he has	authority & has
ZC	has	authority &		has
EMS	has	authority, and	it is known to the church that he has	authority, and has
BC	has	authority, and	it is known to the church that he has	authority, and has
JW	has	authority, and		has
D&C35	has	authority, and	it is known to the church that he has	authority, and has
D&C44	hath	authority, and	it is known to the church that he has	authority, and has

DATING REVELATIONS

We are now able to date the revelations with greater precision than ever attempted before. Most of those in the Doctrine and Covenants are dated accurately, but there are some that we have found to be in error—not major, for the most part—however, still important and interesting. In the following listing of these revelations, the date given in parentheses is the one found in the current edition of the Doctrine and Covenants.

> Section 10 (summer 1828). Although the two dates assigned to this revelation were first May 1829 and then summer 1828, we now feel confident that if it is not a composite of more than one revelation combined later, the correct date is April 1829, shortly after the arrival of Oliver Cowdery on April 5. Even if it is a composite, April 1829

best fits the date when it was brought together to form the revelation as we know it today.

Section 20 (April 1830). Although the essentials of section 20 were written over the span of almost a year, we now know that the version found in the current printing of the Doctrine and Covenants was written April 10, 1830.

Section 23 (April 1830). This section is actually a composite of five revelations first printed in the Book of Commandments. In that book, they were dated April 6, 1830. Although that specific date was not duplicated in later printings of section 23, it is important that we now know that April 6 could not have been the date of reception, and what was printed in the Book of Commandments was in error. This removes part of the basis for the argument used by some that the location of the organization of the Church was in Manchester, not Fayette, New York.

Section 27 (August 1830 and the remainder in the following September). This section is a composite of at least two separate revelations, and the dates attached to it have varied from July through September 1830. We can say with certainty that the first part was received in the forepart of August 1830. There is no complete version extant, either manuscript or printed, before the version in the 1835 edition; however, evidence does point to September 1830 as the date for the second part.

Section 35 (December 1830). We now have sufficient evidence that this revelation was received December 7, 1830.

Section 36 (December 1830). We now know that this revelation was received December 9, 1830.

Section 40 (January 1831). The first revelation to James Covill (D&C 39) was received January 5, 1830, and we now know that this one was received the following day—January 6. We also have evidence that James Covill was a Methodist preacher, not a Baptist.

Section 42 (February 9, 1831). Students of the Doctrine and Covenants have always known that Doctrine & Covenants 42 is a composite of two revelations, one received February 9, 1831, and the other on February 23, but what is not generally known is that there is a portion of this section that has never been published and another portion that has been deleted from the printing in the Book of Commandments.

Section 48 (March 1831). We can now accurately date this section on March 10, 1831.

Section 49 (March 1831). Although the current Doctrine and Covenants dates this revelation in March 1831, we can show it was actually received May 7, 1831.

Section 50 (May 1831). The precise date of this revelation is May 9, 1831.

Section 51 (May 1831). We can now show that this revelation is dated May 20, 1831.

Section 52 (June 7, 1831). We now accept June 6, 1831, as the date of this revelation, not June 7 as in the current Doctrine and Covenants.

Section 53 (June 1831). We now date this section June 8, 1831.

Section 54 (June 1831). This section can be dated June 10, 1831.

Section 55 (June 1831). The accepted date is now June 14, 1831.

Section 56 (June 1831). We can now date this revelation June 15, 1831.

Section 63 (late in August 1831). There is evidence that this revelation was given August 30, 1831.

Section 65 (October 1831). We can now establish this date as October 30, 1831.

Section 66 (October 25, 1831). We now know the date to be October 29, 1831.

Sections 1, 67–70; a portion of section 107; and section 133. These revelations were received during a lengthy conference in the forepart of November 1831. Through extensive research, we can now show that they were received in the following order:

Section 68 (November 1831)	November 1
Section 1 (November 1, 1831)	November 1
Testimony of the Witnesses of the Book of Commandments	November 1
Section 67 (November 1831)	November 2
Section 133 (November 3, 1831)	November 3
Section 69 (November 1831)	November 11
Section 107:59–100 *passim* (March 25, 1835)	November 11
Section 70 (November 12, 1831)	November 12

The Testimony of the Witnesses of the Book of Commandments was not included in the unfinished book; however, a modification of it was included in the 1835 edition of the Doctrine and Covenants as the Testimony of the Twelve Apostles.[2] Both testimonies were included in the Explanatory Introduction of the Doctrine and Covenants in the 1921 edition and all of its later printings. The Testimony of the Witnesses to the Book of Commandments was removed beginning with the 1981 edition.

> Section 74 (January 1832). This is a real surprise to those who thought this revelation was received in connection with the work Joseph Smith was doing in correcting the text of the Bible. This section was actually received sometime in the last part of 1830, and not January 1832 as found in all editions of the Doctrine and Covenants. It probably stemmed from discussions about infant baptism.
>
> Section 78 (March 1832). We now date this section March 1, 1832.
>
> Section 79 (March 1832). This section is now dated March 12, 1832.
>
> Section 80 (March 1832). Correct this date to March 17, 1832.

Section 81 (March 1832). March 15, 1832.

Section 84 (September 22 and 23, 1832). Doctrine & Covenants 84 has always been dated this way, but we now know the breaking point is between verses 102 and 103.

Section 94 (May 6, 1833). The date of reception now reads August 2, 1833.

Section 95 (June 1, 1833). We now accept June 3, 1833, as the correct date.

Section 99 (August 1832). We now accept August 29, 1832, as the correct date.

Section 101 (December 16, 1833). This revelation was written on December 16 and 17, 1833.

Revelations following section 101 were received after 1833; hence they are beyond the work we have done on the revelations from 1828 to 1833.

Linking the Revelations with Historical Events

The following is only a sampling of the understanding gained when one connects the events surrounding the reception of each revelation with the message of the text.

Section 20. Question: How could a revelation written during the same month the Church was organized have information concerning presiding elders, traveling bishops, high councilors, high priests, presidents, high council, and bishops (verses 66–67) when those offices were not revealed until years later?

Answer: In editions from 1876 until 1920, there was an asterisk preceding verse 65 with an accompanying note at the bottom of the page that read: "Verses 65, 66, and 67 were added sometime after the others." There are no manuscript versions of section 20 that include these verses, and the earliest printed version with them is the 1835 edition of the Doctrine and Covenants.

Section 45. Question: What is the relationship between Doctrine & Covenants 45 and Matthew 24, now printed in the Pearl of Great Price? With even a cursory reading, it is obvious section 45 also reports the Mount Olivet prophecy in Matthew 24.

Answer: Section 45 was received on March 7, 1831, and was not given in connection with the work Joseph Smith was doing on the Joseph Smith Translation but to counter "false reports and foolish stories" (see introduction to D&C 45). At the time, Joseph Smith was working on the text of the Old Testament, not the New Testament.

Many of the 1830–31 converts to the Church in Ohio had formerly followed Alexander Campbell in his rejection of the creeds of Christianity and his efforts to restore the ancient order of things. Known as "Disciples," they believed that the reformations launched by Campbell would bring about the Millennium. According to Amos S. Hayden, one of the preachers and historians of the movement, "The restoration of the ancient gospel was looked upon as the initiatory movement, which, it was thought, would spread so rapidly that existing denominations would almost immediately be deorganized; that the *true people,* of whom it was believed Christ had a remnant among the sects, would at once, on the presentation of these evidently scriptural views, embrace them, and thus form the union of Christians so long prayed for," which would constitute the Millennium.[3] Those Disciples who became Latter-day Saints had their faith confirmed in the imminent expectation of the Millennium, for they now believed that God had intervened and had restored the true "ancient order" through Joseph Smith.

Many of the early revelations received by Joseph Smith, including this one, dealt with eschatological matters. Latter-day Saint eschatology, with its vision of the imminent destruction of the wicked and the millennial triumph of the righteous, provided powerful reassurance in the face of opposition. The skeptical local press of the day occasionally published "false reports, lies, and fo[o]lish stories" and members of the Church "had to struggle against every thing that prejudice and wickedness could invent," but Joseph Smith wrote that this revelation was received "to the joy of the saints," with its thematic focus on the end times.[4]

What makes this revelation significant is that it represents another recounting of the Savior's message to His disciples on the Mount of Olives (Matthew 24), in which the longstanding Christian controversy about the timing of these events is resolved. One view was that the predicted events had all been fulfilled in the New Testament generation; another interpretation placed them at the end of time. This revelation made clear that some of the events occurred shortly after the Savior's death and that others would happen just prior to the Millennium. The vividness and specificity of the revelation also served to confirm the converts in their sense that they really were living in the latter, even the last, days.

However, in verses 60 and 61 of section 45 the following is revealed: "And now, behold, I say unto you, it shall not be given unto you to know any further concerning this chapter, until the New Testament be translated, and in it all these things shall be made known; wherefore I give unto you that ye may now translate it, that ye may be prepared for the things to come." The next day, March 8, Joseph Smith and Sidney Rigdon began work on the New Testament, and in a matter of days they reached Matthew 24. Evidently they felt the need to communicate this portion of the Joseph Smith Translation to the Saints as soon as practicable, so a broadsheet was published and distributed. Early missionaries took copies to England, and when Franklin D. Richards first published the Pearl of Great Price in 1851, the broadsheet was included and has had a place in that volume ever since.

Sections 48 and 68. Question: How can these two revelations include text referring to the Presidency of the Church in 1831 when the Presidency of the High Priesthood was formed a year later in March 1832 and the First Presidency of the Church in March 1833?

Answer: Prior to 1835, section 48 read: "And then ye shall begin to be gathered with your families, every man according to his family, according to his circumstances, and as is appointed to him by the bishop and *elders of the church,* according to the laws and commandments, which ye have received, and which ye shall hereafter receive; even so: Amen" (v. 6; emphasis added).[5]

Similarly, section 68 read: "Wherefore it shall be an high priest who is worthy; and he shall be appointed by *a conference of high priests*" (v. 5; emphasis added).[6] Verses 16–21 also mention this presidency, but these verses were added to the revelation in March 1835. Verses 22 and 23 read: "And again, no bishop or judge, which shall be set apart for this ministry, shall be tried or condemned for any crime, save it be before *a conference of high priests;* and in as much as he is found guilty before *a conference of high priests,* by testimony that cannot be impeached, he shall be condemned or forgiven, according to the laws of the church" (emphasis added).⁷ Such alterations to the revelations reflect a growing organization as the Church expanded in territory and numbers.

Section 64, verse 27. Verse 27 reads: "Behold, it is said in my laws, or forbidden, to get in debt to thine enemies." Question: Where is this counsel found in the revelations?

Answer: It was originally part of section 42 but was later deleted. It reads: "4th How far it is the will of the Lord that we should have dealings with the wold [*sic*] & how we should conduct our dealings with them? Thou shalt contract no debts with them & again the Elders & Bishop shall Council together & they shall do by the directions of the spirit as it must be necessary."⁸

Section 77. Question: Why does section 77 give interpretation only to the first eleven chapters of the book of Revelation?

Answer: On February 16, 1832, while working on the Joseph Smith Translation of the Bible, the Prophet and Sidney Rigdon received "A Vision" (see D&C 76). This revelation was given as they were revising John 5, and because the message of the twenty-ninth verse caused them "to marvel." From the beginning of the project, they had written out each verse in its entirety. For some reason, they altered this time-consuming process in the very next chapter, and from that point onward the Joseph Smith Translation manuscript contains only new or emended text. This change enabled them to accelerate their revision of the Bible, and in the following five weeks they nearly completed work on the New Testament. On March 20 they completed the first eleven chapters of the book of Revelation. Also on that date, Joseph Smith received a revelation never published in the Doctrine and Covenants. In part it reads:

> Second shall we finish the translation of the New Testament before we go to Zion or wait till we return
> It is expedient saith the Lord that there be no delays and this saith the Lord for the greatest good and benefit of the church wherefore omit the translation for the present time
> 20 March 1832 at Hyrum⁹

Joseph Smith wrote, "'In connection with the translation of the Scriptures, I received the following explanation of the Revelation of St. John'" (see introduction to D&C 77). Since section 77 is dated March 1832, it likely came in the days just prior to March 20, as the two men wrestled with how to understand and correct this highly symbolic book. It includes interpretations for only the first eleven chapters because the rest of the book was corrected after the Prophet's return from Missouri in June. Parenthetically, there is no manuscript for additional interpretations of the latter chapters.

Sections 81, 90, 107. Question: How can we reconcile the inverse sequence of events in these revelations?

Answer: In section 81, dated March 1832, Frederick G. Williams is given his duties as a counselor to the President of the High Priesthood. In section 90, verse 6, given a year later, March 1833, he is called to that position. In section 107, dated March 28, 1835, the Lord reveals in verses 65–66 that there should be a President of the High Priesthood. (By inference, any counselor to the President would be called after the office was revealed.) Hence, the sequence is just opposite of what we would expect: the position revealed, the person called, and then a delineation of his duties.

The last sentence of the introduction to section 107 alerts us that this section is really a composite of several revelations, with a portion of it written as early as November 1831. Verses 65–66 are part of that portion, and so the office of President of the High Priesthood was revealed in November 1831. Less than three months later, on January 25, 1832, at a conference of the Church at Amhurst, Ohio, Joseph Smith was sustained and ordained President of the High Priesthood (see introduction to D&C 75). Less than two months later, Joseph Smith called two counselors in the Presidency, Jesse Gause and Sidney Rigdon.[10] During the same month, on March 15, 1832, Joseph Smith received section 81 explaining to Jesse Gause, not Frederick G. Williams, his duties as a counselor (see introduction to D&C 81). Gause apostatized during the latter part of 1832, and Williams was called to replace him in March 1833 (see D&C 90:6). Then Gause's name was removed from D&C 81 and Williams's name was inserted. (Parenthetically, one could write in the name of a current counselor in the First Presidency because the duties apply to any of those who have served over the years.)

Though the sequence appears in the Doctrine and Covenants to be just the opposite, historical events show that the office and callings within the Presidency of the High Priesthood did take place in their proper order.

UNPUBLISHED REVELATIONS

Several revelations have never been published, which will now be more accessible to the members of the Church through the Joseph Smith Papers Project. These include the following:

1. Revelation concerning Joseph Smith Sr., Ezra Thayre, and Frederick G. Williams. Williams, a Kirtland farmer and herb doctor, was converted by the "Lamanite Missionaries" in November 1830 and then accompanied them on their mission to Missouri. Land records for Kirtland in 1830 show Williams owning 75 and 67 acres respectively in two adjacent 105–acre "blocks." Before leaving for Missouri in the fall of 1830, Williams apparently made his property available to the Church for its purposes. Although Joseph Smith did not meet Williams until July 1831, when he arrived in Missouri to dedicate the place for the New Jerusalem (see section 57), this revelation advises the Prophet to utilize some of the Williams's farmland in specific ways.

In late August 1831, when Joseph Smith returned from Missouri, land problems involving Williams, Ezra Thayre, and Joseph Smith Sr. needed resolution. A revelation received on September 11 (D&C 64:21) further addressed those problems. Finally, at a conference of elders held in Kirtland on October 10, 1831, matters were resolved. Only the decisions, not the details, of the dispute survive in conference minutes. The Church was to provide the Williams family with a comfortable dwelling. Joseph Smith Sr. was to oversee to the management of the farm and the distribution of its products. The Thayre family could remain where they were until spring. And the conference reproved both the Prophet's father and Ezra Thayre "for the unwise course they have taken in this affair." That solutions were not easily reached is revealed by the decision that Thayre "be sharply rebuked for the disrespect with which he had treated this conference." The conference authorized bishop's agent Newel K. Whitney (see D&C 63:42–45) to present the Williams family's case "before the church" and ensure they were provided with comfortable dwellings "according to the commandment of the Lord," wording that clearly refers to this revelation.[11]

2. Oliver Cowdery's Articles of the Church of Christ. This is a three-page manuscript in Oliver Cowdery's handwriting quoting extensively from the Book of Mormon, particularly from the book of Moroni. The document begins, "A commandment from God unto Oliver how he should build up his church & the manner thereof," and concludes with the words, "Written in the year of our Lord & Saviour 1829—A true copy of the articles of the Church of Christ."[12]

This document has an unmistakable connection to section 20, the Articles and Covenants of the Church of Christ. All of the quotations and paraphrasing from the Book of Mormon in this document are also found in section 20.

In early June 1829, with the translation of the Book of Mormon almost finished and an awareness of recent revealed declarations that Christ's church would again be established on earth, Joseph Smith dictated a revelation containing "instructions relative to building up the church of Christ, according to the fulness of the gospel" (D&C 18). Part of the revelation was directed to Oliver Cowdery. He was instructed to lead in preaching the gospel, having received "that same calling with which [Paul] was called" (D&C 18:9), and, in anticipation of the future "building up the church of Christ," he also seems to have been invited to prepare a précis of Church polity by "rely[ing] upon the things . . . written" in the Book of Mormon.

3. Evidently a revelation was received relative to obtaining the copyright of the Book of Mormon in Canada, hence in all the United Kingdom. The text of this revelation has never been available, so those who have written about it have had to argue with incomplete facts. We can now shed additional light on this revelation that has never been published before. Further explanation will have to wait until the volume is published.

4. There is a supposed revelation dated July 17, 1831, in which the elders of the Church are invited to intermarry with the "Lamanites." It is a reconstruction made thirty years later with many anachronistic

inconsistencies. In the Joseph Smith Papers Project, this revelation is printed only in the appendix because its provenance cannot be satisfactorily established. Arguments accompany the document in the appendix showing the reasons for rejecting it as it is written.

Conclusion

The volumes of the Joseph Smith Papers Project will be published over the course of a decade or more. Fortunately, the first two volumes of the Documents Series, which contain most of the revelations, will be among the early publications. Well-documented evidence and details in those volumes will verify what we have surveyed here as well as many topics beyond the scope of this paper. Future students and researchers will have the most comprehensive resource concerning the reception, recording, and publishing of the revelations ever available. Though scholarly in presentation, those who acknowledge Joseph Smith as a prophet of God will also find in these volumes much evidence to confirm their faith.

Notes

1. Personal communication, Royal Skousen. For more information, see his *History of the Text of the Book of Mormon*, volume 3 of the critical text of the Book of Mormon (forthcoming from the Maxwell Institute at BYU).

2. Doctrine and Covenants, 1835 edition, 256.

3. Amos S. Hayden, *Early History of the Disciples in the Western Reserve* (Cincinnati: Chase & Hall, 1876), 183.

4. Dean C. Jessee, ed., *Papers of Joseph Smith* (Salt Lake City: Deseret Book, 1989), 1:350.

5. Book of Commandments 51:6.

6. *Evening and Morning Star*, October 1832, 35.

7. *Evening and Morning Star*, October 1832, 35.

8. Symonds Ryder Manuscript, MS 4583, box 1, folder 13, 1831, Church History Library, Salt Lake City.

9. One-page manuscript in handwriting of Sidney Rigdon, Newel K. Whitney Papers, L. Tom Perry Special Collections, Harold B. Lee Library, Brigham Young University.

10. Kirtland Revelation Book, 10–11.

11. For further information, see Frederick G. Williams, "Frederick Granger Williams of the First Presidency of the Church," *BYU Studies* 12, no. 3 (Spring 1972): 243–60.

12. MS 1829, Church History Library.

3

ONE CONTINUOUS FLOW: REVELATIONS SURROUNDING THE "NEW TRANSLATION"

Kerry Muhlestein

We often underestimate both the complexity and continuity of Joseph Smith's revelatory life. His visions rolled, he said, "like an overflowing surge before [his] mind."[1] Now that they have been compartmentalized into different sections, chapters, and books, we tend to compartmentalize them in our minds.[2] Such a practice, however, limits our ability to see how powerful and continuous this "overflowing surge" really was. Nevertheless, if we read his revelations in the order in which they came, we find ourselves better able to understand not only the revelations themselves but also their interrelations with each other and the context from which they arose. In the infancy of the Church, Joseph's revelatory work on translating the Bible and his other concurrent revelations laid, stone by stone, a doctrinal foundation upon which the Church would firmly stand. The revelations resulting in the Joseph Smith Translation, which he called the New Translation, and those in the Doctrine and Covenants are not two separate sides of this

---

Kerry Muhlestein is an assistant professor of ancient scripture at Brigham Young University.

foundation but are instead many individual stones that overlay and interlock.

To understand this interaction, we must first establish a time line for the revelations. While the entire process of creating the New Translation is worthy of study, that would be too large a project for the current venue. Instead we will focus on the material that represents Old Testament Manuscript 1 (OT1),[3] or Joseph's first pass through the first twenty-four chapters of Genesis. This material contains the revelations and corrections he received until the Lord directed him to stop translating the Old Testament and begin with the New Testament. This period is associated with great new revelations, such as those found in the book of Moses. Afterward, while many important changes were made during the translation, including small bursts of completely new passages, it was not of the same magnitude as the beginning of the work.[4] For these reasons, we will consider the revelations in the Doctrine and Covenants that took place just before, during, and after the time in which the Prophet was creating OT1.

We must also keep in mind that the revelations the Prophet Joseph received were not immediately published. The eventual publication would come in various forms, including the Book of Commandments and several serial publications such as the *Evening and Morning Star,* the *Messenger and Advocate,* and *Times and Seasons.* Yet often these publications were designed to make the revelations available to Saints who had joined the Church after their reception. We know that early on some people, such as John Whitmer and Edward Partridge, made their own copies of portions of the New Translation.[5] We are also sure that Franklin Richards obtained copies in some way.[6] While we cannot know how many people had some personal portion of the translation, the existence of personal copies is indicative that some Saints wanted, obtained, and shared the information flowing from the Prophet. We can assume that as the revelations were received they were read or made known in some way to many Church members of the time. At the very least, the doctrine learned by those who had access to the revelations was imparted to others in sermons, conversations, and preaching. Thus, the revelations surely had immediate impact on the doctrinal understanding of the Church as a whole. Furthermore, when Joseph Smith speaks of the happiness of the "little flock"[7] upon receiving a revelation that was part of the New Translation, it indicates that at least many members of the fledgling Church had indeed received the revelation. Indeed, when Joseph said that the flock received the revelation, he simultaneously noted that the total membership was about seventy people, which suggests that most, if not all, of those members knew the contents of the revelation.

When we see and teach the relationships between these various revelations, it will enhance our study and understanding of the gospel. As Elder Neal A. Maxwell said, "Sometimes I fear that we teach the scriptures in isolation from each other, when in fact, if you will make multiple use of them . . . you will not only make the teaching moment more significant but you will also be witnessing to the congruency and relevance of all the scriptures. You will find, as one would expect, a powerful conceptual consistency that flows throughout all the scriptures, sometimes even verbatim language, because they come from the same source."[8] Among other things, our understanding of Joseph Smith, Church history, certain gospel doctrines, and the Lord's methods of teaching His people will be enhanced by correctly understanding the interrelationship of the New Translation and Joseph Smith's other revelations.

It must also be noted that the work done here is only possible because of that which has already been done by others. While this is true of all scholarship, it is particularly true of this topic. One cannot work on the New Translation without learning that *every* path has been paved by Robert J. Matthews.[9] Additionally, his work in conjunction with Scott H. Faulring and Kent P. Jackson in providing a critical edition of the New Translation manuscripts[10] opens up completely new avenues of possible research, including the current article.

Seeing the Continuous Flow

In early April 1830, several revelations clarified the organization of the Church and questions relating to various people joining it shortly thereafter. These revelations are Doctrine and Covenants sections 21–23 and seemingly portions of 20.[11] We are aware of no significant revelations coming during the rest of that month, nor in all of May. But sometime in June a wonderful flood of light sprang forth as Joseph began the New Translation of the Bible. As the spectacular vision in Moses 1 was unfolded to him, it apparently flowed "from the Prophet's lips without the slightest contemplation, hesitation, or uncertainty."[12] Following this, sections 24–26 were received in July, section 27 in August, sections 28 and 29 in late September,[13] sections 30 and 31 on September 28,[14] and section 32 in mid-October.[15] Of particular note is the Lord's command to Joseph Smith, Oliver Cowdery, and John Whitmer to devote their time to studying the scriptures (see D&C 26:1). Along with the reception of Moses 1, this urge may have served as an impetus to continue the New Translation.

During the same months these revelations were given (June–October), the Prophet also received revelations that became Moses 2–5:43. He grouped this material into two separate topics. On page 3 of OT1, just above the beginning of Moses 2, the heading states, "A Revelation given to the Elders of the Church of Christ On the First Book of Moses."[16] Written on page 8 of this manuscript above what is now Moses 4 is "A Revelation concerning Adam after he had been driven out of the garden of Eden."[17] These two headings indicate that Moses 2–3 was received separately from Moses 4–5:43. While we know that all this translation was done by October 21, 1830, we do not know precisely when these verses were received and recorded. It is possible that their translation was spread over a number of days and received on a number of occasions. However, the Prophet seems to have worked on the New Translation in great bursts of communion with the divine, which, combined with the two topical headings, suggests that Moses 2–3 was received as one great revelation and Moses 4–5:43 as another, though we cannot be certain.

One small clue may enable a more refined dating of the reception of these revelations. As noted above, the heading of Moses 2 states that the revelation was "given to the Elders of the Church of Christ." The wording suggests that several elders were present either at the reception of the revelation or that the revelation was intended to be read to several elders shortly after its reception. This may even indicate that the revelation was associated with a conference. The timing of the Church's second conference on September 26–28 coincides with the time Moses chapters 2–3 were received. Section 28 was received just days before the conference. President Joseph Fielding Smith believed (though he provided no explanation as to how he came to this conclusion) that the Lord also revealed section 29 just days before the conference.[18] However, the Prophet Joseph Smith noted that section 29 was received in the presence of six elders.[19] There were six elders (besides the Prophet) attending the conference held in September,[20] so it is likely these were the same six elders present when the revelation was received,[21] signaling it may have been received *at* the conference instead of *before* the conference. This may be confirmed by Newel Knight's record, which states that they received three revelations after the conference began (he notes the reception of section 28 before the conference but mentions no other revelations until the conference had convened).[22]

It is difficult to tell what revelations Knight may have been referring to. Sections 30 and 31 were revelations received at the conference, and by this count section 29 may be the third to which he referred. However, originally section 30 was regarded as three separate revelations (comprising chapters 30–32 of the original Book of Commandments), which would mean that these three and section 31 comprise *four* revelations received at the conference. We cannot be certain precisely when section 29 and Moses 2–3 were received. It is plausible that they were both given in the presence of the same elders and that this was either during or just before the September 26 conference. Certainly section 29 was read at the conference, and perhaps Moses 2–3 as well. Whether or not this is an accurate scenario, it seems quite likely they were both received close together. Thus it is probable that Moses 2–3 was received around the same time as sections 28–31, with Moses 4–5:43 coming shortly after Moses 2–3. Undoubtedly Moses 2–5:43 and sections 28–31 were received within (at most) months of each other. At this point the "surge" of revelation had begun in earnest, but it was only a forerunner to the deluge on the way.

Shortly thereafter the Lord poured out revelations upon the Saints. Moses 5:43b–5:51 was received on October 21 according to John Whitmer's handwritten annotation in the text[23] (Whitmer had just taken over scribal duties from Oliver Cowdery). The Prophet received section 33 in late October[24] and section 34 on November 4. The end of November through the beginning of December was a period during which Joseph received a flood of revelations. On November 30 he received Moses 5:52–6:18.[25] The next day he brought forth Moses 6:19–52.[26] Sometime in the next nine (possibly six) days, he also dictated Moses 6:52–7:1.[27] Sections 35 and 36 came on December 10 (possibly the 7).[28] Section 35 is particularly meaningful for the New Translation because it said Joseph had been given "keys of the mystery of those things which have been sealed" (D&C 35:18), and Sidney Rigdon was commanded by the Lord to "write for him; and the scriptures shall be given, even as they are in mine own bosom, to the salvation of mine own elect" (D&C 35:20). Sidney Rigdon's service as scribe allowed the torrent of translation to continue with the reception of Moses 7:2–8:12 sometime during the rest of that month.[29] It is remarkable to note that the Prophet provided 156 completely new verses of Genesis in one month or less, surely observing the Christmas holiday in the midst. Section 37 was also received sometime in late December.[30] Combining the Doctrine and Covenants revelations with those of the New Translation allows us to understand that Joseph gave the fledgling Church 195 new scriptural verses during the last month of the Church's first year. The reception of sections 38 (January 2) and 39 (January 5) within the next few days brings the total to 261 verses in a five-week period. Without considering the place of the New Translation, we could easily pass over the fact that this was one of the greatest periods of revelation the Church has experienced, an overflowing surge.

After this, the New Translation efforts took a brief respite while the Prophet and Sidney moved to Ohio, where they arrived in early February. Sometime in January the Lord gave Joseph the revelation that is now section 40. Then recorded revelation ceased for about a month. However, upon arrival in Kirtland the prophetic flow resumed. Section 41 came on February 4, section 42 on February 9, section 43 sometime in the middle of the month, and section 44 late in the month. Section 45, wherein the Prophet was instructed to temporarily stop translating the Old Testament and begin translating the New Testament, came on March 7, 1831. By that time the translation had reached Genesis 24:41.[31] This means that all the material between Moses 8:12 (equivalent to

Genesis 5:32) and Genesis 24:41 was received during a five-week period. Thus, the translation process seems to have happened in great bursts of prophetic energy. To be sure, there was less new material received in these chapters of Genesis than those that preceded, yet the Prophet still worked through every verse, and Sidney still wrote out each entire verse by hand.[32] This means that the two men labored together as the Prophet received inspiration regarding 470 verses (with an additional 221 received that would make their way into the Doctrine and Covenants, totaling 691 verses in five weeks, though many of the Genesis verses comprised nothing new). While this work may have largely taken place on certain days with gaps between, the work must have gone forward somewhat consistently and steadily to cover so many verses in a mere thirty-five days. Thus, while we cannot know for certain the exact dates on which the Prophet translated specific verses, we can deduce fair approximations within definite time limits.

During this five-week period, the translation process averaged ninety-four verses a week. Again, some weeks may have seen more translation than others, but the rapid and extended pace demands that it could not have been far off this mark. If the average is close, we can estimate that after one week of being in Kirtland, on February 8, Joseph and Sidney had probably gone through most of Genesis chapter 9, coinciding roughly with the reception of sections 41 and 42. By February 15 they had likely worked their way through Genesis 12 and would then have been midway through chapter 17 by February 22. Section 43 was seemingly received sometime during this process. By March 1, they were likely about halfway through Genesis 20, enabling them to have progressed to Genesis 24:41 by March 7, the day the Lord revealed section 45. We can use these approximations as rough guidelines as we look at the interrelationships of the revelations.

One Continuous Flow 47

Concurrence of Revelations

1830–31	D&C Revelations	JST Material
March	Section 19	
April	Sections 20–23	
May		
June		Moses 1
July	Sections 24–26	Moses 2–3 (July–September)
August	Section 27	
September	Sections 28–31	Moses 4–5:43 (September–October 20)
October	Sections 32–33	Moses 5:43b-51
November	Section 34	Moses 5:52–6:18
December	Sections 35–37	Moses 6:19–8:12
January	Sections 38–40	
February	Sections 41–44	Moses 8:13–30 Gen. 6:14–mid-Gen. 20
March	Section 45	Mid-Gen. 20–Gen. 24:41

Time Line of Revelations

March 1830
Section 19

April 1830
Section 20 (parts composed in 1829)
Section 21 (April 6)
Section 22
Section 23

June 1830
Moses 1

July 1830
Section 24
Section 25
Section 26

July–August 1830
Moses 2–3

August 1830
Section 27

September 1830
Section 28
Section 29
Section 30

Section 31

September–October 20, 1830
Moses 4–5:43

October 1830
Section 32 (mid-October)
Moses 5:43b–5:51 (October 21)
Section 33 (late October)

November 1830
Section 34 (November 4)
Moses 5:52–6:18 (November 30)

December 1830
Moses 6:19–52 (December 1)
Moses 6:52–7:1 (between December 1 and 10)
Section 35
Section 36

Moses 7:2–8:12 (in December, after December 10)
Section 37 (late December)

January 1831
Section 38 (January 2)
Section 39 (January 5)
Section 40

February 1831
Section 41 (February 4)
Section 42 (February 9)
Moses 8:13–30; Gen. 6:14–mid-Gen. 9
Section 43 (mid-February)
Mid-Gen. 9–mid-Gen. 17
Section 44 (late February)
Mid-Gen. 9–mid-Gen. 17

March 1831
Mid-Gen. 20–Gen. 24:41
Section 45 (March 7)

The time line not only allows us to gain a clearer idea of just how continuous the "overflowing surge" of revelation was which the Prophet received, as well as the magnitude of this flow, but also permits us to more fully examine how the process of the New Translation is connected with other revelations received, providing fascinating insights and greater understandings of both groups of revelations. Although we cannot touch on all the many aspects of Joseph's revelations that impact one another, we will visit some important highlights.

Understanding Prophethood

As noted, the April revelations comprising sections 20–23 are almost entirely concerned with the organization of the Church and the entrance and duties of members thereto. It was months before the Prophet received another revelation that would make its way into the Doctrine and Covenants. In the meantime God gave him a striking and powerful vision (or recounting of a previous vision) now known as Moses 1. We know nothing of the background of the reception of this revelation. It may have been the result of thoroughly going through the Bible or may have been the impetus for doing so. We do, however, know how grateful Joseph was for the vision because he testified, "Amid all trials and tribulations we had to wade through, the Lord, who well knew our infantile and delicate situation, vouchsafed for us a supply, and granted us 'line upon line, here a little and there a little,' of which the following [Moses 1] was a precious morsel."[33]

We will never know all that was going through the Prophet's mind and heart at this time, but we can understand some of the significance of this revelation. While the Prophet had already experienced several visions and revelations and was by now confident as a translator, his role as revelator for the Church was still being established, probably in his mind as well as in others. During this "infant" period, Joseph became part of a prophetic experience regarding *the* great prophet of Israel: Moses. This vision expanded our understanding of just how prophetic and revelatory Moses was. The light that shone from this vision not only illuminated the wonderful doctrines conveyed about God, His creations, and His relations with man but also elucidated what it meant to be a prophet. When the question of prophetic ability and authority arose in connection with Hiram Page shortly thereafter, the Lord outlined the special and unique position that Joseph the Prophet held in the Church: "No one shall be appointed to receive commandments and revelations in this church excepting my servant Joseph Smith, Jun., for he receiveth them *even as Moses*" (D&C 28:2; emphasis added). Coming about two months after receiving Moses 1, this last phrase meant far more than it could have before, for they had a new and substantially elevated perception of Moses's prophetic experiences. The revelation five months later, wherein God told the Church that Joseph was the only one "whom I have appointed unto you to receive commandments and revelations from my hand" (D&C 43:2) would also have been enriched by the recent reception of Moses 1. The Saints would have understood Brother Joseph as one who gave commandments after he had been likened unto Moses, for Moses was renowned as the lawgiver. For those who had access to the account of Moses's glorious vision, they now had a new understanding of how Moses was also a revelator, thus better understanding Joseph's role as one "like unto Moses" (2 Nephi 3:9; see also D&C 28:2). Thus, both the Prophet's and the Saints' reading of section 43 were informed and enhanced by the earlier reception of Moses 1. The reception of Moses's vision in concert with Joseph's revelations raised the stature of both Moses and Joseph.

Satan, Creation, Fall, and the Gospel

It seems that after this glorious glimpse of what was missing from the Bible, the New Translation began in earnest. As mentioned, in the next three and one-half months, Moses 2–5:43 were received. Sometime early in this process, perhaps even before the reception of those chapters had begun and perhaps midstream, Joseph, Oliver, and John Whitmer were told to "let your time be devoted to the studying of the scriptures" (D&C 26:1). Surely this command gave further impetus to the New Translation. As part of that translation process, Joseph and the Church learned a great deal more about the Creation, Adam, Eve, and the Fall than they had previously known. In Moses 3–4 we gain a tremendous amount of knowledge regarding spiritual aspects of the Creation, how Satan became the devil, Adam's and Eve's roles in the Fall, and the nature of the Fall in general.

As noted, while we cannot be certain, it is likely Moses 3 and 4 had been translated about the same time as the reception of section 29 in late September. This context changes the way we read certain verses in the section. Consider the great understanding imparted by the reception of Moses 3:5, wherein we learn that the Lord God created all things "spiritually, before they were naturally upon the face of the earth." Seemingly a short time later, the Lord further explained to the Prophet that He created "all things both spiritual and temporal—first spiritual, secondly temporal" (D&C 29:31–32). This was not particularly new given the Moses revelation, but the Lord went on to explain more. He first reminded Joseph that these creations had no end, nor beginning (see D&C 29:33), reinforcing what had just been communicated in Moses 1. Lest any think that when Adam had been cast out of the garden his whole experience had become temporal or that the commands he was given to sacrifice animals were concerned only with things temporal, the Lord explained that "all things unto me are spiritual, and not at any time have I given unto you a law which was temporal; neither any man, nor the children of men; neither Adam, your father, whom I created" (D&C 29:34). We wonder if this particular verse was not in response to some speculation members might have engaged in after the reception of Moses 3–5. The Lord hastened to add that Adam had agency, and "I gave unto him commandment, but no temporal commandment gave I unto him, for my commandments are spiritual; they are not natural nor temporal, neither carnal nor sensual" (D&C 29:35). It could have been natural to view all those things in which the Lord had instructed Adam after he left the garden as temporal commands, dealing with the newly temporal and changed earth. But shortly after giving the Church more details concerning what Adam had been commanded, the Lord taught the Church that these were *not* merely temporal commands (see D&C 29).

While He was on the subject of Adam's agency, the Lord expounded on the process of how Satan became the devil and how that impacted Adam's agency. He had recently (or contemporaneously) revealed new knowledge that Satan had offered universal redemption, seeking to obtain God's glory in the process and that "because that Satan rebelled against me, and sought to destroy the agency of man, which I, the Lord God, had given him, and also, that I should give unto him mine own power; by the power of mine Only Begotten, I caused that he should be cast down" (Moses 4:3). Then, after discussing Adam's agency, the Lord revealed that Satan had "rebelled against me, saying, Give me thine honor, which is my power; and also a third part of the hosts of heaven turned he away from me because of their agency; and they were thrust down, and thus . . . came the devil and his angels. . . . And it must needs be that the devil should tempt the children of men, or they could not be agents unto themselves; for if they never should have bitter they could not know the sweet—wherefore, it came to pass that the devil tempted Adam" (D&C 29:36–37, 39–40).

Robert Matthews has said of the relationship between Moses 4 and section 29 that the Doctrine and Covenants material "is a brief statement of doctrinal principles—without the story—actually a summary of the doctrines found in the longer narrative of JST Genesis 1–5."[34] It can be supposed that the New Translation spurred on the reception of section 29, but that would be only half the story. By looking at the larger time scale, we note what the Lord had done in teaching the Church about the Fall. When the Book of Mormon came forth in early 1830, the Saints learned from Lehi something of Satan's pre-earth actions, that there must be opposition and that Satan was a part of that opposition so that we might know the bitter and sweet (see 2 Nephi 2:17–23). In mid-1830 they received a more full version of the story of the Fall, including more about who Satan was and what he did (see Moses 4:1–12). Around the same time, the Lord again taught something of Satan's pre-earth actions, that he was a needed part of opposition, which was necessary to know both the bitter and the sweet (see D&C 29:36–40). The Lord hastened to add that while Adam was cast out, he had the gospel taught to him and redemption made known (see D&C 29:41–43), something just being made known to the Saints in narrative form (see Moses 5:4–15). Furthermore, about two months later, even more was revealed on how Adam and his children were taught the gospel and how to overcome the Fall (see Moses 6:51–68).

By combining the Book of Mormon material with the interlaced revelations of the New Translation and those that became the Doctrine and Covenants and by assuming section 29 came just after Moses 4, we see that the Lord gave them a doctrinal discourse on the Fall (2 Nephi 2), then a narrative (Moses 4), then another doctrinal discourse (D&C 29), then more narrative (Moses 6:51–68), all in two four-month intervals. Thus, within about eight months, the Saints learned more about the Fall than any had for well over a thousand years, with multiple lessons, explanations, reminders, and reinforcements. These doctrinal foundation stones interlocked integrally. A Restoration understanding of the Fall was an important part of the overflowing surge that came to the Prophet during 1830 and early 1831.

The Concept of Zion before Moses 7

Today we cannot speak of Zion without bringing to mind the great prophet Enoch. But it has not always been so. I will not go into great detail about the process of learning about Zion here, for Robert Matthews has already done significant work on this subject.[35] Instead I will offer a few additional insights.

While undoubtedly the city of Zion became a central theme in the movement of the Church,[36] if we are to understand the learning process the Saints went through as they came to a clearer understanding of Zion, we must begin with what they knew from the Book of Mormon, coupling it with knowledge gained from the New Translation and other revelations. The Book of Mormon mentions Zion forty-five times. All of these are either by Isaiah or by someone expounding on Isaiah, most notably Nephi. Because of this, the Book of Mormon did not add anything to the Saints' understanding of Zion beyond what they had gathered from the Bible.[37] Most of the times Isaiah uses the term *Zion* he does so as a synonym for Jerusalem; thus his Zion usage imparts very little information about what we now know. Nephi's continual use of the term may have heightened its importance in their minds, but the Book of Mormon would not have caused them to understand anything more about Zion other than that it was a term referring to God's covenant people in some way.

The Savior said that a New Jerusalem would be built in the Americas and that He would gather His people unto it (see 3 Nephi 20:22; 21:23–24). Ether and Moroni spoke extensively about the New Jerusalem as well, also noting America as its location (see Ether 13). But the New Jerusalem had not yet been scripturally equated with something called Zion. Because we view the scriptures with hindsight, we typically equate Zion and New Jerusalem in our minds and assume that the early Saints did as well. However—and we seem to have missed this point up until now—there is nothing in the Book of Mormon that would have led the Saints to believe Zion and New Jerusalem were the same thing. The closest thing is in 3 Nephi 21, wherein the Saints learned Israel would be gathered together and the Lord would establish His Zion among them. Many verses later the Lord also explained that gathered Israel would build a New Jerusalem. Again the reference to Zion is to a vague, ethereal idea not specifically connected with a concrete city or order. While they may have had their own ideas, even after reading the Book of Mormon the Saints knew little about what the Lord meant by the term *Zion*.

The revelations preceding the New Translation did not significantly alter this. Oliver Cowdery, Joseph Knight Sr., Hyrum Smith, and David Whitmer were all told in revelations to "seek to bring forth and establish the cause of Zion" (D&C 6:6; see also D&C 11:6; 12:6; 14:6). This confirmed Zion had something to do with God's work and people and indicated Zion had not yet been established, while clarifying that they would need to do so. A slight refinement of the idea came in several revelations having to do with the Prophet, wherein the Lord indicated that Joseph was inspired to move the cause of Zion forward and that He had been weeping for Zion (see D&C 21:7–8). The Prophet was also admonished to devote all his service to Zion (see D&C 24:7), as was John Whitmer (see D&C 30:11). Emma Smith was informed that she would have an inheritance in Zion (see D&C 25:2), while Sidney Rigdon was assured that if he kept the commandments and covenants, Zion would rejoice and flourish (see D&C 25:24). While the Saints were to build up Zion, they knew little other than the Church was somehow equated with Zion.

Perhaps the most curious pre–New Translation revelation concerning Zion came in late September, some three months before the revelations concerning Enoch were received. At this point the Lord told the Prophet that no one knew where the city of Zion would be built (see D&C 28:9). This is the first modern scriptural statement identifying

Zion with a geographic location. While the "inheritance in Zion" phrase from section 25 could be interpreted as a geographic reference, it could just as easily have fit with the "Zion as the kingdom of God" references already received. We must ask ourselves why the Lord was suddenly so specific about the geography of Zion in what seems to be an abrupt way. There are several possible answers to this question.

It is possible that the idea of Zion as a specific city was native to the Saints' understanding as New Englanders.[38] For many years the idea of an American Zion, or New Jerusalem (and some equated the two), had been prominent among Puritan and other Protestant groups.[39] Certainly this idea had been a driving force behind many Puritan actions and teachings, eventuating in the concept of creating the holy "city upon a hill" written across much of the American cultural landscape and filtering its way into most American religious denominations in one form or another.[40] Some towns were even held to be the New Jerusalem by their Protestant inhabitants.[41] This type of idea was particularly fervent in upstate New York around the time of the organization of the Church, where the establishment of a New Jerusalem was an idea touted by several groups.[42] A "New Zion" was established just before this time near Palmyra.[43] A similar group established a holy city around the same time in New Lebanon[44] and felt this was part of the return to the "primitive church."[45] Moreover, Harmony, Pennsylvania, derived its name from the Harmonists, who tried to establish a communal group in that town to achieve unity and holiness.[46] Their environment was such that Joseph Smith and other early Church members could have easily carried with them the cultural idea of establishing Zion as a specific geographic location.[47] This idea may have included equating Zion with the New Jerusalem, a city the Book of Mormon had proclaimed would be built in the Americas.

It is also possible that the Saints equated the New Jerusalem with the Jerusalem of old,[48] thus adopting the Zion ideas of the Old Testament. This by itself might explain the idea of Zion as a city or may be combined with the cultural ideas presented above.

There is an additional possibility that section 28 was given in response to the supposed revelations that Hiram Page had been receiving. We know little of the content of these revelations, other than that they had to do with the "upbuilding of Zion" and "the order of the Church";[49] these revelations may have even dealt with the location of Zion.[50] This would certainly explain why the Lord, in the midst of addressing Joseph's place as the revelator for the Church, and the spuriousness of Page's revelations, would mention that no one yet knew the location of Zion. Moreover, if Page had been purporting a location for Zion, the statement that Zion would be in the general area of the borders of the Lamanites (D&C 28:9) may have corrected this false location.[51] The concept of Zion as a city might have been first introduced to the Saints by Page, with the Lord confirming the idea in this way; or it may have been present among the Saints already, with the idea added to by Page and then addressed by the Lord.

Thus there are at least three options as to how the Saints came to the concept of Zion as a city: (1) As a product of New England society, they assumed that Zion was a city to be built in the Americas. (2) They had equated Zion with the New Jerusalem the Book of Mormon prophesied would be in this land. (3) Hiram Page's purported revelations contained information about Zion as a city, and Doctrine and Covenants 28:9 dealt with specific aspects of these "revelations."

Enoch, Latter-day Saints, and Zion

What is curious about section 28's Zion reference is that many have assumed the first real exposure to Zion as a city came in the revelation about the city of Enoch in Moses 7.[52] Yet paying close attention to the chronology reveals that the mention of Zion in section 28 precedes the translation of Moses 7. This is not to diminish the role the story of the city of Enoch would play in the concept of Zion in the Church. Before Joseph received the revelation about Enoch in December, the Saints knew precious little as to what establishing Zion really meant. But the reception of Moses 7 brought several important aspects of such a work vividly to the forefront: (1) God would protect His people against great wickedness as they established Zion (see Moses 7:13). (2) The people of Zion must be of one heart and mind (see Moses 7:18). (3) The people of Zion would have no poor among them (see Moses 7:18). (4) Zion was also known as the City of Holiness (see Moses 7:19). (5) Zion would be blessed when the rest of the earth was cursed (see

Moses 7:20). (6) The goal of Zion was to become so righteous it would be taken up to abide with the Lord (see Moses 7:21). (7) Zion had existed for 365 years before being taken up (see Moses 7:68). (8) Before Zion was taken into the bosom of the Lord, her inhabitants walked with God, and He dwelt in their midst (see Moses 7:69). (9) Zion was the New Jerusalem (the first scriptural equation of the two terms), would be established again in the last days, would eventually meet Enoch's Zion in a great day of reunion and rejoicing, and would become a city where the Lord would again abide (see Moses 7:62–64). This represented an overwhelming flood of knowledge about Zion. It fundamentally changed the vision of what it was that they had been counseled to seek to bring forth and establish. It seems that this revelation became the blueprint for what the Prophet would spend the rest of his life trying to accomplish. The profound impact that this revelation had on Joseph and the Church is probably beyond our ability to understand. Certainly the Prophet felt that building Zion was one of his greatest personal missions[53] and that the future of the kingdom of God hinged upon his ability to build Zion.[54] He likely looked to Enoch as a role model in this work, even choosing Enoch as his code name when he first published section 78. In many ways the work of Enoch defined the mission in which the Saints have been engaged from December of 1830 until now. It is no wonder that the revelation was received "to the joy of the little flock."[55] The grandeur of the God-given vision matched the magnitude of the divinely appointed task.

The timing of the reception of this revelation is crucial. It was received just before the Prophet and Sidney were instructed to halt the work while they moved to Ohio (see D&C 37:1). In this same revelation the Saints as a whole were also commanded to gather to Ohio (see D&C 37:3). This would prove to invoke a new phase in establishing Zion. Within days of the directive to gather, the Prophet received a revelation during a conference which commanded the initial phases of creating a Zion that included having no poor among them. At the beginning of this revelation, which would be difficult for many to receive, the Lord reminded them of just who was asking this of them: "The Lord your God, even Jesus Christ, the Great I Am, Alpha and Omega, the beginning and the end, the same which looked upon the wide expanse of eternity, and all the seraphic hosts of heaven, before the world was made; the same which knoweth all things, for all things are present before mine eyes; I am the same which spake, and the world was made, and all things came by me. I am the same which have taken the Zion of Enoch into mine own bosom" (D&C 38:1–4).

This last line, referring to Zion and Enoch, would have had little meaning to the Saints a few weeks earlier. But here, at the very moment the Lord would ask them to care for the poor in a Zionlike way, He referred to Himself with a term that would remind those assembled of the glorious Zion and her characteristics, which must have so inspired them just days before. The Lord reminded them that Enoch and his people were in His bosom, bringing to the fore the great blessings available to those who chose to live in a Zionlike way. This type of juxtaposition was only possible because of the New Translation material they had just received with such great joy.

The use of Moses 7 imagery continued. Immediately after mentioning Enoch, the Lord said He would plead for those who believed in His name, "but behold the residue of the wicked have I kept in chains of darkness until the judgment of the great day, which shall come at the end of the earth" (D&C 38:5). Here the Lord contrasts the blessed state of those who will believe in Him with those who remain in chains of darkness, which surely suggested to the Saints the recently received vision Enoch had beheld of Satan standing with "a great chain in his hand, and it veiled the whole face of the earth with darkness; and he looked up and laughed, and his angels rejoiced" (Moses 7:26). This chilling allusion underscored the need to obey the new and strenuous commands the Lord was about to deliver. For those who did not, a laughing Satan awaited, chain in hand.

Moreover, when the Lord told the assembled Saints that "I am in your midst and ye cannot see me" (D&C 38:7), it undoubtedly gave them a surge of hope that they *were* approaching the type of Zion where the Lord could abide, mingling with its inhabitants. Additionally, the promise that the Lord would give them a land flowing with milk and honey where they would have no laws but His when He came (see D&C 38:18–22) must have added to the swelling desire and hope to establish a city like unto Enoch's. Surely the command to "be one; and if ye are not one ye are not mine" (v. 27) must have reminded them that Zion consisted of those who were "of one heart and one mind" (Moses 7:18). Moreover, the way that the Lord had protected Enoch's Zion would have lent a sense of urgency and understanding to the Lord's warning that the earth was going to shake and that only those who gathered to Ohio would have power to escape the enemy (see D&C 38:30–32).[56] The insistent imagery of section 38 is redoubled in light of the epic episodes of Moses 7.

All of this would help the Saints accept what the Lord was asking of them, namely, that they should gather to Ohio (see D&C 38:32), and appoint men to govern the affairs and property of the Church in such a way that the poor and needy would be taken care of (vv. 34–36), that all things should be preserved and eventually "gathered unto the bosom of the church" (v. 38), and that they should labor with their might to accomplish these things (v. 40).

From the outset, section 38 divided some Saints. John Whitmer, who was likely not present at the meeting, reported that the revelation created some divisions among the people and that some would not receive it as coming from God.[57] Another account recorded that the Saints received the revelation with "unshaken confidence" and "all rejoiced under the blessings of the gospel."[58] Given these accounts, it is difficult to know exactly how the revelation was received, but we know that as the difficulties of the move and of caring for the poor pressed upon the Saints, many forsook the revelation, even in the face of the grandeur of Enoch's Zion. We can only wonder how many more would have done so had they not possessed such a beacon to see them through their trials.

A little more than a month later, on February 9, the Lord revealed many more specifics as to how Zion was to have no poor (see D&C 42). These detailed directions, such as consecrating properties to the bishop, were integrally tied to Joseph's other revelations. When speaking of what the bishop would do with consecrated properties, the Lord said that surplus (or residue) should be kept in the storehouse to administer to the poor and to purchase lands for the "building up of the New Jerusalem" (D&C 42:35), which had so recently been identified with the latter-day imitation of the city of Enoch (Moses 7:62–64). The

Lord then explained more of how consecration would take place, immediately followed by the instructions "thou shalt ask, and my scriptures shall be given as I have appointed, and they shall be preserved in safety" (D&C 42:56). The Lord Himself then juxtaposed the process of the New Translation and the other revelations Joseph received, as we have been doing, by telling Joseph he would receive more revelations and by tying them in with New Jerusalem: "Thou shalt receive revelation upon revelation, knowledge upon knowledge. . . . Thou shalt ask, and it shall be revealed unto you in mine own due time where the New Jerusalem shall be built" (D&C 42:61–62).

While there were probably many reasons for the Lord to associate the New Translation with other of the Prophet's revelations he was about to receive, many of which would have to do with the New Jerusalem, here we will identify one specific reason. As noted above, we cannot tell exactly when in February 1831 Joseph translated various verses of Genesis. But if our approximation is correct, then he translated Genesis 14 not long after section 42 but a little while before receiving other important Zion revelations, such as sections 45 (March 7, 1831), 48 (March 1831), 49 (March 1831), 51 (May 1831), 56 (June 1831), 57 (July 20, 1831), 58 (August 1, 1831), and 59 (August 7, 1831). This is significant because of the material contained in the New Translation of Genesis 14. While Moses 7 must have provided a surge of hope and excitement about building Zion, it must have been somewhat deflating as members met their own shortcomings head on as they tried to implement this order. It is likely that many questioned whether or not it was possible to ever duplicate what Enoch had done. In the midst of this the Prophet learned that men who came to God in an Enochlike way "were translated and taken up into heaven" and that Melchizedek "and his people wrought righteousness, and obtained heaven, and sought for the city of Enoch" (Joseph Smith Translation, Genesis 14:32, 34). How comforting this must have been, to know that others had attempted and succeeded in imitating that which Enoch had done. In the face of day-to-day-induced doubt, the Lord supplied the Saints with a vision of accomplishing their lofty ideal, an assurance that Enoch could be imitated, a knowledge that such a difficult task was possible.

Zion and the Second Coming

The theme of building Zion is intertwined with another motif that appears in both Moses 7 and the other revelations received around that time, and on which we can touch only lightly here. That is the theme of the signs of the times and the troubling days and events associated with the Second Coming.[59] In Enoch's vision he not only saw the horrible wickedness that happened in and just after his day but also similar events to happen just before the Second Coming. The vision clearly casts these eras in parallel, highlighting their similarities. Similarly, the Doctrine and Covenants revelations received about this same time stress the signs of the times and the need to prepare, such as in sections 29, 34, 43, and 45. The last section explicitly ties those things learned of Enoch's day to the need to establish Zion in the last days.

In Moses 7, as iniquity grew, the wicked hated and fought against the righteous, yet the righteous were protected as they gathered to Zion. The Saints learned of Enoch's causing the earth to tremble and rivers to turn from their course as Zion was defended. Zion's enemies feared them so much that while among the wicked there was great bloodshed, those same iniquitous people stood afar off from Zion, which flourished beneath the glory of the Lord during all this chaos (see Moses 7:13–17). How edifying this must have been for the Saints as they compared this comforting and inspiring story with that which the Lord told them of their own day.

The Lord Himself encouraged this comparison, telling them, "Hearken ye [to] . . . the wisdom of him whom ye say is the God of Enoch, and his brethren, who were separated from the earth, and were received unto myself—a city reserved until a day of righteousness shall come" (D&C 45:11–12). The Lord then told the Saints of terrible things that would come forth upon the earth, noting some of the most horrific of the signs of the times, such as the love of men waxing cold, earthquakes, wars in their own land, an overflowing scourge, and a desolating sickness covering the land (see D&C 45:27–33, 63). To prepare against this, the Lord urged them to gather together "and with one heart and with one mind, gather up your riches that ye may purchase an inheritance which shall hereafter be appointed unto you. And it shall be called the New Jerusalem, a land of peace, a city of refuge, a place of safety for the saints of the Most High God; and the glory of the Lord shall be there, and the terror of the Lord also shall be there, insomuch that the wicked will not come unto it, and it shall be called Zion" (D&C 45:65–67).

The Lord warned the Saints that if they did not want to be part of the fighting and wickedness, they must gather to Zion and that the wicked would be afraid to go against Zion (D&C 45:68–70). In a symbiotic circle, the vision of Enoch, his Zion, and prophecies concerning the last days must have cast light on this revelation and helped the Saints understand the relevancy of Enoch's message. Moses 7 added to both the horror and glorious comfort that the Lord propounded in section 45, and the Lord specifically used language to help the Saints feel this connection. We see again the unity of the Prophet's revelatory experiences and of God's communication with His children.

The timing and sequence of these Zion revelations were important. In September 1830 the Lord noted that Zion would be built in the borders by the Lamanites. In October He sent Oliver Cowdery and others on a mission that would open doors in Ohio and Missouri. In December the Lord gave the Prophet both the wonderful revelation concerning Enoch and the command to move to Ohio. Rising persecution necessitated that the Saints begin to move, and it seems that the Lord intended that when they did so, it would commence the gathering that was part of establishing Zion. Thus in January He commanded them to gather to Ohio and later to Missouri as well. These gatherings would require land, which would require the implementation of consecration. Both gathering and living consecration were arduous efforts, and the revelations that came about Enoch and Melchizedek must have been immensely helpful and important in this process. Again we see one revelation interlocking with another as the Lord carefully and systematically built up an understanding of Zion. He provided many custom-fitted stones to create the proper foundation for this great work.

Why would the Lord have Joseph start translating Genesis and in the middle abruptly instruct him to stop and begin translating the New Testament, as he did on March 7, 1831? (see D&C 45:60–61). Why not just have the Prophet begin translating the New Testament in the first place? There are probably many answers. It is likely that the Saints needed to know of Enoch and Melchizedek as they began gathering. The time was approaching in which the Saints *had* to move, and thus they *had* to have lands to move to. Physical necessities dictated that the gathering begin in early 1831, so before that time the Lord gave the Saints an inspiring scriptural vision of what He was going to ask them to do. The events of early 1831 were facilitated by the sequence of revelations provided during late 1830 and early 1831. In His omniscience, the Lord had instructed His servants to do that which would fortify them in their hour of need. After providing this much needed revelation, it was time for the Prophet to move on to the New Testament.

Clearly the relationship between the Doctrine and Covenants and the New Translation was more intimate than we have generally realized. The Prophet experienced this revelatory surge as a continuous, connected flow, not as separate streams that we must force together. As we see the timing of the New Translation, its interrelationship with Joseph's other revelations and with the events which became an every day reality for the early Saints, we join with Lehi in proclaiming, "Great and marvelous are thy works, O Lord God Almighty! Thy throne is high in the heavens, and thy power, and goodness, and mercy are over all the inhabitants of the earth; and, because thou art merciful, thou wilt not suffer those who come unto thee that they shall perish!" (1 Nephi 1:14). We also stand in admiration of the "overflowing surge" Joseph received during the infancy of the Church, a surge that was stronger and larger than most of us had supposed.

NOTES

1. Joseph Smith, *History of the Church of Jesus Christ of Latter-day Saints*, ed. B. H. Roberts, 2nd ed. rev. (Salt Lake City: Deseret Book, 1957), 5:362.

2. For other discussions on this, see Scott H. Faulring, Kent P. Jackson, and Robert J. Matthews, eds., *Joseph Smith's New Translation of the Bible: Original Manuscripts* (Provo, UT: Religious Studies Center, Brigham Young University, 2004); 17; and Robert J. Matthews, "The Joseph Smith Translation: A Primary Source for the Doctrine and Covenants," in *Sperry Symposium Classics: The Doctrine and Covenants*, ed. Craig K. Manscill (Provo, UT: Religious Studies Center, Brigham Young University; Salt Lake City: Deseret Book, 2004), 142–43.

3. On the relationship between OT1 and OT2, see Kent P. Jackson, *The Book of Moses and the Joseph Smith Translation Manuscripts* (Provo, UT: Religious Studies Center, Brigham Young University, 2005), 7–12.

4. For information on how these bursts may have come, see Kent P. Jackson and Peter M. Jasinski, "The Process of Inspired Translation: Two Passages Translated Twice in the Joseph Smith Translation of the Bible," *BYU Studies* 42, no. 2 (2003): 61–62.

5. Jackson, *The Book of Moses*, 12. Whitmer's copy is sometimes referred to as OT3.

6. Jackson, *The Book of Moses*, 18.

7. Smith, *History of the Church*, 1:132.

8. Neal A. Maxwell, "The Old Testament: Relevancy within Antiquity," in *A Symposium on the Old Testament* (Salt Lake City: The Church of Jesus Christ of Latter-day Saints, 1979), 9.

9. See, for example, Robert J. Matthews, "Doctrinal Connections with the Joseph Smith Translation," in *The Doctrine and Covenants, A Book of Answers, The 25th Annual Sidney B. Sperry Symposium*, ed. Leon R. Hartshorn, Dennis A. Wright, and Craig J. Ostler (Salt Lake City: Deseret Book, 1996), 27–42; Robert J. Matthews, *A Bible! A Bible!* (Salt Lake City: Bookcraft, 1990); and Robert J. Matthews, *"A Plainer Translation": Joseph Smith's Translation of the Bible: A History and Commentary* (Provo, UT: Brigham Young University Press, 1985).

10. See Faulring, Jackson, and Matthews, *Joseph Smith's New Translation*.

11. See Stephen E. Robinson and H. Dean Garrett, *A Commentary on the Doctrine and Covenants, Volume 1* (Salt Lake City: Deseret Book, 2000), 126–28, for a discussion on the timing of the reception of this section.

12. Kent P. Jackson, "New Discoveries in the Joseph Smith Translation of the Bible," *Religious Educator* 6, no. 3 (2005): 154.

13. For dates, see Robinson and Garrett, *Commentary*, 188, 195. While many sources could be cited regarding the dating of Doctrine and Covenants sections, Robinson and Garrett's work represents the most up-to-date information.

14. Robinson and Garrett, *Commentary*, 211, 214.

15. Robinson and Garrett, *Commentary*, 219.

16. Faulring, Jackson, and Matthews, *Joseph Smith's New Translation*, 86.

17. Faulring, Jackson, and Matthews, *Joseph Smith's New Translation*, 92.

18. Joseph Fielding Smith, *Church History and Modern Revelation* (Salt Lake City: The Church of Jesus Christ of Latter-day Saints, 1947), 130.

19. Joseph Smith, *History of the Church*, 1:111.

20. *Far West Record: Minutes of the Church of Jesus Christ of Latter-day Saints, 1830–1844*, ed. Donald Q. Cannon and Lyndon W. Cook (Salt Lake City: Deseret Book, 1983), 3.

21. Robinson and Garrett, *Commentary*, 195.

22. Newel Knight, "Newel Knight's Journal," in *Classic Experiences and Adventures* (Salt Lake City: Bookcraft, 1969), 65.

23. Faulring, Jackson, and Matthews, *Joseph Smith's New Translation*, 95.

24. Robinson and Garrett, *Commentary*, 223–24.

25. Faulring, Jackson, and Matthews, *Joseph Smith's New Translation*, 95–96.
26. Faulring, Jackson, and Matthews, *Joseph Smith's New Translation*, 98–101.
27. Faulring, Jackson, and Matthews, *Joseph Smith's New Translation*, 101–2.
28. Robinson and Garrett, *Commentary*, 236.
29. Kent P. Jackson and Scott H. Faulring, "Old Testament Manuscript 3: An Early Transcript of the Book of Moses," in *Mormon Historical Studies* 5, no. 2 (Fall 2004): 114–16.
30. Robinson and Garrett, *Commentary*, 250.
31. Faulring, Jackson, and Matthews, *Joseph Smith's New Translation*, 64.
32. This process continued until they had gotten through John 5, when they switched to only writing out the changes and making marks in Joseph's Bible (see Jackson, "New Discoveries," 151). For information about the Bible Joseph used, see Kent P. Jackson, "Joseph Smith's Cooperstown Bible: The Bible Used in the Joseph Smith Translation in Its Historical Context," *BYU Studies* 40, no. 1 (2001): 41–70.
33. *Times and Seasons*, January 16, 1843, 71.
34. Matthews, "JST as Primary Source," 146.
35. Matthews, "JST as Primary Source," 147–50.
36. See Steven L. Olsen, "Joseph Smith's Concept of the City of Zion," in *Joseph Smith: The Prophet, the Man*, ed. Susan Easton Black and Charles D. Tate Jr. (Provo, UT: Religious Studies Center, Brigham Young University, 1993), 204–5.
37. On how little was known from only the biblical account, see Robert L. Millet, "Enoch and His City," in *The Pearl of Great Price, Studies in Scripture, Vol. 2*, ed. Robert L. Millet and Kent P. Jackson (Salt Lake City: Deseret Book, 1985), 131. For a sample of the ideas that biblical scholars have come up with on the meaning of Zion based on the Bible alone, see Christopher R. Seitz, *Zion's Final Destiny: The Development of the Book of Isaiah, a Reassessment of Isaiah 36–39* (Minneapolis: Fortress Press, 1991); John H. Hayes, "The Tradition of Zion's Inviolability," in *The Journal of Biblical Literature* 82, no. 4 (1963): 419–23; and B. C. Ollenburger, *Zion the City of the Great King: A Theological Symbol of the Jerusalem Cult*, JSOT Supplemental Series 41 (Sheffield: JSOT Press, 1987).
38. I am grateful to Scott Esplin, Richard Bennett, and Spencer Fluhman for their valuable aid in regard to this section.
39. Craig S. Campbell, *Images of the New Jerusalem, Latter Day Saint Faction Interpretations of Independence, Missouri* (Knoxville: University of Tennessee Press, 2004), 2–4.
40. See Donald E. Pitzer, *America's Communal Utopias*, ed. Donald E. Pitzer (Chapel Hill: The University of North Carolina Press, 1997), 5–6.
41. Pitzer, *America's Communal Utopias*, 5.
42. Pitzer, *America's Communal Utopias*, 10.
43. Ruth Bloch, *Visionary Republic: Millennial Themes in American Thought, 1756–1800* (Cambridge: Cambridge University Press, 1985), 167.
44. See J. Spencer Fluhman, "Early Mormon and Shaker Visions of Sanctified Community," *BYU Studies* 44, no. 1 (2005): 85–86; and Campbell, *Images*, 11.
45. Fluhman, "Early Mormon and Shaker Visions," 97.

46. See Karl J. R. Arndt, "George Rapp's Harmony Society," in *America's Communal Utopias*, 62–66.

47. See also Lyndon W. Cook, *Joseph Smith and the Law of Consecration* (Provo, UT: Grandin Book, 1985), 1–4; and Leonard J. Arrington, Feramorz Y. Fox, and Dean L. May, *Building the City of God: Community and Cooperation Among the Mormons* (Salt Lake City: Deseret Book, 1976), 1–4.

48. See David B. Galbraith, D. Kelly Ogden, and Andrew C. Skinner, *Jerusalem, The Eternal City* (Salt Lake City: Deseret Book, 1996), 15, 41; Karen Armstrong, *Jerusalem, One City, Three Faiths* (New York: Alfred A. Knopf, 1996), 6, 27, 38.

49. Joseph Smith, *History of the Church*, 1:109–10.

50. As is assumed by Robinson and Garrett, *Commentary*, 192; and Dennis Wright, "The Hiram Page Stone: A Lesson in Church Government," in *The Doctrine and Covenants, A Book of Answers, The 25th Annual Sidney B. Sperry Symposium*, ed. Leon R. Hartshorn, Dennis A. Wright, and Craig J. Ostler (Salt Lake City: Deseret Book, 1996), 89.

51. As is assumed by Wright, "Hiram Page Stone," 89.

52. As was done by Robinson and Garrett, *Commentary*, 192.

53. See Smith, *History of the Church*, 1:207.

54. Smith, *History of the Church*, 2:517.

55. Smith, *History of the Church*, 1:132.

56. See also Steven C. Harper, "Every Man Walketh in His Own Way: Individualism, Revelation, and Authority in the Ohio Period," in *Regional Studies in Latter-day Saint Church History: Ohio and Upper Canada*, ed. Guy L. Dorius, Craig K. Manscill, and Craig J. Ostler (Provo, UT: Religious Studies Center, Brigham Young University, 2006), 39.

57. John Whitmer, *An Early Latter-day Saint History: The Book of John Whitmer, Kept by Commandment*, ed. F. Mark McKiernan and Roger D. Launius (Independence, MO: Herald Publishing House, 1980), 33–34.

58. Robinson and Garrett, *Commentary*, 254.

59. See also Keith W. Perkins, "The JST on the Second Coming of Christ," in *The Joseph Smith Translation: The Restoration of Plain and Precious Things*, ed. Monte S. Nyman and Robert L. Millet (Provo, UT: Religious Studies Center, Brigham Young University, 1985), 237–49.

4

THE JOSEPH SMITH REVELATIONS AND THE CRISIS OF EARLY AMERICAN SPIRITUALITY

J. Spencer Fluhman

Returning from his mission to western Missouri in spring 1831, Elder Parley P. Pratt found the Ohio branches of the Church boiling over with dramatic spiritual displays. He wrote that in the various Church gatherings

> Some very strange spiritual operations were manifested, which were disgusting, rather than edifying. Some persons would seem to swoon away, and make unseemly gestures, and be drawn or disfigured in their countenances. Others would fall into ecstasies, and be drawn into contortions, cramp, fits, etc. Others would seem to have visions and revelations, which were not edifying. . . . All these things were new and strange to me, and had originated in the Church during our absence, and previous to the arrival of President Joseph Smith from New York.[1]

J. Spencer Fluhman is an assistant professor of Church history and doctrine at Brigham Young University.

Elder Pratt's description of the rather raucous spirituality that developed during his absence from the infant Latter-day Saint community in northeast Ohio was vivid but by no means one of a kind. Ohio convert John Corrill told a similar tale. During that winter, he remembered many young Latter-day Saints "became very visionary."[2] John Whitmer summed up the display by describing the goings-on as "vain and foolish manoeuvers, that are unseeming, and unprofitable to mention. Thus the devil blinded the eyes of some good and honest disciples."[3] Commentators from other faiths offered even less flattering appraisals of the Saints' spiritual expressions. Writing to the *Painesville* [Ohio] *Telegraph* in February 1831, a concerned critic of the new Church blasted away at the Saints' behavior. Soon after the missionaries had converted Sidney Rigdon and most of his congregation, the critic fumed that "a scene of the wildest enthusiasm was exhibited." Members of the fledgling faith would

> fall, as without strength, roll upon the floor, and, so mad were they that even the females were seen in a cold winter day, lying under the bare canopy of heaven, with no couch or pillow but the fleecy snow. At other times they exhibited all the apish actions imaginable, making grimaces both horid and ridiculous, creeping upon their hands and feet, &c. . . . At other times they are taken with a fit of jabbering that which they neither understand themselves nor any body else, and this they call speaking foreign languages by divine inspiration. . . . They say much about working miracles, and pretend to have that power.[4]

Whether within or outside the Latter-day Saint community, witnesses agreed that something had gone awry in Ohio. Corrill's reminiscences made short work of the episode in a telling line: a revelation given after Joseph Smith's arrival in Ohio put an end to "these visionary spirits, and gave rules for judging of spirits in general. After a while these spirits were rooted out of the Church."[5]

These Ohio encounters encapsulate early Church history in significant ways. First, the boldness with which participants publicized these charismatic outbursts reminds us that the Church's first generation came of age in what one historian has called the "antebellum spiritual hothouse"—a period of unparalleled religious revival, creativity, and expressiveness.[6] Second, the Saints were even more prone than others to provoke difficult questions about religious experiences because a central theme of their message related to the paucity of spiritual gifts in contemporary Christianity and, by contrast, the necessary abundance of those very powers in what they considered a restoration of the ancient church. Third, the conflicts resulting from these experiences revealed the explosive combination of shared assumptions and differing perceptions held by biblical believers within and outside the Church; both traditional Christians and the early Saints agreed about the reality of biblical spiritual "gifts" and the real threat of spiritual deception, but they disagreed in important ways about how and when those gifts might manifest themselves. Finally, though questions persisted after 1831, the resolution of the earliest clashes over religious experiences within the Church indicates that Joseph Smith's revelations charted something of a middle way, a balance between various degrees of denying modern spiritual gifts and, on the other hand, an unrestrained cacophony that might have submerged the young Church in waves of divisive, albeit exciting, spiritual reverie.

In pressing their case for restoration, not only of doctrinal truth and lost scripture but of the apostolic church's spiritual potency, early Latter-day Saints found themselves in an extended conversation within Christendom about the applicability of spiritual gifts in a modern world. Skeptics, in fact, were most often struck by strands of Latter-day Saint religiosity that had troubled orthodox Christians for centuries. "The distinguishing feature of Mormon Faith," wrote Thomas Kirk, "is, that its devotees profess to be in possession of a certain *power of the spirit,* which places them in direct communication with God and his angels, endowing them with the gifts of revelation and prophecy, healing and tongues, &c."[7] Where some might expect the greatest opposition to the early Church to relate to distinctive doctrines, much that was levied at rank-and-file Saints in the early years thus pertained to inter-Christian wrangles over religious experience that had been fomenting for some time. In fact, skeptical preoccupation with the Saints' spirituality was so common that, after surveying early criticisms of the Church, Hugh Nibley considered spiritual gifts, along with claims to being God's chosen people, the central reason "the Mormons were formally ostracized by the churches of America."[8] So while the experiences that caused the greatest stir served to alienate early Saints from more traditional Christians, theirs seem to have been curiously *standard* forms of Christian "deviance." Because some experiences embraced by early Saints had long been considered controversial by many Christians, antagonistic Christians reassured themselves that the Saints suffered from an age-old spiritual delusion, and thus the godly could weather outbursts of religious enthusiasm now as in the past.[9] Untangling early American thinking about religious experience not only sharpens our understanding of the intellectual and religious worlds from which early Latter-day Saint converts came, but it helps clarify both the meaning and significance of the revelations that guided, and still guide, the spirituality of the Latter-day Saints.

The controversy over the Saints' religiosity was not limited to Ohio, of course. With each Latter-day Saint gathering came critiques of the Saints' vibrant spirituality. Missouri residents, for instance, first encountered the Latter-day Saints in 1831, and by 1833 they had seen enough. Meeting in July, non-Mormon residents drafted a list of grievances and demands before making their point with tar, feathers, and some rough handling of the Latter-day Saint printing press. The "gentlemen" of the county insisted that the Saints were "characterized by the profoundest ignorance, the grossest superstition, and the most abject poverty. . . . Elevated . . . little above the condition of . . . blacks," they wrote, the sect of "pretended Christians" had a corrupting influence on slaves, boasted of their imminent possession of the whole of the county, and even offered free blacks a share in their new Zion. Of the Saints' "pretended revelations from heaven—their personal intercourse with God and His angels—the maladies they pretend to heal by the laying on of hands—and the contemptible gibberish with which they habitually profane the Sabbath, and which they dignify with the appellation of unknown tongues," the Missourians had "nothing to say"—though in fact they said a great deal by listing those particular "errors," as the following pages reveal—but they warned that the growing "swarms" of Latter-day Saints would not long hence wrest civil government from civil hands.[10]

This list nicely summarizes the mantra that the Church's critics would sound throughout the nineteenth century, but what of the Saints as religionists? What of their distinctive brand of Christianity, of which the Missourians had so little to say? Taken at face value, the Missourians' report designates Latter-day Saint religiosity as a relatively minor irritant. The document is complicated, though, by the fact that several "secular" grievances seem downright disingenuous. The alleged overture to free blacks, for instance, appeared in the local Latter-day Saint paper and seemed innocuous enough to some historians to prompt hypotheses that it was perhaps deliberately exaggerated.[11] Moreover, upon hearing that some had taken offense at the warning to missionaries that Missouri state law made the "gathering" of free blacks to "Zion" problematic, the editor promptly ran an apologetic explanation.[12] And as for tampering with slavery, it is true that many Saints came to Missouri from the Northeast and brought anti-slavery sentiments with them, but, as Richard Bushman has noted, overtly abolitionist Germans in Missouri were never harassed. Furthermore, the Saints, like many Northerners, had early and often repudiated abolitionism as too drastic a solution to the slavery problem.[13] So, while some historians have rightly called attention to the real cultural divide separating the primarily New York–, New England–, or Ohio-hailing Saints and their upper-South-transplanted Missouri neighbors, others have emphasized the contradictions within opposition rhetoric and have narrated the conflict as Protestant "orthodoxy" loathing a threatening "heresy" existing within a political climate, given American ideals of religious toleration, that made attacks leveled in wholly religious terms problematic.[14]

Such problems complicate efforts to categorize hostility to the early Saints as either "religious" or "secular." Historian Kenneth Winn finds that "the Missourians displayed a relative indifference to the actual content of Mormon theology," but his point has merit only if one limits the discussion of theology to exclude religious practice.[15] If skeptical Christians sometimes exhibited little or no interest in the nuances of Latter-day Saint thought, they were likely to harbor deep misgivings about the Saints' religiosity, as with those who composed the 1833 Missouri grievances. More to the point, Americans worried over various aspects of the Saints' religious expression and were repulsed by their claims to spiritual power. The Saints, after all, gravitated towards beliefs and practices that were controversial or heretical in Protestant formulations, and, as the ubiquity of the epithets "delusion" or "enthusiasm" might suggest, some were troubling enough to prompt worries about the Saints' mental fitness. "I sincerely believe," wrote a prominent critic in a characteristic formulation, "the Mormons are in a perfect hallucination of mind."[16] As opponents emphasized the more striking elements of the Saints' religiosity or wrestled with claims of translated ancient records, angels, and miracles, they found themselves making claims about the cessation of biblical supernaturalism in modern times, the reasonableness of Christianity, and the nature of God's postbiblical influence in human lives. If one draws too stark a line between the secular and the religious in early Church history, in other words, one risks clarifying with contemporary lenses what was comfortably muddled for historical subjects themselves. Whatever political, economic, or cultural divides existed between the Saints and the skeptical, religion clearly remained in the mix.

In making sense of Latter-day Saint claims, commentators fixed the Saints on the radical end of a spectrum that had been taking discursive shape for some time before 1830. At one end was what some Protestants described as "formalism," by which most meant religious life that was largely devoid of God's Spirit and had thus devolved into lifeless form, cultural habit, or intellectual abstraction. At the other end of the gamut was "enthusiasm," a term detractors used to designate various forms of religious craziness—from those religiously "insane" to those who were in some way falsely inspired. In her delineation of the various interpretive battles over religious experience in early nineteenth-century America, Ann Taves rightly suggests that false experience proved as troubling to Anglo-American Protestants as false belief: "In contrast to sectarian and schismatic, which were linked to false ecclesiology, and heresy, which was linked to false doctrine, enthusiasm defined illegitimacy in relation to false inspiration or, more broadly, false experience. Enthusiasm, unlike schism or heresy, located that which was threatening not in challenges to ecclesiology or doctrine but in challenges to that most fundamental of Christian categories—revelation."[17]

At least as early as the English Civil War, English-speaking Christians had exchanged charges of enthusiasm and formalism, all the while contesting what constituted legitimate religious experience. By the early nineteenth century, Protestants had consecutively exercised themselves over the religiosity of the Quakers, French Prophets, Methodists, Shakers, and successive waves of revivalists; not surprisingly, earlier "enthusiasts" often served as the denunciatory model for later targets.[18] John Taylor, for instance, remembered that after hearing Parley P. Pratt preach, he was warned by concerned acquaintances with tales "about the French prophets—I was told about Matthias, Johanna Southcote, and of all the follies that had existed for centuries; and then they put 'Mormonism' at the end of them all."[19] Early American evangelicals, for their part, found that they had to walk a fine line, arguing for a more prominent place for the miraculous infusion of the Holy Spirit in the "new birth" but at the same time warding off charges of enthusiasm. Importantly, the most confirmed opponents of enthusiasm tended to be intellectual elites, and though they rarely decried religious experience generally, they tended to oppose particular practices or groups in naturalistic terms. Protestants thus found themselves employing Enlightenment strategies for discrediting enthusiasm and superstition in their sectarian contests, and eighteenth- and nineteenth-century religious polemics offer an often confused mingling of rationalistic, historical, and doctrinal arguments as a result.[20]

The most controversial elements of the early Saints' religiosity were the same ones that had figured in Anglo-American thinking about religious experience for at least the previous two centuries: speaking in tongues, angelic visitations, bodily agitations, and faith healing. Unitarian Jason Whitman astutely summed up both the Latter-day Saint message of spiritual power and the challenge it presented to Bible-believing Protestants. Writing in 1834, Whitman lamented that Mormonism was on the rise but admitted that the fact of its spreading "with some degree of rapidity . . . cannot be disputed."[21] By reviewing the contents of the Book of Mormon, he hoped to discover for his audience "the peculiarities which are calculated to give it success," and, additionally, offered to illustrate how "the course pursued by the preachers in setting forth their views" might have also abetted Mormonism's ascent. His summation of Latter-day Saint claims was sound. "They state," he wrote, "what all admit to be facts, that, in the primitive ages of the church, there was among the disciples the power of speaking with tongues and of working miracles; that, at the present day, no denomination of Christians possesses this power." Armed with claims of speaking in tongues and healing, Latter-day Saints could then reason from "these *facts,* as they call them . . . that *they* are the members of the true church of Christ." Whitman abhorred the Saints' arguments, but he conceded, given biblical precedents, that "some degree of plausibility" attended their message.[22] Opponents of Mormonism, like the Protestants who had preceded them in decrying enthusiasm, thus found themselves in a prickly interpretive situation: they felt impelled to discredit expressions on the religious "fringe" but had to do so without disgracing religious experience generally. Moreover, they, like their antienthusiast predecessors, found ready interpretive tools in Enlightenment narratives but learned they had to wield them gently so as not to touch the validity of biblical miracles or more conventional experiences with the divine.

Perhaps no aspect of the Saints' religion disturbed nonbelievers more than did speaking in tongues. The early Saints considered the gift of an "unknown" or "heavenly" tongue (glossolalia) and the miraculous ability to speak in an ordinary language the speaker had not previously known (xenoglossia) to be profound manifestations of divine power. Scholars disagree about the origins of the practice in the early Church, but it is clear that many understood it to be evidence that God was once again pouring out His spirit, this time on the new Israel. The Book of Mormon, after all, railed against those who would deny the miraculous in the last days. The following passage so neatly sums up how early Saints came to relate tongues with other spiritual phenomena, the Bible, modern Christianity, and a "restoration" of God's power, that it merits extended quotation:

> And again I speak unto you who deny the revelations of God, and say that they are done away, that there are no revelations, nor prophecies, nor gifts, nor healing, nor speaking with tongues, and the interpretation of tongues;
>
> Behold I say unto you, he that denieth these things knoweth not the gospel of Christ; yea, he has not read the scriptures; if so, he does not understand them. For do we not read that God is the same yesterday, today, and forever, and in him there is no variableness neither shadow of changing?
>
> And now, if ye have imagined up unto yourselves a god who doth vary, and in whom there is shadow of changing, then have ye imagined up unto yourselves a god who is not a God of miracles. . . .
>
> And these signs shall follow them that believe—in my name shall they cast out devils; they shall speak with new tongues. (Mormon 9:7–10, 24)

Joseph Smith remembered that Brigham Young had first introduced him to speaking in tongues in 1832 in Ohio, but the practice appears to have prevailed in Ohio before that time, perhaps even in the infant Church's first months in New York.[23] Sidney Rigdon, whose congregation made up the core of the early Mormon harvest in Ohio, had split with onetime ally Alexander Campbell in part because of a disagreement over the modern restoration of spiritual gifts, including tongues. Rigdon's congregation was thus ripe for Parley P. Pratt and the other missionaries traveling from New York, armed with the conviction according to a skeptical Ohio editor, that "'there would be as great miracles wrought'" through their preaching "'as there was at the day of Pentecost.'"[24] Indeed, the Ohio Saints experienced an outpouring of spirituality in the time before the Prophet's arrival from New York and after, and glossolalia figured prominently among the gifts. John Corrill recalled an early Ohio meeting where he first witnessed the gift:

> The meeting lasted all night, and such a meeting I never attended before. They administered the sacrament, and laid on hands, after which I heard them prophecy and speak in

tongues unknown to me. Persons in the room, who took no part with them, declared, from the knowledge they had of the Indian languages, that the tongues spoken were regular Indian dialects, which I was also informed, on inquiry, the persons who spoke had never learned. I watched closely and examined carefully, every movement of the meeting, and after exhausting all my powers to find the deception, I was obliged to acknowledge, in my own mind, that the meeting had been inspired by some supernatural agency."[25]

Corrill, though skeptical, had at least initially found in the gift what the other early Saints had found, namely, evidence of God's restoration of the apostolic church's spiritual power.

Future Church President Wilford Woodruff recalled that it was in the spring of 1832 that he had first read of the new sect "that professed the ancient gifts of the gospel they healed the sick cast out devils and spoke in tongues."[26] His statement reflects the fact that, scarcely two years into Latter-day Saint history, speaking in tongues had become a headline-grabbing curiosity.[27] The Saints' tongues probably caused them the greatest trouble in Missouri. The Missourians had "little to say" about tongues in their polished list of grievances quoted earlier, but their "secret constitution" (dubbed the "mob manifesto" by the Saints) written sometime before (probably early July 1833; the Saints discovered it by the middle of the month) provided a more candid appraisal of the Saints' spirituality. "They openly blaspheme the Most High God," Jackson County citizens wrote, "and cast contempt on His holy religion, by pretending to receive revelations direct from heaven, by pretending to speak unknown tongues, by direct inspiration, and by divers pretenses derogatory to God and religion, and to the utter subversion of human reason."[28] The violence that ensued in western Missouri that July and in the months following had myriad causes, but at least one participant reduced the trouble to the Saints' spiritual gifts. David Pettigrew had joined the Church in 1832 after reading the Book of Mormon and thereafter moved his family to Missouri. Recalling the turbulent summer and fall of 1833, he wrote that the "gift of tongues, I think was the cause, or means of the excitement." Pettigrew went on to reason that "when they heard little children speaking tongues, that they did not themselves understand," the non-Mormons became convinced the Saints were up to no good—especially once a Mr. Poole of Independence joined the Church after witnessing a display of speaking in tongues. Pettigrew recognized the Missourians' fears of being "over run" by the sheer size of the Saints' gathering, but his statement is nevertheless indicative of the deep suspicion occasioned by this aspect of the Saints' spirituality.[29]

Antagonistic appraisals of speaking in tongues differed little from standard Christian accounts of the practice in postbiblical Christian history. Hannah Adams, writing years before Mormonism, noted that the infamous French Prophets had not only exhibited "strange fits, which came upon them with tremblings and faintings" but had "trances" that provided the prophets (false) prophecies and visions of the afterlife. Moreover, she wrote, the "prophets also pretended to the gift of languages, of discerning the secrets of the heart; the power of conferring the same spirit on others, and the gift of healing by the laying on of hands." She went on to note that the Shakers had in her own time imbibed the very same extravagances.[30] (Indeed, as much as prophetic leadership, tongues provoked both curiosity about Shakerism and the polemical association of Latter-day Saints with Shakers.[31]) In 1782, Amos Taylor cautioned against the Shaker "delusion" by showing that they were "bewitched, as it were, or enchanted with the splendid shew of perfection." Taylor wrote that this beguiling display of false religious power, "truly distinguished from pure and vital religion," featured "a perpetual scene of trembling, quivering, shaking, sighing, crying, groaning, screaming, jumping, singing, dancing and turning" and a propensity to "utter forth their unknown mutter, so gibberish that a person not deluded would imagine they were a company of madmen, by whom their passions in different colours are artfully displayed; this they call the gift of new tongues."[32] Anticipating the American encounter with tongues in the Pentecostal movement of the twentieth century by three-quarters of a century, early Latter-day Saints found themselves embroiled in a controversy over glossolalia that had been ongoing in Christianity since antiquity (see, for example, 1 Corinthians 12–14).

The fact that much of the early speaking in tongues was initiated by ordinary Saints hints at its constituting a grassroots religious expression and a potential challenge to ecclesiastical order. Joseph Smith, for instance, while never invalidating the practice, tended to favor xenoglossia over glossolalia as the most useful expression of the gift. (His preference is clear, for instance, in the fact that, in his "new translation" of the Bible, the Prophet stipulated that all instances of "unknown toungue" in 1 Corinthians 14 be rendered "<and> other toungues."[33]) A revelation dated March 8, 1831, legitimized the already prevalent practice of tongues-speaking but also cautioned that spiritual phenomena, including glossolalia, could be deceptive and that Church leaders were given the power to "discern all those gifts lest there shall be any among you professing and yet be not of God" (D&C 46:27; see also vv. 24–25). Joseph Smith found himself sometimes encouraging the gift while at other times endeavoring to curtail it. In the end, the Prophet's growing awareness of the problems glossolalia posed to spiritual authenticity and priesthood authority eventually prompted firmer direction about its place in the Church. Speaking at an Ohio Church conference in 1834, the Prophet asserted that the gift "was particularly instituted for the preaching of the Gospel to other nations and languages, but it was not given for the government of the Church."[34] At a meeting of the Twelve Apostles in 1839, the Prophet added that "tongues were given for the purpose of preaching among those whose language is not understood; as on the day of Pentecost, etc., and it is not necessary for tongues to be taught to the Church particularly, for any man that has the Holy Ghost, can speak of the things of God in his own tongue as well as to speak in another."[35] At another meeting the following month, he charged Church leaders to "speak not in the gift of tongues without understanding it, or without interpretation. The devil can speak in tongues; . . . Let no one speak in tongues unless he interpret, except by the consent of the one who is placed to preside."[36] Speaking to the Nauvoo Relief Society in 1842, he advised the women: "If you have a matter to reveal, let it be in your own tongue; do not indulge too much in the exercise of the gift of tongues, or the devil will take advantage of the innocent and unwary. You may speak in tongues for your own comfort, but I lay this down for a rule, that if anything is taught by the gift of tongues, it is not to be received for doctrine."[37]

The Prophet's efforts to circumscribe glossolalia and to emphasize xenoglossia apparently succeeded; historians of the phenomenon note that though glossolalia had flourished in every previous Latter-day Saint center, little or no evidence of glossolalia can be found for the Nauvoo period.[38] As with Latter-day Saint spirituality generally, Joseph Smith's "middle way," in this case his simultaneous affirmation and circumscription of tongues-speaking, validated some individual experiences but kept expressions generally under the watchful care of the Church community and its priesthood leadership in particular.

If the Prophet displayed some ambivalence about glossolalia, the same cannot be said of his feelings about the bodily exercises that coincided with the first manifestations of tongues in Ohio. The fits, shakes, swoons, and other physical expressions that had animated American revivals before and after Mormonism's advent found their way into the Church meetings in Ohio and caused no small stir within and outside the Church. Joseph Smith, Parley P. Pratt, and other Church leaders denounced such exercises as false—generally, the Prophet supported only those manifestations for which some biblical precedent could be found—but were aware that such examples could be used by critics to discredit other spiritual gifts Church leaders deemed legitimate. Careful "filtering," then, of the false from the real became an important task of early Church teaching about spirituality. A *Times and Seasons* editorial attributed to Joseph Smith left no question as to whether or not the bodily revival expressions had any place in the Church of Jesus Christ:

> The "French Prophets," were possessed of a spirit that deceived. . . . Now God never had any prophets that acted in the is way; there was nothing indecorous in the proceeding of the Lord's prophets in any age. . . . Paul says "let every thing be done decently and in order;" but here we find the greatest disorder and indecency in the conduct of both men, and women. . . . The same rule would apply to the falling, twitchings swooning, shaking, and trances of many of our modern revivalists.[39]

Non-Latter-day Saint observers, of course, rarely made such distinctions between true and false spiritual gifts when commenting on Church practices and tended, rather, to lump them together under the heading of religious enthusiasm.

Like speaking in tongues, Latter-day Saint claims of healing by faith were notable in part because such assertions were, at least ostensibly, amenable to outside observation and evaluation—internal experiences with the Spirit, in other words, were less open to empirical verification than were the Saints' outward "signs." For their part, the Saints, ever convinced that God would heal the sick when faith was sufficient, nevertheless came to recognize that their proselytizing efforts could be severely hampered if the elders tried to answer every skeptic with an attempt to heal by faith. Some early Church preachers learned that lesson the hard way, in fact, much to the delight of skeptics. In the wake of what one critic described as a failed healing, the Saints received prophetic caution in the form of a revelation dated February 1831, in which the Lord instructed that "he that hath faith in me to be healed, and is not appointed unto death, shall be healed" (D&C 42:48).[40] Another followed in August 1831, in the aftermath of the first Ohio controversies over tongues and healing. It warned that "faith cometh not by signs" but, rather, that signs would "follow those that believe." The Lord further advised that he was "not pleased with those" who had "sought after signs and wonders for faith" (D&C 63:9, 12). These themes were underscored yet again in a revelation on priesthood issued the following year. Cautioning again that signs "follow them that believe," the revelation warned the Saints against boasting of such things and against even speaking of them "before the world" (D&C 84:65–73). The revelations, then, sounded a moderating note. The message was clear: yes, the Saints would experience miraculous infusions of God's power, but such were for their own benefit and were not intended to convince the unbelieving (see D&C 63:9–12).[41]

Antagonistic dismissal of such cautions—one skeptic sarcastically derided the Saints for keeping their miracles "all to themselves"—skirted the problem of attested spiritual manifestations.[42] An inquisitive group from neighboring Portage County, Ohio, visited Joseph Smith at Kirtland to ascertain the truth about his claims. When the conversation turned to the spiritual powers of the apostolic age, the Prophet surprised the party by approaching one of their number, Elsa Johnson, whose arm had been withered by what contemporaries assumed was chronic rheumatism, and in the name of Jesus commanded her to "be whole." Not only did she impress the group by being able to immediately lift her arm but she resumed household tasks thereafter without difficulty.[43] The event was evidence enough for Ezra Booth, a Methodist minister from Mantua, who, after his later disaffection from the Church, explained how observable evidence could as easily gather new converts as "expose" Mormonism. In justifying his earlier "beguilement," he succinctly explained that his faith in Mormonism had been "built upon the testimony of my senses."[44] In another example, Mary Ettie V. Smith recalled that her family's conversion to Mormonism resulted from the healing of her mother's deafness. Promised by a "Mormon Elder" that the Saints could "heal the sick, and . . . if she would consent to be baptized, the deafness with which she was afflicted . . . would in a very short time be removed," Smith's mother consented to baptism. The family was convinced of the Mormons' message when "immediately after" the event, "her hearing was improved, and soon, it was entirely restored." A short time later, Joseph Smith himself healed Smith's brother's leg. "With all these astonishing evidences before us," Smith concluded, "how could we doubt Mormonism?"[45] So, while most Americans remained skeptical of manifestations like those described by Smith, many witnesses felt duty bound—in part because of the very Enlightenment strategies others used to discredit spiritual phenomena—to trust "empirical" sensory evidence of Mormonism's spiritual power.

Added to the discomfort occasioned by tongues and healing was the fact that the Saints maintained more or less regular interaction with supernatural beings. Joseph Smith's first religious experiences were with Gods and angels, but less-prominent Saints too found themselves in company with beings from the unseen world.[46] Manifestations of supernatural beings struck a chord with antebellum Americans because they found biblical precedents for such visitations, yet many felt that enlightened reason demanded they toss such experiences onto the trash heap of antiquated superstition.

This tension between biblical precedent and "modern" discomfort reveals itself in the two ways Latter-day Saint visionary experiences figured in oppositional literature: on the one hand, such experiences prompted discussions of visions generally and addressed their reliability as evidence for religious claims or, acknowledging the presence of visions in the Bible, their applicability in a postbiblical context; on the other hand, they also were lumped together with belief in witches, ghosts, and the like, inferring that belief in angelic visitations was tantamount to folksy fascination with goblins and fairies. In 1829 the *Painesville Telegraph* reported that Joseph Smith claimed to have been visited by a "spirit," and editor E. D. Howe no doubt chose his words carefully.[47] Unlike Latter-day Saints, who typically preferred the word "angel," skeptics often chose words that effectively distanced such experiences as far as possible from the Bible. Similarly, the *Vermont Telegraph* reported that the Mormon prophet claimed to enjoy communication with "celestial spirits" at will.[48] Howe wrote in 1834 that the Smiths' neighbors knew them to be "ignorant and superstitious—having a firm belief in ghosts and witches."[49] E. G. Lee wrote that Martin Harris "had always been a firm believer in dreams, and visions, and supernatural appearances, such as apparitions and ghosts."[50] Howe, admittedly borrowing material from the *Palmyra* [New York] *Freeman*, also reported that Joseph Smith had seen the spirit "in a dream." Ironically, the Prophet could have saved himself considerable trouble with skeptics had he maintained that his visitations were wholly visionary, but he typically did not. Indeed, he would eventually give the Saints a way to distinguish between a heavenly angel and a dark spirit merely posing as one: shake his hand and see if you feel anything. In 1843 the Prophet explained that angels were in fact "resurrected personages" with "bodies of flesh and bones" (D&C 129:1). Methodist Tobias Spicer attended a meeting where Latter-day Saint preaching turned to angelic visitations. Spicer recalled that one speaker asserted that "many angels had appeared" to confirm "the truth of Mormonism" and that they "had heard these angels with their own ears, and seen them with their own eyes." Spicer found the assertions "strange" and considered the Mormons deceived; he wrote that he would like to smell such angels as well as see them, "to be sure they had not come from heaven by the way of hell."[51] In *Mormonism Unvailed* (1834), Howe ruminated on the relationship between belief in such fantasies as "spirits" and the spread of religious fanaticism. He wrote that one's "faculties are always improved by embracing simple philosophical truths," and, alternately, in rejecting them "we become depraved, and less capable of discriminating between falsehood and error."[52] For Spicer, Howe, and many other critics, intimate contact with supernatural beings was evidence not of blessedness but of evil or an unsound mind.

While most American Protestants saw no conflict in the twin commitments to Protestant Christianity and the march of enlightened reason, Mormonism's spiritual "extravagances" nevertheless forced tough questions to the fore. Chief among them was the question of biblical interpretation. After all, early Latter-day Saints offered proof texts for their religiosity and indeed prided themselves on the "self-evident" biblical premises on which their faith rested. This line of Latter-day Saint reasoning was both blasphemous and confounding for Protestant skeptics, and the question of the Saints' being either too biblical or not biblical enough runs through their writing. To inoculate believers against the Mormon threat, the *Gospel Messenger* advised a simple return to the Bible: "When will men learn from example & experience that all pretences to discoveries in religion, all plans for instructing men in the way to Heaven not upon the basis of the Revelation of Christ, and the model left by his Apostles, must be productive of mischief and mortification?"[53] The Carthage, Ohio, *Evangelist* agreed: "A people ignorant of the Bible are always an easy prey to the ministers of delusion and error."[54] But, as Tyler Parsons found out in a Boston debate with Latter-day Saint Freeman Nickerson, it was not exactly that simple. Parsons claimed victory in their 1841 debate before Boston's Free Discussion Society and described it in *Mormon Fanaticism Exposed,* published the same year. After hearing the opposing positions, two men in the audience came forward in defense of the Mormon argument, no doubt much to Parsons's consternation. Indeed, a "Mr. S." remarked that "it was the duty of the christians to come out in support of the Mormon faith," reasoning that the "Mormons supported all their books and dogmas." Ultimately, Mr. S. argued, "all the difference ... between them was, the Mormons believed the Bible to the very letter, while the christians believed it figurative and spiritual." Parsons's self-proclaimed vindication followed, but he concluded his narration of that particular exchange by noting that at least one of the sympathizers "intended to become a christian of the Mormon stamp."[55] Thus, what the literalist hermeneutic Mark Noll has ably described as characterizing antebellum Protestant approaches to the Bible not only colored much oppositional literature, it also made some American Protestants susceptible to the logic of Mormon religiosity, resonating as it did with what the Saints believed to be biblical patterns (prophets, revelation, spiritual gifts, and so forth), and left the Saints and their antagonists alike wondering why the other would not simply follow the Bible.[56]

The Holy Spirit was paramount among the interpretive issues prompted by early Latter-day Saint religiosity. Whereas the Saints tended to think that the Bible was a cornerstone of their spirituality, anti-Mormons charged that false spirituality had led the Mormons to do violence to biblical Christianity. The editor of the *Christian Palladium* associated the Saints with both Quakers and Shakers, asserting that each group so emphasized the Spirit that each had been led to "undervalue and discard the *Book of God.*"[57] E. D. Howe found that religious imposters had been waging their war on true religion for some time under the false banner of the Spirit:

> Here is the sure refuge, the fast hold, of every imposter. This something, which is the *Spirit,* or the *Holy Spirit,* has been the standing, unequivocal, incontrovertible and true witness for at least 24 false Messiahs, for Mahomet, who is considered the prince of impostors, and for nearly fifty others who have come with pretended comissions from Heaven. They all had, and may still have, numerous followers, whose faith was wrought and confirmed by what they supposed to be the Spirit.[58]

The popular evangelical preacher Nancy Towle concurred. After reading the Book of Mormon, she was willing to grant that Saints' attempts at "healing the sick, raising the dead, [and] casting out devils" were "according to the attainment of the primitive disciples," but she was convinced they had misconstrued the influence of the Spirit and had thus failed to attain their desired spiritual potency.[59] She related an experience at a Latter-day Saint meeting in which Joseph Smith "turned to some women and children in the room; and lay his hands upon their heads; (that they might receive the Holy Ghost;)." Eliza Marsh, one of those blessed under the hand of the Prophet, immediately turned to Towle and, according to the latter, remarked, "What blessings, you do lose!—No sooner, his hands fell upon my head; than I felt the Holy Ghost,—as *warm-water,* go over me!" Towle was disgusted with Marsh's report: "I was not such a stranger, to the spirit of God, as she imagined;—that I did not know its effects, from that of *warm-water!*" Joseph Smith, though, bore the brunt of her revulsion: "I turned to Smith, and said 'Are you not ashamed, of such pretensions? You, who are no more than any ignorant plough-boy of our land! Oh! blush at such abominations! and let shame, forever cover your face!'" The Prophet's response was characteristic: "The gift," he countered, "has returned back again, as in former times, to illiterate fishermen."[60]

Christian commentators had long sought a balance between formalistic and enthusiastic religion along a fictive spectrum that ranged from disbelief to hyperbelief, and Latter-day Saints functioned for antebellum Christians as the far end of the gamut.[61] Often placed just beyond the "enthusiasm" of the more ecstatic revivals, Mormonism ironically numbered some of its most committed opponents among the evangelicals. Indeed, Joseph Smith, by his own account, was drawn as a youth to Methodist camp-meeting piety but could never acclimate to the evangelical temperament. A German convert recorded a conversation with the Prophet in Nauvoo in which the latter detailed his early strivings for a conversion experience. He recalled a "Revival meeting" where his mother and a brother and sister "got Religion"—he "wanted to feel & shout like the Rest," but in the end "could feel nothing." A turn to the Bible prompted a secluded prayer and subsequent vision that took his religious life in a markedly different direction. The Prophet told of "a fire towards heaven" and "a personage" joined by another "person" shortly thereafter. In answer to the first question, he posed to the personages—"must I join the Methodist Church[?]"—he was told that "none . . . doeth good no not one" and that the Methodists were "not my People." The Prophet's disaffection was complete when, shortly after the vision, he "told the Methodist priest" of his experience and was answered that the modern age was not one "for God to Reveal himself in Vision" and that "Revelation [had] ceased with the New Testament."[62] Undeterred, Joseph Smith insisted on a revelation of spiritual power aimed at a religious world that both craved and feared it. Those who heard the call rejoiced—and are still rejoicing—in a new age of miracles and a restoration of the ancient church's gifts.

NOTES

1. Parley P. Pratt, ed., *Autobiography of Parley P. Pratt* (Salt Lake City: Deseret Book, 1938), 61. Original spelling and grammar retained in quoted material unless otherwise noted. The author thanks Grant Underwood and David Holland for their suggestions and support.

2. John Corrill, *A Brief History of the Church of Christ of Latter Day Saints, (Commonly Called Mormons)* (St. Louis: printed for the author, 1839), 16.

3. Bruce N. Westergren, ed., *From Historian to Dissident: The Book of John Whitmer* (Salt Lake City: Signature Books, 1995), 57.

4. M. S. C., "Mormonism," *Painesville* [Ohio] *Telegraph*, February 15, 1831, 1.

5. Corrill, *Brief History*, 17. Corrill's account, in positing an easy "resolution" of such matters, hints at the significance of Joseph Smith's revelations in the development of Latter-day Saint thinking about spirituality but also obscures the fact that questions and problems persisted after 1831.

6. See Jon Butler, *Awash in a Sea of Faith: Christianizing the American People* (Cambridge: Harvard University Press, 1992), 225.

7. Thomas J. Kirk, *The Mormons and Missouri: A General Outline of the History of the Mormons, From Their Origin to the Present, (including the late disturbance in Illinois); and a Particular Account of the Last Mormon Disturbance in Missouri, or the Mormon War: With an Appendix, Containing an Epitome of the Book of Mormon, with Remarks on the Nature and the Tendency of Mormon Faith* (Chillicothe, MO: J. H. Darlington, Printer, 1844), 62–63.

8. Hugh Nibley, *The World and the Prophets*, ed. John W. Welch, Gary P. Gillum, and Don E. Norton, 3rd ed. (Salt Lake City: Deseret Book; Provo, UT: FARMS, 1987), 295.

9. The quotation, derived from Ecclesiastes 1:9, is from M.S.C., "Mormonism," 3. "Enthusiasm" in early American usage constituted an epithet relating to alleged false inspiration.

10. As reported in the *Western Monitor* [Fayette, MO], August 2, 1833; reprinted in Joseph Smith Jr., *History of the Church of Jesus Christ of Latter-day Saints*, ed. B. H. Roberts, 2nd ed. rev., (Salt Lake City: Deseret Book, 1948), 1:395–98.

11. See, for instance, B. H. Roberts, *A Comprehensive History of the Church of Jesus Christ of Latter-day Saints* (Provo, UT: Brigham Young University Press, 1965), 1:328.

12. "Free People of Color," in Smith, *History of the Church*, 1:378; "Extra," *Evening and Morning Star* [Independence, MO], July 18, 1833; reprinted in Smith, *History of the Church*, 1:379.

13. Richard L. Bushman, "Mormon Persecution in Missouri, 1833," *BYU Studies* 3 (Autumn 1960): 11–20.

14. For characteristic examples of these two perspectives on the Mormon/anti-Mormon conflict, see Terry L. Givens, *The Viper on the Hearth: Mormons, Myths, and the Construction of Heresy* (New York: Oxford University Press, 1997); Kenneth H. Winn, *Exiles in a Land of Liberty: Mormons in America, 1830–1846* (Chapel Hill: University of North Carolina Press, 1989). Whereas Givens casts the conflict as a religious struggle, Winn narrates it as a contest between competing versions of American political republicanism.

15. Winn, *Exiles in a Land of Liberty*, 89.

16. Tyler Parsons, *Mormon Fanaticism Exposed: a Compendium of the Book of Mormon, or Joseph Smith's Golden Bible* (Boston: printed for the author, 1841), 68.

17. Ann Taves, *Fits, Trances, and Visions: Experiencing Religion and Explaining Experience From Wesley to James* (Princeton, NJ: Princeton University Press, 1999), 17–18.

18. For a discussion of the French Prophets and, especially, their influence on Shaker religiosity, see Clarke Garrett, *Spirit Possession and Popular Religion: From the Camisards to the Shakers* (Baltimore: Johns Hopkins University Press, 1987); see also David S. Lovejoy, *Religious Enthusiasm in the New World: Heresy to Revolution* (Cambridge, MA: Harvard University Press, 1985).

19. See John Taylor's 1857 sermon in *Journal of Discourses*, 26 vols. (Liverpool: F. D. and S. W. Richards, 1854–86), 5:239.

20. Taves, *Fits, Trances, and Visions*, 3–5, 15, 19. "Confused" to modern eyes, that is. Most nineteenth-century subjects saw no contradiction between Enlightenment thought and traditional Christianity (see Henry F. May, *The Enlightenment in America* [New York: Oxford University Press, 1976]).

21. Jason Whitman, "The Book of Mormon," *Unitarian* (January 1834): 45; see also pp. 40–50.

22. Whitman, "The Book of Mormon," 45–46.

23. Joseph Smith wrote: "About the 8th of November [1832] I received a visit from Elders Joseph Young, Brigham Young, and Heber C. Kimball of Mendon, Monroe county, New York. They spent four or five days at Kirtland, during which we had many interesting moments. At one of our interviews, Brother Brigham Young and John P. Greene spoke in tongues, which was the first time I had heard this gift among the brethren; others also spoke, and I received the gift myself" (*History of the Church*, 1:295–97). Brigham Young recalled the Prophet's reaction to his prayer in tongues: "As soon as we arose from our knees, the brethren flocked around him, and asked his opinion concerning the gift of tongues that was upon me. He told them it was the pure Adamic language. Some said to him they expected he would condemn the gift Brother Brigham had, but he said, 'No, it is of God.'" (Young's reminiscence was recorded in his "Manuscript History" and reprinted in Smith, *History of the Church*, 1:297.) David Whitmer recalled in 1887, long after his exit from Mormonism, that the early Saints had in New York

experienced "all the signs which Christ promised should follow the believers," including speaking in tongues. David Whitmer, *An Address to all Believers in Christ* (Richmond, MO: David Whitmer, 1887), 33. A partially crossed-out portion of Joseph Smith's effort to narrate the early history of the Church included a description of its first meeting on April 6, 1830, in Fayette, New York. In it, the Prophet wrote that "the Holy Ghost was poured out upon us all to a greater or less degree. Some prophecied, many spoke with new tongues, and some of our number were completely overpowered for a time, that we were obliged to lay them upon beds" (Dean C. Jessee, ed., *The Papers of Joseph Smith: Autobiographical and Historical Writings* [Salt Lake City: Deseret Book, 1989], 1:242–43). For early speaking in tongues, see Lee Copeland, "Speaking in Tongues in the Restoration Churches," *Dialogue: A Journal of Mormon Thought* 24, no. 1 (Spring 1991): 13–34; Dan Vogel and Scott G. Dunn, "'The Tongue of Angels': Glossolalia Among Mormonism's Founders," *Journal of Mormon History* 19, no. 2 (1993): 1–34.

24. *Painesville Telegraph*, December 14, 1830; Copeland, "Speaking in Tongues," 17.

25. Corrill, *Brief History*, 9.

26. Woodruff is quoted in Copeland, "Speaking in Tongues," 19.

27. See, as an example, "The Mormons in Trouble," *Boston Recorder*, September 11, 1833, 148.

28. Smith, *History of the Church*, 1:374–76. At precisely the same time, the Prophet expressed deep concerns about the Missouri Saints' controversial tongues-speaking. "As to the gift of tongues," the Prophet wrote, "all we can say is, that in this place [Ohio], we have received it as the ancients did: we wish you, however, to be careful lest in this you be deceived.... Satan will no doubt trouble you about the gift of tongues, unless you are careful; you cannot watch him too closely," he concluded, "nor pray too much" (Smith, *History of the Church*, 1:369).

29. David Pettigrew, "A History of David Pettigrew (n.d.)," *David Pettigrew Papers* 1840–1857, microfilm, Church History Library, The Church of Jesus Christ of Latter-day Saints, Salt Lake City, Utah, 15–17. In the end, speaking in tongues proved controversial enough that the Missouri high council, an ecclesiastical body charged with oversight of the Saints in the state, forbade the practice there for an extended period following the 1833 mobbing (see Donald Q. Cannon and Lyndon W. Cook, eds., *Far West Record: Minutes of The Church of Jesus Christ of Latter-day Saints, 1830–1844* [Salt Lake City: Deseret Book, 1983], 63; Vogel and Dunn, "'Tongue of Angels,'" 15–17).

30. Hannah Adams, *A Dictionary of All Religions and Religious Denominations, Jewish, Heathen, Mahometan, and Christian, Ancient and Modern*, 4th ed. (New York: James Eastburn and Company, 1817), 84–85, 268–69.

31. For examples, see Thomas Branagan, *A Concise View of the Principal Religious Denominations in the United States of America, Comprehending a General Account of Their Doctrines, Ceremonies, and Modes of Worship* (Philadelphia: printed by John Cline, 1811), 45; Valentine Rathbun, *An Account of the Matter, Form, and Manner of a New and Strange Religion, Taught and Propagated by a Number of Europeans, Living in a Place Called Nisqueunia, in the State of New-York* (Providence, RI: Bennett Wheeler, 1781), 4; Benjamin West,

Scriptural Cautions against Embracing a Religious Scheme, Taught by a Number of Europeans, Who came from England to America, in the Year 1776, and Stile Themselves a CHURCH, &c. &c. (Hartford, CT: Bavil Webster, 1783), 14.

32. Amos Taylor, *A Narrative of the Strange Principles, Conduct and Character of the People Known by the Name of Shakers: Whose ERRORS Have Spread in Several Parts of North-America, but Are Beginning to Diminish, and Ought to Be Guarded against* (Worcester, MA: printed for the author, 1782), 12–13.

33. Scott H. Faulring, Kent P. Jackson, and Robert J. Matthews, eds., *Joseph Smith's New Translation of the Bible: Original Manuscripts* (Provo, UT: Religious Studies Center, Brigham Young University, 2004), 507.

34. Smith, *History of the Church*, 2:162.
35. Smith, *History of the Church*, 3:379.
36. Smith, *History of the Church*, 3:392.
37. Smith, *History of the Church*, 4:607.
38. Vogel and Dunn, "'Tongue of Angels,'" 22–23.
39. *Times and Seasons*, April 1, 1842, 745.

40. For the critical appraisal of the revelation's context, see "Mormonism," *The Spirit of Practical Godliness, Devoted to the Present and Future Happiness of Mankind* 1, no. 1 (May 1832): 95–96.

41. This direction revised earlier instructions. In July 1830, elders were to "require not miracles, except I shall command you, except casting out devils, healing the sick, and against poisonous serpents, and against deadly poisons; and these things ye shall not do, except it be required of you by them who desire it, that the scriptures might be fulfilled; for ye shall do according to that which is written" (D&C 24:13–14).

42. James H. Hunt, *Mormonism: Embracing the Origin, Rise and Progress of the Sect, With an Examination of the Book of Mormon; also, Their Troubles in Missouri, and Final Expulsion from the State* (St. Louis: Ustick and Davies, 1844), 279.

43. Milton V. Backman Jr., *The Heavens Resound: A History of the Church of Jesus Christ of Latter-day Saints in Ohio, 1830–1838* (Salt Lake City: Deseret Book, 1983), 83.

44. Booth's nine letters criticizing Mormonism, sent to the *Ohio Star* between October and December 1831, were republished in Eber D. Howe, *Mormonism Unvailed: or, A Faithful Account of That Singular Imposition and Delusion, from Its Rise to the Present Time. . . .* (Painesville, OH: Howe, E. D., 1834), 175–221 (quoted material appears on page 176).

45. Some in Smith's family, including Mary herself, eventually left the Church. See Nelson W. Green, *Fifteen Years Among the Mormons; Being a Narrative of Mrs. Mary Ettie V. Smith, Late of Great Salt Lake City; a Sister of one of the Mormon High Priests, She Having Been Personally Acquainted with Most of the Mormon Leaders, and Long in the Confidence of the "Prophet" Brigham Young* (New York: C. Scribner, 1858), 19, 52.

46. For a discussion of the context of LDS visionary claims, see Richard L. Bushman, "The Visionary World of Joseph Smith," *BYU Studies* 37, no. 1 (1997–98): 183–204.

47. "'Golden Bible,'" *Painesville Telegraph*, September 22, 1829, 3.

48. "The Mormon Delusion," *Vermont Telegraph*, December 6, 1831, 44.

49. Howe, *Mormonism Unvailed*, 11.
50. E. G. Lee, *The Mormons; or, Knavery Exposed* (Philadelphia: E. G. Lee, Frankford, Pa., 1841), 8.
51. Tobias Spicer, *Autobiography of Rev. Tobias Spicer: Containing Incidents and Observations; Also Some Account of His Visit to England* (Boston: C. H. Pierce and Company, 1851), 113.
52. Howe, *Mormonism Unvailed*, 37.
53. "Mormonism," *Gospel Messenger*, June 1, 1833, 67.
54. Matilda Davison, A.C., and W. Scott, "The Mormon Bible," *Evangelist* [Carthage, OH], July 1, 1839, 160.
55. Parsons, *Mormon Fanaticism Exposed*, 55–56.
56. See Mark A. Noll, *America's God: From Jonathan Edwards to Abraham Lincoln* (New York: Oxford University Press, 2002), chapter 18. For the Saints' attachment to and uses of the Bible, see Philip Barlow, *Mormons and the Bible: The Place of the Latter-day Saints in American Religion* (New York: Oxford University Press, 1991).
57. "The Spirit," *Christian Palladium*, September 1, 1834, 148.
58. Howe, *Mormonism Unvailed*, 130–31.
59. Nancy Towle, *Vicissitudes Illustrated, In the Experience of Nancy Towle, in Europe and America* (Portsmouth, NH: printed for the authoress, by John Caldwell, 1833), 152–53.
60. Towle, *Vicissitudes Illustrated*, 156–57.
61. Interestingly, antebellum commentators cast the Saints as occupying both ends of the spectrum. For a discussion of the ways skeptics considered early Mormonism to both reflect and promote atheism, see J. Spencer Fluhman, "Anti-Mormonism and the Making of Religion in Antebellum America," (PhD dissertation, University of Wisconsin–Madison, 2006), 132–37.
62. Alexander Neibaur Journal, May 24, 1844, reprinted in Jessee, ed., *Papers of Joseph Smith*, 1:461. Joseph Smith and early Mormonism thus mirror the Revolutionary-era prophets Susan Juster describes as having both "fed on and repudiated the evangelical ethos" (Susan Juster, *Doomsayers: Anglo-American Prophecy in the Age of Revolution* [Philadelphia: University of Pennsylvania Press, 2003], 5).

5

JOHN THE BELOVED IN LATTER-DAY SCRIPTURE (D&C 7)

Frank F. Judd Jr. and Terry L. Szink

In the New Testament, there are two main persons named John. One is John the Baptist, who baptized the Savior of the world. The other man has many different titles: John the Beloved, John the Apostle, John the brother of James, John the Evangelist, and John the Revelator.

John the Beloved is a key figure in the Restoration of the gospel of Jesus Christ in the latter days and has an entire section of the Doctrine and Covenants devoted to him (see D&C 7). It is vital that Latter-day Saints understand what we know about John the Beloved from modern revelation. In this paper we will discuss the historical background of section 7, followed by possible situations giving rise to the revelation on John the Beloved, including the possibility that questions arose while translating the Book of Mormon. We will also explore the traditional

---

Frank F. Judd Jr. is an assistant professor of ancient scripture at Brigham Young University.

Terrence L. Szink is an assistant professor of ancient scripture at Brigham Young University.

date for the revelation in section 7 and a theory for another possible date of the revelation. We will then examine John's mission, the doctrine of translation, and additional light and understanding gleaned from latter-day sources. It is hoped that this paper will help Latter-day Saints appreciate the wealth of additional truth the Restoration provides about this wonderful disciple of Christ.

Historical Context of Section 7

The traditional date for the reception of the revelation in section 7 is April 1829. This is the date given in the 1833 Book of Commandments, the 1835 Doctrine and Covenants, and every subsequent edition of the Doctrine and Covenants, including the current 1981 edition.[1] In a letter written to W. W. Phelps in 1834, Oliver Cowdery explained that he arrived in Harmony, Pennsylvania, on April 5, 1829.[2] He and Joseph spent the remainder of April translating the Book of Mormon.

In his 1839 "History of Joseph Smith," the Prophet Joseph Smith stated the following about the reception of section 7: "During the month of April [1829] I continued to translate, and he [Oliver Cowdery] to write, with little cessation, during which time we received several revelations. A difference of opinion arising between us about the account of John the Apostle, mentioned in the New Testament, John, as to whether he died or continued to live, we mutually agreed to settle it by the Urim and Thummim and the following is the word which we received."[3]

Possible Situations Leading to the Discussion of John

Joseph does not explicitly state how the issue of John's mortality arose. A few scenarios could have led up to such a conversation. Perhaps the topic spontaneously came up during one of what must have been many heartfelt discussions between Joseph and Oliver. We know that the issue of what happened to John was a popular subject of debate in the early nineteenth century.[4]

Another possibility is that Joseph and Oliver were reading John 21, which prompted the discussion about John. In a slightly ambiguous conversation between the resurrected Savior and His chief Apostle,

Jesus explained that Peter would eventually be martyred for his testimony of Christ (see John 21:18–19). Peter then asked, referring to John, "What shall this man do?" (John 21:21). The Savior responded with a question, "If I will that he tarry till I come, what is that to thee?" (John 21:22). The next verse shows that there was confusion about the precise fate of John from the very beginning: "Then went this saying abroad among the brethren, that that disciple should not die: yet Jesus said not unto him, He shall not die; but, If I will that he tarry till I come, what is that to thee?" (John 21:23). The reading of this account may have been the catalyst for the reception of section 7.

Yet because Joseph and Oliver were so busy translating the Book of Mormon during this period, it is unlikely that they had time to peruse the Bible in April 1829. The Lord stated in March 1829 that He had given the Prophet "a gift to translate the plates" and further instructed Joseph, "You should pretend to no other gift until my purpose is fulfilled in this; for I will grant unto you no other gift until it is finished" (D&C 5:4).

Another theory is that a discussion of John's fate was sparked by the translation of the Book of Mormon, as were a number of other sections in the Doctrine and Covenants. For example, section 6 grants Oliver Cowdery permission to translate, rather than just act as scribe for Joseph (see D&C 6:25–27). Section 8 gives him instructions on how to translate (see D&C 8:1–2). Section 9 consoles Oliver after his unsuccessful attempt at translating the Book of Mormon (see D&C 9:1–10). All three sections are directly related to the early translation period of the Book of Mormon.[5] Except for a brief trip to Colesville for provisions, Joseph and Oliver spent virtually all their time translating the plates.[6] Their urgent focus on translation opens up the possibility for this third theory.

Robert J. Matthews said that "many of the revelations that comprise the Doctrine and Covenants have a direct relationship to the translation of the Bible which the Prophet Joseph was making at the time the revelations were received."[7] Dr. Matthews was referring to the Prophet's work on the Joseph Smith Translation, but the principle could also apply to his translation of the Book of Mormon.

In another instance of revelation prompted by translation, the question of Joseph and Oliver concerning baptism—which resulted in the restoration of the Aaronic Priesthood at the hands of John the Baptist—was sparked by the translation of the plates. Concerning this, the Prophet stated, "We still continued the work of translation, when, in the ensuing month (May, 1829), we on a certain day went into the woods to pray and inquire of the Lord respecting baptism for the remission of sins, that we found mentioned in the translation of the plates" (Joseph Smith—History 1:68). In addition, John W. Welch has shown that the manifestation of the Three Witnesses in June 1829 was likely "prompted by the translation of 2 Nephi 27:12," which mentions that Three Witnesses would behold the plates.[8] Based on this model, it is possible that section 7 may have been revealed because of questions that arose while translating the Book of Mormon.

Book of Mormon Translation as Catalyst

If section 7 was indeed prompted by translation, what passages in the Book of Mormon might have functioned as catalysts for questions relating to the fate of John the Beloved? One such passage might be Alma 45:18–19, which states:

> And when Alma had done this he departed out of the land of Zarahemla, as if to go into the land of Melek. And it came to pass that he was never heard of more; as to his death or burial we know not of.
> Behold, this we know, that he was a righteous man; and the saying went abroad in the church that he was taken up by the Spirit, or buried by the hand of the Lord, even as Moses. But behold, the scriptures saith the Lord took Moses unto himself; and we suppose that he has also received Alma in the spirit, unto himself; therefore, for this cause we know nothing concerning his death and burial.

While it does not specifically mention John, this account may have reminded Joseph and Oliver of the Beloved Disciple. The phrase, "the saying went abroad in the church that he was taken up by the Spirit," is similar to a phrase in John 21:23 concerning the fate of John: "Then went this saying abroad among the brethren, that that disciple should not die." It is therefore possible that the translation of Alma 45:18–19 served as a springboard into a discussion about what happened to John.

Another possible candidate from the Book of Mormon is 3 Nephi 28, where the resurrected Savior asks the Nephite disciples, "What is it that ye desire of me?" (v. 1). Nine of the twelve desired to return to be with the Lord at the end of their lives (see 3 Nephi 28:2). Jesus discerned the desire of the remaining three: "Behold, I know your thoughts, and ye have desired the thing which John, my beloved, who was with me in my ministry, before that I was lifted up by the Jews, desired of me" (3 Nephi 28:6). Jesus then explained that they would not die but would remain on the earth until His return (see 3 Nephi 28:7–8). One can see how translation of this chapter could lead to questions about the fate of John.

Some Latter-day Saint scholars have pointed out similarities between 3 Nephi 28 and section 7 but have not posited an explicit causal connection.[9] This possibility merits exploration.[10] In 3 Nephi 28, nine of the twelve Nephite disciples, like Peter the chief Apostle in section 7, desired to immediately return to the Savior at the conclusion of their mortal lives.[11] They were all told that their desire was a good one.[12] John and the Three Nephites were asked what they desired, and they all wanted to continue to live on earth so they might continue to preach the gospel, which desire was subsequently granted unto them.[13] Although there are differences—for example, the Savior spiritually discerned the desire of the Three Nephites, and John verbally declared his desire[14]—the similarities are striking.

Close parallels in the language of 3 Nephi 28 and section 7 are noteworthy. Nine of the Nephite disciples expressed their desire "that we may *speedily come unto thee in thy kingdom*" (3 Nephi 28:2; emphasis added). Likewise, the Lord explained to Peter, "Thou desiredst that thou mightest *speedily come unto me in my kingdom*" (D&C 7:4; emphasis added). There are no other places in the standard works that employ this phraseology.

Furthermore, when the resurrected Lord spoke to the Three Nephites, He declared: "Ye shall live to behold all the doings of the Father unto the children of men, even until all things shall be fulfilled according to the will of the Father, when *I shall come in my glory* with the powers of heaven. And ye shall never endure the pains of death; but when *I shall come in my glory* ye shall be changed in the twinkling of an eye from mortality to immortality" (3 Nephi 28:7–8; emphasis added). When the Savior responded to John's desire, He said: "Because thou desirest this thou shalt tarry until *I come in my glory*" (D&C 7:3; emphasis added). Significantly, the phrase "come in my glory" appears in these two passages and twice in section 45, but nowhere else in scripture (see D&C 45:16, 56).

What is the significance of these parallels between 3 Nephi 28 and section 7? It is likely that the Savior simply used the same phraseology when speaking to the Nephite disciples and also the Apostles Peter and John. But it is also possible that these similarities may suggest more. Speaking of analogous parallels between 3 Nephi 9–21 and section 10, Max Parkin concluded, "This similarity does not claim literary dependency, but rather concurrent rendering."[15] In other words, the similarities may indicate both were received during the same time period. These similarities in phraseology open up the possibilities that the discussion of the fate of John was triggered by the translation of 3 Nephi 28 and, further, that when the Lord revealed section 7 to Joseph Smith, the revelation reflected familiar language from the catalyst.

Another Possible Date for Section 7

The theory that 3 Nephi 28 may have been the catalyst for the reception of section 7 suggests we reexamine the traditionally accepted date for that revelation. As stated above, Joseph Smith said that he received section 7 in April 1829.[16] It must be remembered, however, that Joseph Smith's history was dictated to James Mulholland one decade later.[17] There are difficulties in precisely dating events from this time period, including the reception of section 10 and the restoration of the Melchizedek Priesthood.[18]

Further, we must consider whether Joseph Smith would likely have been translating 3 Nephi 28 by the end of April, if he began on April 7. It is well known that after the Prophet translated 116 pages of manuscript with Martin Harris in 1828, he allowed the manuscript pages to leave his possession, and they were lost (see D&C 10:1–3). It is not as well known, however, that when Joseph Smith received permission to recommence translation, he likely continued in the translation from the point where he had ended with the lost manuscript. In other words, Mosiah 1 was probably translated first, not 1 Nephi 1.[19] The Lord subsequently instructed Joseph: "You shall translate the engravings which are on the [small] plates of Nephi, down even till you come to the reign of king Benjamin, or until you come to that which you have translated, which you have retained [not lost]" (D&C 10:41).[20]

The Prophet Joseph made little progress in translation between the return of the Urim and Thummim on September 22, 1828, and the arrival of Oliver Cowdery on April 5, 1829.[21] Once Oliver arrived, however, they resumed translating—probably somewhere near the beginning of the book of Mosiah. To get a sense of the speed of translation this would have required, the beginning of the book of Mosiah through the end of 3 Nephi takes up 360 pages in the 1830 edition of the Book of Mormon. In order to finish translating that material by the end of April, Joseph and Oliver would have had to translate the equivalent of about fifteen pages per day.

A statement by Oliver Cowdery, however, could have bearing on the dating of the translation of 3 Nephi 28 and the possibility of this theory. Oliver stated that he and Joseph completed the translation "of the Savior's ministry to the remnant of the seed of Jacob, upon this continent . . . not long" before the time of the restoration of the Aaronic Priesthood, which was not until May 15, 1829.[22] The ambiguity of the phrase "not long" opens the possibility that the translation of 3 Nephi was completed during the first half of May—still with miraculous speed but at a more moderate rate of translation, between nine and ten pages per day.

The traditional understanding of the origin of section 7 suggests that the question concerning the fate of John arose in April—either independently of the translation of the Book of Mormon or possibly as a response to translating Alma 45:18–19. If, on the other hand, the discussion of what happened to John was prompted by the translation of 3 Nephi 28, it is possible that the date for section 7 might be the first half of May 1829, rather than April.

The Text of Section 7

Doctrine and Covenants 7 is one of seven sections received by means of the Urim and Thummim (see D&C 3; 6; 7; 11; 14; 15; 16). After the 116 pages of manuscript were lost in June 1828, the Lord took away the plates as well as the Urim and Thummim from Joseph Smith. A few months later, the Lord restored Joseph's gift and authorized him to resume translation (see D&C 10:1–3). At some point after Oliver Cowdery began assisting the Prophet in early April 1829, they were discussing the fate of John the Beloved and sought understanding through the Urim and Thummim.[23]

The heading to this revelation in the 1833 Book of Commandments states that it was "translated from parchment, written and hid up by himself [John]."[24] There is no further information available about this parchment. Lyndon W. Cook surmised, "The parchment would not have been in the Prophet's possession, rather, it would have been seen and translated by means of the Urim and Thummim."[25] Presumably Joseph used the Urim and Thummim to translate the parchment similar to the way that he used it to translate the gold plates.

Two versions of this revelation exist. The original, shorter version was published in the 1833 Book of Commandments. An expanded version was published in the 1835 Doctrine and Covenants.[26] The current 1981 edition of the Doctrine and Covenants follows the 1835 expanded version, with slight alteration to the numbering of the verses. Both versions contain the same basic information: the Savior asks John what he wants; John expresses his desire to bring souls unto Christ; the Savior informs John that he will remain on earth until the Second Coming. Much of what was added in 1835 is a more detailed elaboration of these basic concepts, especially concerning the specifics of John's future mission as a translated being.

For example, the original edition declares that John would "tarry until I come in my glory" while the current version adds "and shalt prophesy before nations, kindreds, tongues and people" (D&C 7:3). In addition, the shorter version simply states to Peter that John "has undertaken a greater work," but the expanded edition illustrates in greater detail what that mission would entail: "I will make him as flaming fire and a ministering angel; he shall minister for those who shall be heirs of salvation who dwell on the earth" (D&C 7:6).[27]

How does one account for this additional information? Concerning this, Stephen E. Robinson and H. Dean Garrett concluded: "Verses 6–7 were added to the text of section 7 in the 1835 edition of the Doctrine and Covenants under the supervision of the Prophet Joseph Smith, and the wording of other verses was revised at that time by the Prophet. Because Joseph worked on the Joseph Smith Translation after section 7 was received, it may be that he obtained additional insights on John 21:20–23 from that labor, which he then added to this revelation in the 1835 edition."[28]

Although the Joseph Smith Translation does not change the text of John 21:20–23, it is interesting to note that while work on the Joseph Smith Translation led Joseph Smith to receive further inspiration, that revealed information was not always included in the translation but sometimes in the Doctrine and Covenants.[29] For instance, while the Prophet and Sidney Rigdon were working on the Joseph Smith Translation, Joseph read John 5:29 and they began to wonder about the resurrections of the just and the unjust (see D&C 76:15–18). As a result they received the wonderful revelation contained in section 76 (see D&C 76:19). The information received in section 76 is not reflected in the Joseph Smith Translation, but the study of John 5 led to additional revelation on the subject. Regardless of the exact source for the additional information in the expanded version, however, the current edition of section 7 contains valuable insights that illuminate our understanding of John's mission.

Past Perspectives on the Fate of John

Without the additional truth that modern revelation supplies, the information contained in John 21:20–23 is ambiguous enough to have fostered a great deal of confusion concerning the fate of John the Beloved. It is important to note that there is evidence of scribal editing in our current edition of the Gospel of John.[30] Some editorial comments seem to have made their way into the text itself. For instance, following the Savior's declaration that John would "tarry till I come" (John 21:22), the narrative continues: "Then went this saying abroad among the brethren, that that disciple should not die: yet Jesus said not unto him, He shall not die; but, If I will that he tarry till I come, what is that to thee?" (v. 23). Taken at face value, the second part of this statement seems to discount the idea of John's being translated. Those words likely reflect an editor's view of the speculation about John.[31]

Whether those particular words are to be attributed to John or an editor, they have been a key factor in the traditional interpretation of the Savior's statement over the past two millennia; namely, it may have sounded like Jesus said John would not die, but He did not really say that John would not die. The Christian leader Papias, who probably lived sometime between A.D. 60 and 130, is reported to have said that John and his brother James were both killed by Jews.[32] Tertullian, an early Christian theologian from around A.D. 200, taught that "John underwent death, although concerning him there had prevailed an ungrounded expectation that he would remain alive until the coming of the Lord."[33] This same conclusion was common among other early Christian writers down to the fifth century.[34]

Furthermore, interest in the fate of John was alive and well in the days of Joseph Smith. For example, Adam Clarke, a scholar who published a comprehensive commentary on the Bible at the beginning of the nineteenth century, stated: "Some have concluded from these words [in John 21:22] that John should *never die*. Many eminent men, *ancients* and *moderns,* have been and are of this opinion. . . . For nearly eighteen hundred years, the greatest men in the world have been puzzled with this passage. It would appear intolerable in me to attempt to *decide,* where so many eminent doctors have disagreed, and do still disagree."[35]

With Joseph's and Oliver's interest in religion, they had likely already been exposed to this debate. Hence, when the topic came up again—either spontaneously or as a result of translating the Book of Mormon—they naturally wanted to know what had happened to John.

The Doctrine of Translation

Latter-day scripture not only confirms that John did not die but also provides valuable information about translated beings. During His mortal ministry, the Savior declared to His Apostles, "There be some standing here, which shall not taste of death, till they see the Son of man coming in his kingdom" (Matthew 16:28; see also Mark 9:1; Luke 9:27). John apparently desired to fulfill this prophecy. According to the translated parchment, John asked the Savior for "power over death" so that he might "live and bring souls unto thee" (D&C 7:2). The Lord responded by confirming to John that he would "tarry until I come in my glory" (D&C 7:3)—in other words, he would be translated. Use of the English word *translated* to describe someone who was taken to heaven without tasting death can be traced all the way back to the first English version of the Bible by John Wycliffe in the year 1380.[36] The King James Version of the Bible describes Enoch in the following way: "By faith Enoch was *translated* that he should not see death; and was not found, because God had *translated* him: for before his *translation* he had this testimony, that he pleased God" (Hebrews 11:5; emphasis added).

What does it mean to be translated? The Greek verb used in Hebrews 11:5 is *metatithemi* and can mean "to effect a change in state or condition" as well as "to convey from one place to another."[37] Because of its association with the biblical story of Enoch, by the time of the Prophet Joseph Smith the word *translated* was understood not only to mean "conveyed from one place to another" but specifically "removed to heaven without dying."[38] It is noteworthy that when discussing the doctrine of translation, latter-day scripture includes important information concerning changes to the condition of an individual's body (see 3 Nephi 28:7, 37–38).

Although the Book of Mormon does not provide details about John's translation, the resurrected Savior's words to the Three Nephites link their translation to that of John, declaring that they "desired the thing which John, my beloved, who was with me in my ministry, before that I was lifted up by the Jews, desired of me" (3 Nephi 28:6). Thus, the information we learn about the translation of the Three Nephites illuminates us about the translation of John as well. In other words, 3 Nephi 28 is essentially a commentary on Doctrine and Covenants 7 (and John 21:21–23).[39]

John requested "power over death" (D&C 7:2) and was promised by the Savior that he would "tarry until I come in my glory" (D&C 7:3). The Savior taught in more detail to the Three Nephites: "Ye shall never taste of death; but ye shall live to behold all the doings of the Father unto the children of men, even until all things shall be fulfilled according to the will of the Father, when I shall come in my glory with the powers of heaven" (3 Nephi 28:7). Further, the editor Mormon explained, "That they might not taste of death there was a change wrought upon their bodies" (3 Nephi 28:38).

What kind of change? Mormon continued, "This change was not equal to that which shall take place at the last day; but there was a change wrought upon them" so that "they were sanctified in the flesh, that they were holy" (3 Nephi 28:39). Translated beings are not celestial or resurrected, but they are immortal. The Prophet Joseph Smith taught that the bodies of translated individuals are changed from their mortal or telestial state to an immortal or terrestrial state.[40]

The Three Nephites were further told that they would "not have pain" while they continued to live, nor would they have "sorrow save it be for the sins of the world" (3 Nephi 28:9; see also v. 39). When comparing the glory and peace associated with the Resurrection with that of translation, Joseph Smith explained, "Translation obtains deliverance from the tortures and sufferings of the body, but their existence will prolong as to the labors and toils of the ministry, before they can enter into so great a rest and glory."[41] This change also made it possible that "Satan could have no power over them, that he could not tempt them" (3 Nephi 28:39). Translated beings are perfectly suited to devote themselves to the service of the Lord: they have power over death, they cannot be harmed physically, and they are immune to the temptations of the devil.

The Mission of Translated Beings

The primary mission of translated beings is sharing the gospel. John's request included the desire to "live and bring souls unto [Christ]" (D&C 7:2). The Savior promised John that he would "prophesy before nations, kindreds, tongues and people" (D&C 7:3) and then explained to Peter that John would "minister for those who shall be heirs of salvation who dwell on the earth" (D&C 7:6).

The missionary experiences of the Three Nephites may provide a glimpse into the experiences of John the Beloved. As they went forth to preach the gospel, the Three Nephites baptized those who "would believe in their preaching" (3 Nephi 28:18). They encountered opposition and dangerous situations—such as prisons, pits, furnaces, or dens of wild beasts—but they were always delivered in a miraculous manner (see 3 Nephi 28:18–22). In addition, the Three Nephites prayed unto the Father and received power to "show themselves unto whatsoever man it seemeth them good" (3 Nephi 28:30) so that they were able to "preach the gospel of Christ unto all people upon the face of the land" (3 Nephi 28:23). The prophet Mormon explained that the Three Nephites would minister among the Jews and the Gentiles (see 3 Nephi 28:27–28). We know that John was given a mandate to "prophesy before nations, kindreds, tongues and people" (D&C 7:3) as he continued to "minister for those who shall be heirs of salvation who dwell on the earth" (D&C 7:6). Perhaps John the Beloved was also given special protection from harm and divine power as he went forth "as flaming fire and a ministering angel" (D&C 7:6).[42]

The Lord explained that John the Beloved would continue his ministry until the Second Coming (see D&C 7:3). At the time of the Savior's triumphant return, translated beings will "receive a greater change" (3 Nephi 28:40; see also v. 39), namely instantaneous resurrection. The Savior instructed the Three Nephites that when He would return in His glory, they would be "changed in the twinkling of an eye from mortality to immortality" (3 Nephi 28:8). At that point they would "be received into the kingdom of the Father to go no more out, but to dwell with God eternally in the heavens" (3 Nephi 28:40), and there they would experience a "fulness of joy" (3 Nephi 28:10).

John in the Latter Days

In the latter days, we have greater revealed knowledge about John the Beloved, yet verifiable eyewitness accounts are extremely limited.[43] There is an important reason for this. Concerning the translated Three Nephites, the prophet Mormon explained that as they preached the gospel, the Jews and the Gentiles "shall know them not" (3 Nephi 28:27–28). The fact that the Three Nephites appeared to the prophet Mormon as well as to his son Moroni illustrates that translated beings "can show themselves unto whatsoever man it seemeth them good" (3 Nephi 28:30), especially to the prophets (see 3 Nephi 28:24–26;

Mormon 8:10–11). But the implication of 3 Nephi 28:27–28 remains that translated individuals will not normally be recognized by the general populace.

We know that the chief Apostles of the ancient church—the translated John, together with the resurrected Peter and James—appeared to the Prophet Joseph Smith in the spring of 1829 to restore the Melchizedek Priesthood.[44] The Lord declared to the Prophet Joseph: "Peter, and James, and John, whom I have sent unto you, by whom I have ordained you and confirmed you to be apostles, and especial witnesses of my name, and bear the keys of your ministry and of the same things which I revealed unto them" (D&C 27:12; see also D&C 128:20).

In June 1831, Church historian John Whitmer recorded the following: "The spirit of the Lord fell upon Joseph [Smith] in an unusual manner. And prophesied that John the Revelator was then among the ten tribes of Israel."[45] Oliver B. Huntington, an early Latter-day Saint, later reported that Joseph met with John the Beloved in 1834 during the march of Zion's Camp and that the Prophet stated that John was on his way to visit the ten tribes of Israel.[46] After ordinances had been performed in the Kirtland Temple in 1836, Elder Heber C. Kimball reported that "the beloved disciple John was seen in our midst by the Prophet Joseph, Oliver Cowdery, and others."[47]

If one desires to actually pinpoint the location of John the Revelator, these statements are actually less helpful than they may seem. The Book of Mormon clearly teaches that the ten tribes of Israel are scattered all over the world: "The house of Israel, sooner or later, will be scattered upon all the face of the earth, and also among all nations . . . and whither they are none of us knoweth, save that we know that they have been led away" (1 Nephi 22:3–4).[48]

Conclusion

John had the sacred honor of being known as "the disciple whom Jesus loved" (see John 13:23; 20:2; 21:7, 20). He was devoted to his Master, Jesus Christ, and desired to serve Him. So strong was John's desire and so great was his commitment that he did not want to cease bringing souls unto Christ. John received a special commission according to his desire and continues to bless countless lives as the message of the gospel of Jesus Christ floods the earth. The Melchizedek Priesthood that he helped restore brings with it the authority to act in the name of God. As we have demonstrated, the Restoration of the gospel in the latter days has provided us with crucial information about the mission of John, which confirms his translation, describes his authority, and documents his continuing involvement in preparing for the Savior's glorious return.

Although we may not receive the same specific call as John, we can still follow his example in our lives. The Lord has invited all of us, "If ye have desires to serve God ye are called to the work" (D&C 4:3). If we respond to the call to lose ourselves in the Lord's work, we have been promised, "How great will be your joy if you should bring many souls unto me!" (D&C 18:16). Every Latter-day Saint has the opportunity to follow John's example of love, discipleship, and missionary work.

NOTES

1. Robert J. Woodford, "The Historical Development of the Doctrine and Covenants," 3 vols. (PhD diss., Brigham Young University, 1974), 1:179.

2. Oliver Cowdery to W. W. Phelps, *Messenger and Advocate*, October 1834, 14.

3. Joseph Smith, *History of the Church of Jesus Christ of Latter-day Saints* (Salt Lake City: Deseret Book, 1955), 1:35–36. For a transcript of the original document, see *The Papers of Joseph Smith*, ed. Dean C. Jessee (Salt Lake City: Deseret Book, 1989), 1:289.

4. For example, see Adam Clarke, *The New Testament of our Lord and Savior Jesus Christ*, vol. 5, *Matthew to the Acts* (Nashville, TN: Abingdon, 1977), 663. This commentary was originally published in the early nineteenth century.

5. For a detailed chronology, see John W. Welch, "The Miraculous Translation of the Book of Mormon," in *Opening the Heavens: Accounts of Divine Manifestations 1820–1844*, ed. by John W. Welch and Erick B. Carlson (Salt Lake City: Deseret Book, 2005), 90–93.

6. Welch, "The Miraculous Translation of the Book of Mormon," 92.

7. Robert J. Matthews, *"A Plainer Translation," Joseph Smith's Translation of the Bible: A History and Commentary* (Provo, UT: Brigham Young University Press, 1975), 255–56.

8. Welch, "The Miraculous Translation of the Book of Mormon," 97. It is also possible that the translation of Ether 5:2–4 prompted the manifestation to the Three Witnesses, but Professor Welch persuasively argues that the translation of 2 Nephi 27 is the more likely scenario (Welch, "The Miraculous Translation of

the Book of Mormon," 113). Because of the similarity of language between 3 Nephi and D&C 10, Max H. Parkin has shown how D&C 10 could possibly be dated to the time of the translation of 3 Nephi (Max H. Parkin, "A Preliminary Analysis of the Dating of Section 10," *The Seventh Annual Sidney B. Sperry Symposium: The Doctrine and Covenants* [Provo, UT: Brigham Young University Press, 1979], 82–83).

9. Keith H. Meservy, "New Testament Items in the Doctrine and Covenants," in *Studies in Scripture, vol. 1: The Doctrine and Covenants*, ed. Robert L. Millet and Kent P. Jackson (Salt Lake City: Randall Book, 1985), 266–68; Jonn D. Claybaugh, "As Flaming Fire and a Ministering Angel," *Ensign*, October 1999, 56.

10. The only other Book of Mormon references to John discuss his role as the author of the New Testament book of Revelation and do not mention his desire or his fate (see 1 Nephi 14:19–27; Ether 4:16).

11. Compare 3 Nephi 28:2 with D&C 7:4.

12. Compare 3 Nephi 28:3 with D&C 7:5.

13. Compare 3 Nephi 28:4–7 with D&C 7:1–3.

14. Compare 3 Nephi 28:6 with D&C 7:2.

15. Parkin, "A Preliminary Analysis of the Dating of Section 10," 82.

16. Smith, *History of the Church*, 1:35–36.

17. There are other instances where the Prophet misstated a precise date many years after the fact. For example, when Joseph recounted his First Vision, his 1832 account has "in the 16th year of my age" while the 1835 account has "I was about 14 years old" (see Milton V. Backman Jr., *Joseph Smith's First Vision: Confirming Evidences and Contemporary Accounts*, 2nd ed. [Salt Lake City: Bookcraft, 1980], 157, 159).

18. On the dating of D&C 10, see Parkin, "A Preliminary Analysis of the Dating of Section 10," 68–84; Lyndon W. Cook, *The Revelations of the Prophet Joseph Smith* (Salt Lake City: Deseret Book, 1985), 122–23. On the dating of the restoration of the Melchizedek Priesthood, see Larry C. Porter, "The Restoration of the Aaronic and Melchizedek Priesthoods," *Ensign*, December 1996, 30–47.

19. For evidence of the "Mosiah-first" theory, see Welch, "The Miraculous Translation of the Book of Mormon," 115–17; Richard L. Bushman, *Joseph Smith: Rough Stone Rolling* (New York: Alfred Knopf, 2005), 579–80n63.

20. Assigning a date to D&C 10 is very complicated. Some Latter-day Saint scholars propose that "the revelation was given in 1828 and that some additions were made in 1829" (Joseph Fielding McConkie and Craig J. Ostler, *Revelations of the Restoration* [Salt Lake City: Deseret Book, 2000], 101). On the evidence for the various dates proposed for the reception of D&C 10, see Parkin, "A Preliminary Analysis of the Dating of Section 10," 68–84. Regardless of the precise date, the revelation still implies that after he lost the 116 manuscript pages, Joseph eventually resumed translating at Mosiah 1, rather than at 1 Nephi 1.

21. Welch, "The Miraculous Translation of the Book of Mormon," 88–90.

22. Oliver Cowdery to W. W. Phelps, *Messenger and Advocate*, October 1834, 15; see also a portion of this letter appended to the end of Joseph Smith—History in the Pearl of Great Price.

23. Smith, *History of the Church*, 1:35; emphasis added.

24. Robert J. Woodford mistakenly stated that "the earliest account that indicates this revelation was a translation of an ancient parchment" was the version published in the *Times and Seasons* on July 15, 1842 (Woodford, "The Historical Development of the Doctrine and Covenants," 1:176, 179).

25. Cook, *The Revelations of the Prophet Joseph Smith*, 15; see also H. Michael Marquardt, *The Joseph Smith Revelations: Text and Commentary* (Salt Lake City: Signature Books, 1999), 33.

26. An additional 111 words were added to the revelation in the 1835 expanded version. For a comparison of the two versions, see Marquardt, *The Joseph Smith Revelations*, 33–35.

27. Immediately following this, the current edition also adds: "And I will make thee to minister for him and for thy brother James; and unto you three I will give this power and the keys of this ministry until I come" (D&C 7:7). Although the previous verse was addressing Peter, this verse seems to be addressing John again because it mentions "thy brother James."

28. Stephen E. Robinson and H. Dean Garrett, *A Commentary on the Doctrine and Covenants*, 4 vols. (Salt Lake City: Deseret Book, 2000–2005), 1:59. It should be noted, however, that the Joseph Smith Translation does not make any changes to the text of John 21:20–23. For the Joseph Smith Translation of the New Testament, see Thomas A. Wayment, *The Complete Joseph Smith Translation of the New Testament* (Salt Lake City: Deseret Book, 2005).

29. Matthews, "A Plainer Translation," 255–56.

30. For a study of the work of editors in the Gospels, see Frank F. Judd Jr., "Who Really Wrote the Gospels? A Study of Traditional Authorship," in *How the New Testament Came to Be*, ed. Kent P. Jackson and Frank F. Judd Jr. (Salt Lake City: Deseret Book, 2006), 123–40.

31. C. K. Barrett, *The Gospel According to St. John*, 2nd ed. (Philadelphia: Westminster Press, 1978), 587; George R. Beasley-Murray, *John*, 2nd ed. (Waco, TX: Word Books, 1999), 412.

32. Bart D. Ehrman, trans., *The Apostolic Fathers*, 2 vols. (Cambridge, MA: Harvard University Press, 2003), 2:112–13.

33. Tertullian, *An.* 50. English translation is from Alexander Roberts and James Donaldson, eds., *Ante-Nicene Fathers*, 10 vols. (Peabody, MA: Hendrickson, 1994), 3:228.

34. This includes Clement of Alexandria, Irenaeus, the apocryphal *Acts of John*, Ambrose, Theodore of Mopsuestia, and Augustine. For references, see Joel C. Elowsky, ed., *John 11–21* (Downers Grove, IL: InterVarsity Press, 2007), 393–95; Wilhelm Schneemelcher, *New Testament Apocrypha*, rev. ed. (Louisville, KY: Westminster John Knox Press, 1992), 2:23.

35. Adam Clarke, *The New Testament of Our Lord and Savior Jesus Christ*, 5:663; emphasis in original.

36. The word *translated* was used to describe Enoch in the most prominent early English Bibles, including John Wycliffe (1380), William Tyndale (1534), the Great Bible (1539), the Geneva Bible (1560), Rheims (1582), and King James (1611) (see *The English Hexapla* [London: Samuel Bagster and Sons, 1841]).

37. Frederick W. Danker, *A Greek-English Lexicon of the New Testament and Other Early Christian Literature*, 3rd ed. (Chicago: University of Chicago Press, 2000), 642.

38. Noah Webster, *An American Dictionary of the English Language* (New York: S. Converse, 1828), s.v. "translated."

39. For a full study of the doctrine of translation, see Clyde J. Williams, "The Three Nephites and the Doctrine of Translation," in *The Book of Mormon: Third Nephi 9–30, This Is My Gospel*, ed. Monte S. Nyman and Charles D. Tate Jr. (Salt Lake City: Bookcraft, 1993), 237–51.

40. Joseph Smith, *Teachings of the Prophet Joseph Smith*, comp. Joseph Fielding Smith (Salt Lake City: Deseret Book, 1976), 170.

41. Smith, *Teachings of the Prophet Joseph Smith*, 171.

42. This power, protection, and longevity is possibly what the Book of Mormon prophet Alma longed for when he expressed his desire: "O that I were an angel, and could have the wish of mine heart, that I might go forth and speak with the trump of God, with a voice to shake the earth, and cry repentance unto every people! Yea, I would declare unto every soul, as with the voice of thunder, repentance and the plan of redemption, that they should repent and come unto our God, that there might not be more sorrow upon all the face of the earth" (Alma 29:1–2). For Alma, as for the rest of us, that ultimate wish remains unfulfilled as we utilize the gifts God has given mortals to be "an instrument in the hands of God to bring some soul to repentance" (Alma 29:9).

43. Jonn D. Claybaugh, "What the Latter-day Scriptures Teach about John the Beloved," in *The Testimony of John the Beloved* (Salt Lake City: Deseret Book, 1998), 16–35; Claybaugh, "As a Flaming Fire and a Ministering Angel," 54–60.

44. Porter, "The Restoration of the Aaronic and Melchizedek Priesthoods," 30–44.

45. Bruce N. Westergren, ed., *From Historian to Dissident: The Book of John Whitmer* (Salt Lake City: Signature Books, 1995), 69; see also Smith, *History of the Church*, 1:176.

46. Diary of Oliver B. Huntington, 1847–1900, part 2, 162, typescript in Harold B. Lee Library; cited in Jerry C. Roundy, "The Greatness of Joseph Smith and His Remarkable Visions," *New Era*, December 1973, 12.

47. Orson F. Whitney, *Life of Heber C. Kimball* (Salt Lake City: Bookcraft, 1967), 91–92.

48. On this issue, see Kent P. Jackson, *Lost Tribes and Last Days: What Modern Revelation Tells Us about the Old Testament* (Salt Lake City: Deseret Book, 2005), 62–71.

6

"THE LAWS OF THE CHURCH OF CHRIST" (D&C 42): A TEXTUAL AND HISTORICAL ANALYSIS

Grant Underwood

On January 2, 1831, "in the presence of the whole congregation" of the Church of Christ convened in quarterly conference in Fayette, New York, Joseph Smith received the "word of the Lord."[1] The revelation directed the Saints to gather "to the Ohio" and included the declaration: "There I will give unto you my law" (D&C 38:32). Pursuant to this promise, on February 9, 1831, just days after Joseph and Emma Smith arrived in Ohio, twelve elders "were called together, and united in mighty prayer, and were agreed, as touching the reception of the Law."[2] On that occasion, Joseph received the "Laws of the Church of Christ," or simply "the Law" as it was commonly known among the Saints.[3] Two weeks later, on February 22, Joseph wrote to Martin Harris: "We have received the laws of the Kingdom since we came here and the Disciples in these parts have received them gladly."[4] The following day, February 23, the Prophet and seven elders met to determine "how the Elders of the church of Christ are to act upon the points of the Law."[5]

Grant Underwood is a professor of history at Brigham Young University and an editor of the Joseph Smith Papers.

As a result, several additional paragraphs of instruction, comprising what is now Doctrine and Covenants 42:74–93, were recorded. The revelations of these two days constitute what is now section 42, the subject of this study. What follows is a detailed textual and content analysis of this important document. Throughout this study, while quotations from the revelations are taken from the earliest manuscript sources, for ease of reference, given the variation of versification and revelation numbering in the early years, the current Doctrine and Covenants section and verse numbers will be cited.

Textual Analysis

Although virtually none of the original dictation copies of the revelations Joseph Smith received have survived, in many instances early manuscript copies made before initial publication are extant. At present, five such copies of the Law exist that are known to have been recorded before July 1832, when Church printers in Missouri published the first extract in *The Evening and the Morning Star* (referred to as "the *Star*" by early Latter-day Saints).[6] Only one of the five manuscripts includes all the text given on both February 9 and February 23 (see accompanying chart), but each contains the portion of the February 9 material considered the core of the Law, verses 11–69 in today's Doctrine and Covenants. Of the five manuscripts, three contain revealed text from both days, indicating that the copyists perceived an organic relationship between the initial articulation of the Law on February 9 and instructions regarding how "to act upon" it recorded on February 23. While the Missouri printers chose to publish each day's material separately in the Book of Commandments (though they had not done so in one of the two extracts they published the year before in the *Star*), the First Presidency, in charge of compiling the Doctrine and Covenants in 1835, viewed the two days' revelations as connected and published them as a single section. No mention of its composite nature was included in the section's heading (nor has it been in any subsequent edition of the Doctrine and Covenants), and the reception date was listed simply as February 1831.[7]

Composition of Known Pre-1835 Versions of Section 42

In addition to the little-known fact that section 42 combines material received two weeks apart, another aspect is equally obscure. The portion received on February 9 appears to consist of answers to five specific questions posed by Joseph Smith and his colleagues. Although these questions were not included in published versions of the revelation, two of the five manuscripts contain them, and they offer valuable insight into the organization and content of this section. In order, the five questions and the distinct textual units they frame are:

1. "Shall the Church come together into one place or remain as they are in separate bodies?" (answered in verses 1–10);
2. "[What is] the Law regulating the Church in her present situation till the time of her gathering[?]" (answered in verses 11–69);[8]
3. "How the Elders are to dispose of their families while they are proclaiming repentance or are otherwise engaged in the service of the Church?" (answered in verses 70–73);[9]
4. "How far it is the will of the Lord that we Should have dealings with the wo[r]ld & how we Should conduct our dealings with them?" (answered in several sentences that were eliminated when the Doctrine and Covenants was published);
5. "What preperations we shall make for our Brethren from the East & when & how?" (also answered by text that was eliminated when the Doctrine and Covenants was published).

The latter portion of the Law, recorded two weeks later on February 23, 1831, also falls into discrete units of text: verses 74–77 and 78–93. Before publication in the Doctrine and Covenants, these two units appeared in inverse order in every manuscript or publication that contained both. Thus, verses 74–77 always concluded the document. The chart below shows the different combinations of the seven text units found in each of the extant pre-1835 manuscripts or printed sources. In every instance, the seven individual clusters contain precisely the same textual material, demonstrating that they were consistently perceived as discrete units of text.

Versions[10]	Current Verses					
Ryder (1831)	1–10,	11–69,	70–73,	*, **,	78–93,	74–77
Whitmer (1831)	1–10,	11–69,	70–73,	*,		74–77
Gilbert (1831)	1–10,	11–69,	70–73,	*		
Courier (Sept 1831)	1–10,	11–69				
Coltrin (Jan 1832)		11–69				
Hyde (1832)		11–69,	70–73,	*,	78–93,	74–77
Star (July 1832)		11–69,	70–73,			74–77
Star (October 1832)					78–93	
Book of Commandments chapter 44 (1833)	1–10,	11–69,	70–73,	*		
Book of Commandments chapter 47 (1833)					78–93,	74–77
Williams (1834)						74–77

* Material in the fourth and fifth text units was not included in any printings after the 1833 Book of Commandments.
** This manuscript contains two short paragraphs of unique material.

The Symonds Ryder manuscript is particularly important not only because it is one of the earliest copies of the Law but also because it is unique in two respects. First, as seen in the chart, it is the only manuscript copy containing all the text given on both days. Second, and perhaps more significantly, the Ryder manuscript contains two small paragraphs, some 160 words, of additional text found in no other manuscript or printed version. Though the Ryder manuscript has been in the Church's possession for more than forty years, the two paragraphs have gone unnoticed and appear below in print for the first time.[10] The first paragraph, really just a long sentence, serves as a bridge between the material received on February 9 and that which was recorded on February 23:

February 23d 1831, the rules and regulations of the <Law> How the Elders of the church of Christ are to act upon the points of the Law given by Jesus Christ to the Church in the presents of twelve Elders February 9th 1831 as agreed upon by seven ~~Elders~~ Elders Feby 23d 1831 according to to [*sic*] the commandment of God?"[11]

Brief as it is, this statement offers important insight into the difference between what was recorded on the two days. Though the grammar is somewhat awkward, the statement communicates that the Law proper was received on February 9 in the presence of twelve elders and that what was added on February 23, when seven elders were present, was inspired guidance about how to "act upon" the Law. Moreover, the phrase "as agreed upon by seven Elders" may imply something more than mere ratification of what Joseph Smith received on February 23. It is possible that the seven elders played an active role in helping the Prophet define the procedures recorded that day that would become verses 78–93 and 74–77. This possibility is strengthened by the fact that the statement in the Ryder manuscript says their action was "according to the commandment of God," which seems to refer to a directive given to the elders just days before in section 43 and which may have provided the specific impetus for the meeting: "I give unto you a commandment, that when ye are assembled together ye shall note with a pen how to act . . . upon the points of my law. . . . And thus it shall become a law unto you."[12] This is precisely what occurred on February 23, and because such procedural decisions did become "a law unto" the Church, they were combined with the February 9 material into a single document.

Originally, this composite document consisted of some 2,395 words. Because the dictation copies of the portions of the Law received on February 9 and February 23 have not survived, it is impossible to do an exact word count or to know with absolute certainty how the originals read. However, there is considerable consistency in wording between the five extant manuscript copies. Even in the minority of instances in which there is some disagreement, usually three or four of the manuscripts are identically worded. This allows reasonable confidence about the likely original wording, or at least the wording of a very early version from which these manuscripts were copied. This consensus early wording (CEW) and the word count it enables provide a baseline for the comparisons that follow.

When the Law was published in the Doctrine and Covenants in 1835, it consisted of 2,622 words.[13] That represents a net gain of approximately 230 words from the 2,395 in the CEW. This 9.6 percent gain came from the deletion of some 220 words and the addition of about 450 new words. Most of these revisions were made between September 1834, when the First Presidency was appointed to prepare the Doctrine and Covenants, and September 1835, when the volume came off the press. Some redactions, though, were made no later than November 1831, when the revelations were reviewed and revised in anticipation of their publication in the Book of Commandments. While any assessment of the purpose of particular revisions is subjective, they can be broadly divided between those that *clarify* meaning and those that *change* meaning. In the former category, some 110 words were deleted and replaced with about 300, for a net gain of 190, or an 8 percent gain in the Doctrine and Covenants version of the Law. These revisions range from the grammatical to the conceptual, with the latter type, which endeavors to provide greater clarity or adjust the tone of the message, accounting for the greatest number of new words. About one-fifth of the added words explicitly include the female gender (for example, "he *or she*" or "man *or woman*").

Other revisions change the original meaning, usually by updating the revelation to keep pace with new policies or developing ecclesiastical organization. If the Law's overall size gain between the CEW and the Doctrine and Covenants version is 9.6 percent, and if 8 percent clarifies meaning, that would seem to leave only 1.6 percent that changes meaning. This is misleading, however. In contrast to the "clarifies meaning" category, where virtually all deletions are linked to replacement-verbiage additions, most additions in the "changes meaning" category are new information, unaffected by any previous wording and requiring no deletions. About 150 new words in the Doctrine and Covenants version can be categorized as changing meaning, and they are associated with only 15 deletions from the CEW, for a net gain of

135 words. Thus, actually 5.6 percent of the size increase in the revelation can be attributed to revisions that change meaning. The 4 percent discrepancy between the 9.6 percent overall gain and the 13.6 percent that results from combining the "clarifies meaning" and "changes meaning" percentages is accounted for by the Doctrine and Covenants editors dropping all of text units 4 and 5 (see chart). This represents some 95 words, or 4 percent of the CEW that were deleted to appropriately change the Law. In the final analysis, what is striking is not that some revisions were made, but that more than 85 percent of the Law's content and phraseology were found suitable to a rapidly developing church several years after their initial articulation. Significantly, there is no record of opposition to the changes that were made. The Saints appear to have embraced them as having been made by the same inspiration that produced the original text.[14]

The following sections discuss significant revisions made to produce the final text of the Law, noting interpretations of the time. It is a work of historical reconstruction, not theological prescription. Readers seeking to understand modern Latter-day Saint practice or the latest interpretations of the Law will need to look elsewhere. Within the Latter-day Saint community, authoritative theologizing is understood to be the prerogative of prophets and apostles. Thus, the approach here is historical rather than theological or pastoral.

D&C 42:1–10

We gain significant insight into this first text cluster by returning to the two unique paragraphs in the Ryder manuscript, specifically the second paragraph, which offers a rare glimpse of early understandings by providing a review and restatement of verses 1–10:

> The first commandment in the law teaches that all the Elders shall go unto the regions westward and labour to build up Churches unto Christ wheresoever they shall <find> any to receive them and obey the Gospel of Jesus Christ except Joseph [Smith] & Sidney [Rigdon] and Edward [Partridge] and such as the Bishop shall appoint to assist him in his duties according to the Law which we have received this

commandment as far as it respects these Elders to be sent to the west is a special one for the time being incumbent on the present Elders who shall return when directed by the Holy Spirit!

Summary statements such as this, by their very distilling nature, provide a useful interpretive window into the text. As initially recorded, the "first commandment" in the Law directed the elders to "go forth in my name every one of you except my servant Joseph & Sidney & I give unto them a commandment that they shall go forth for a little Season, & it shall be given by the power of my spirit when they shall return" (v. 4).[15] Who are the "them" that are to go forth for a little season and return when the Spirit directs? The immediate antecedent is Joseph and Sidney, but the summary paragraph in the Ryder manuscript interprets "them" as the elders and excuses Joseph and Sidney from this particular proselytizing mission altogether. Whether the paragraph reflects the proper understanding of a grammatically ambiguous statement or whether there was a change of plans for the Prophet and Sidney Rigdon in the intervening two weeks is unclear. In the end, however, there is no historical evidence that Joseph and Sidney went off on a mission at this time, even for a little season.

The Ryder paragraph contains two other interpretations worth noting. On February 9, the elders were told, "Ye shall go forth in to the regions westward & in as much as ye shall find my diciples ye shall build up my church." A modern Latter-day Saint might read the latter part of this passage as an injunction to seek out geographically isolated converts and organize them into a branch of the Church. Actually, "my diciples" seems to be referring to Christians whom Jesus knew to be His true disciples and who therefore were expected to embrace the restored gospel when it was presented to them. This unusual way of labeling such individuals parallels a similar reference to "my church" in section 10. There "my church," like "my diciples," appears to identify Christ's devout followers in any (or no) religious organization. The revelation promises that "if this generation harden not their hearts, I will establish my church among them" (D&C 10:53). Then it makes this unusual statement: "Now I do not say this to destroy my church, but I say this to build up my church; therefore, whosoever belongeth to my church need not fear, for such shall inherit the kingdom of heaven" (D&C 10:54–55). At the time this was said, there was no restored church on earth, and there would not be for another year. Thus, "my church" seems to refer to a spiritual fellowship known only to God and consisting of people, regardless of their institutional affiliations, whose private beliefs and behaviors qualified them for membership in it and who, like "my diciples," were expected to receive the fullness of the gospel and inherit the kingdom of heaven.

Later, when the Law was being prepared for publication in the Book of Commandments, the phrase "my diciples" was replaced with "them that will receive you." This clarification shifts emphasis from a label, which can be variously construed, to actions, which are unmistakable. It is interesting that a similar clarification first appeared in the Ryder paragraph in which the elders were to "build up Churches unto Christ wheresoever they shall <find> any to receive them."

The Ryder paragraph also states more clearly than the original that the mission assigned to the elders was "incumbent" on them only "for the time being." John Whitmer recorded that "after the above Law or Revelation was received, the elders went forth to proclaim repentance according to commandment, and there were numbers added to the church."[16] One of the elders, John Corrill, reported that he and his preaching companion "went to New London, about one hundred miles from Kirtland, where we built up a Church of thirty-six members in about three weeks time. . . . Other elders proceeded to erect churches in various places, and the work increased very fast."[17]

D&C 42:11–69

This unit of text constitutes the core of the Law. Indeed, some manuscripts and printed sources reserve the designation of "the Law" only for this particular unit. The heading for the Book of Commandments chapter containing the first two text units distinguishes them as "a revelation given to twelve elders assembled in Kirtland, Ohio; *and also* the law for the government of the church, given in the presence of the same."[18] The question that launched this text cluster asks about "the Law regulating the Church in her present situation," and several manuscripts shorten the heading to simply "The Law" or "The Laws." Thus, it is not surprising that of the revealed material recorded on February 9, only this text unit, verses 11–69, is included in all five early manuscripts.

In addition to setting forth the Church's moral code, this text cluster addresses several nettlesome issues that had been troubling the fledgling fold in Ohio. First, in an effort to control the charismatic chaos that Joseph Smith encountered upon his arrival, the Law clarifies that no one can function in the teaching ministry of the Church unless they have been "regularly ordained" by recognized ecclesiastical authority (v. 11). Neither an internal call nor spiritual giftedness was sufficient to appoint one to the ministry, though the properly appointed ministers would be effective only to the degree that they were aided by the Holy Spirit: "Thou shalt be directed by the spirit . . . & if ye receive not the spirit ye shall not teach" (vv. 13–14).

Some months after this revelation was received, recent convert William E. McLellin left a typical description of what it was like to try to teach without the Spirit: "I arose and attempted to preach, but could not, I had no animation in it, no memory, and in truth I had lost the spirit of God. Hence I was confounded, I set down and told bro. H. to preach for I could not."[19] The need for assistance from the Holy Ghost was crucial in a populist church that eschewed formal ministerial training and relied on ordinary individuals to do the work of evangelism. As historian Richard Bushman notes, Joseph Smith was "a plain man himself, inexperienced in preaching, [and he] trusted ordinary men to carry the message. In a democratic time, the Mormons emerged as the most democratic of churches, rivaled only by the Quakers."[20]

After discussing qualifications for the ministry, the revelation turns from the elders to the members: "Now behold I speak unto the church" (v. 18). The ethical vision of the Ten Commandments is here reaffirmed by including specific injunctions against murder, theft, lying, adultery, and harming one's neighbor. The revelation then summarizes such moral codes: "Thou knowest my laws they <are> given in my scriptures. . . . If thou lovest me thou shall serve & keep all my commandments" (vv. 28–29).

Next the Law addresses the economic organization of the Church, in part to correct the well-intended but misguided efforts of some Ohio converts who had formed communal groups called "Families" to imitate the early Christians in having "all things common" (Acts 2:44).[21] Instead of the communalism practiced by these converts, principles were revealed in the Law that were understood to be at the root of how the biblical Enoch brought his people to be "of one heart and of one mind" and have "no poor among them" (Moses 7:18). These principles included the "socialization of surplus incomes, freedom of enterprise, and group economic self-sufficiency."[22] The key to applying these principles was "consecration," a word that in the religious terminology of the day meant to "set apart, dedicate, or devote, to the service and worship of God" one's life or possessions.[23] The Prophet's vision of consecration coincided with an efflorescence of utopian experimentation in American history. In this era, groups as diverse as the Shakers and the Harmony Society sought to improve people's social and economic lives through communitarian association.[24] Consecration provided a theological basis for the necessary resource sharing to bring about the imminent migration and settlement of the New York Saints in Ohio and to lay the foundation for the eventual attempt to replicate Enoch's Zion on the western borders of the United States.

Ultimately, for internal as well as external reasons, implementation fell short of the ideal. Church historian John Whitmer reported that when "Bishop Edward Partridge visited the Church in its several branches, there were some that would not receive the Law. The time has not yet come," he opined, "that the law can be fully established, for the disciples live scattered abroad and are not organized, our members are small and the disciples untaught, consequently they understand not the things of the kingdom." Among the problems Whitmer identified were members "who were flattered into the Church because they thought that all things were to be common, therefore they thought to glut themselves upon the labors of others."[25] As it turned out, the complete consecration of one's property was practiced only during 1831–33 and then only by some Saints and in certain places.[26] Thus, for publication in the 1835 Doctrine and Covenants, the original declaration "thou shalt consecrate all thy propertys" was edited to read "thou *wilt remember the poor, and* consecrate *of* thy properties *for their support"* (D&C 42:30; revelation revisions are italicized here and hereafter).²⁷

The Law stated that such consecration was to be done "with a covenant and deed which cannot be broken" (D&C 42:30). The need for a deed was reiterated several months later when the Colesville (New York) Saints were given the "privilege of organizing themselves according to my laws" (D&C 51:15). Bishop Edward Partridge, who was instructed to so "organize this people" (D&C 51:1), was told that "when he shall appoint a man his portion, give unto him a writing that shall secure unto him his portion" (D&C 51:4). This initial attempt at living the law of consecration unraveled before Partridge could implement the instruction, but he did so the following year in Missouri. Sometime after the Church launched its printing operation in 1832, Bishop Partridge created and began using printed deeds to certify receipt and conveyance of consecrated property. The deeds show how various provisions regarding consecration were actually implemented. Surviving deeds of stewardship, for instance, uniformly illustrate that consecrating individuals were made "steward[s] over [their] own property" (D&C 42:32), rather than over other consecrated property. Though obviously this could not have been universal, because some poor Saints would have required additional property to meet their needs, it does demonstrate that the core of what was "loaned" to a steward as personal property was the very same property he had consecrated initially.

The deeds also preserve the Law's original intent that consecrated property "cannot be taken from you [later clarified to read *the church*]" (v. 32) and that "he that sinneth & repnteth not shall be cast out & shall not receive again that which he hath consecrated" (v. 37). The deeds state that should the steward be excommunicated, he would "forfeit all claim to the above described leased [real] and loaned [personal] property, and hereby bind myself to give back the leased, and also pay an equivalent for the loaned," though most, if not all, had been his own property before consecrating it to the Lord.²⁸

Not surprisingly, this arrangement was challenged in court by disaffected Church members, and the nature of stewardships was modified.²⁹ In May 1833 Joseph Smith wrote to Bishop Partridge instructing him to "give a deed, securing to him who receives inheritances, his inheritance, for an everlasting inheritance, or in other words, to be his individual property, his private stewardship, and if he is found a transgressor & should be cut off, out of the church, his inheritance is his still. . . . But the property which he consecrated to the poor, for their benefit, & inheritance, & stewardship [meaning the "residue" or surplus that stayed in the storehouse (see v. 34)], he cannot obtain again by the law of the Lord[.] Thus you see the propriety of this law, that rich men cannot have power to disinherit the poor by obtaining again that which they have consecrated."[30]

Reflecting this understanding, when section 51 was later edited for publication in the Doctrine and Covenants, a new statement (now v. 5) was added: "*And if he shall transgress, and is not accounted worthy to belong in the church, he shall not have power to claim that portion which he has consecrated unto the bishop for the poor and the needy of my church: therefore, he shall not retain the gift, but shall only have claim on that portion that is deeded to him.*" Because charitable donations were legally safeguarded in a way that communal resource sharing was not, in several places in the Law, wording was added to similarly clarify that the poor were the specific beneficiaries of consecrations. Instead of "thou shalt consecrate all thy propertys that which thou hast unto me," which could be interpreted adversely, the declaration was edited thus: "Thou *wilt remember the poor, and* consecrate *of* thy properties *for their support* that which thou hast *to impart* unto *them*" (D&C 42:30). Likewise, the subsequent statement "that which he hath consecrated unto me" was revised to read, "That which he has consecrated *unto the poor and the needy of my church, or in other words* unto me, *for inasmuch as ye do it unto the least of these ye do it unto me*" (vv. 37–38).

In his letter to Bishop Partridge, the Prophet clarified consecration and stewardship procedures not only with the intention of safeguarding donations to the storehouse as being earmarked for the poor but also to "secure unto [each steward] his portion." After his letter arrived in Missouri, an editorial appeared in the next issue of the *Star* emphasizing that when the Saints "are gathered, instead of becoming a common stock family, as has been said . . . each man receives a warranty deed securing to himself and heirs, his inheritance in fee simple [unrestricted ownership] forever."[31] In July 1833 an anti-Mormon riot broke out in Independence, Missouri, putting the Saints in the area in a precarious position. By year's end they had been driven from their homes in Jackson County. Under such unsettled circumstances, it appears that the envisioned revised deeds granting fee simple ownership were never actually prepared or issued (at least none have survived). Moreover, it is noteworthy that only a half dozen of the earlier deeds are extant, and of those only one (Joseph Knight Jr.'s) is actually signed. The others, which seem to be drafts, exist only because Bishop Partridge retained them and used their blank back sides for copying personal letters. That neither the bishop responsible for managing the consecration and stewardship program nor any of its stewards (other than Knight) would have retained the official "legal" deeds raises questions about how formally or how systematically consecrations were made and even about how widespread the practice of consecration actually was.[32]

Embedded in the Law's consideration of consecration is this unusual statement: "For it shall come to pass that which I spake by the mouth of my prophets shall be fulfilled for I will consecrate the riches of the Gentiles unto my people which are of the house of Israel" (v. 39). This alludes to the prophecy of Isaiah that Israel would one day "eat the riches of the Gentiles, and in their glory shall ye boast yourselves" (Isaiah 61:6). Reiterated in the Law, some Latter-day Saints seem to have entertained grandiose but misguided visions of the prophecy's fulfillment. A disaffected Ezra Booth provided this summary of his perceptions of eschatological expectations among the Saints: Zion was "to be a city of Refuge, and a safe asylum when the storms of vengeance shall pour upon the earth, and those who reject the book of Mormon, shall be swept off as with the besom of destruction. Then shall the riches of the Gentiles be consecrated to the Mormonites; they shall have lands and cattle in abundance, and shall possess the gold and silver, and all the treasures of their enemies."[33] In the face of such misreadings, the Prophet was impressed to make a crucial clarification when he published this passage in the Doctrine and Covenants: "For I will consecrate *of* the riches of *those who embrace my gospel among* the Gentiles, unto *the poor of* my people *who* are of the house of Israel" (D&C 42:39; emphasis added).

Nonetheless, the apocalyptic dream of a great reversal in fortunes and relations between believers and their antagonists died hard. In fall

1838, at the height of tensions between Mormons and Missourians, certain Latter-day Saint zealots recalled the Law's original recapitulation of Isaiah's prophecy and construed it as justification for plundering their enemies. Morris Phelps remembered in this way the charge of Danite leader Sampson Avard to his men: "Know ye not, brethren, that it will soon be your privilege to take your respective companies and go out on a scout on the borders of the settlements, and take to yourselves spoils of the goods of the ungodly Gentiles? for it is written, the riches of the Gentiles shall be consecrated to my people, the house of Israel; and thus you will waste away the Gentiles by robbing and plundering them of their property; and in this way we will build up the kingdom of God."[34] Later, a disaffected John Whitmer accused Nauvoo Saints of doing the same things under the same pretext during the Mormon War in Hancock County, Illinois, in the mid-1840s.[35]

Discussion of consecration concludes in this part of the Law with encouragement to dress simply, cultivate cleanliness, and avoid idleness (see D&C 42:40–42). Such ideals were common among contemporary communitarian societies. Idleness, in particular, was to be avoided at all costs. From the beginning, the Missouri Saints seemed to have had trouble with this. A November 1831 revelation declared, "I, the Lord, am not well pleased with the inhabitants of Zion, for there are idlers among them" (D&C 68:31). Several months later, it was put even more directly: "The idler shall not have place in the church" (D&C 75:29). Even the poor, who are rarely condemned in scripture, were not exempt from admonition: "Wo unto you poor men . . . who will not labour with their own hands" (D&C 56:17).

At this point the revelation turns to matters of sickness and healing. It reiterates the New Testament injunction in James to "call for the elders of the church" when someone is sick to "anoint" with oil and offer a "prayer of faith" on their behalf (James 5:14–15). The early years of Latter-day Saint history are filled with examples of dramatic healings.[36] To cite only one of the more notable examples, not long after this revelation was received, Joseph Smith was instrumental in healing Elsa Johnson's lame arm, a healing that contributed to the conversion of several of her acquaintances.[37]

On the other hand, believers whose faith was insufficient for them to be divinely healed were to be "nourished with all tenderness, with herbs and mild food" (D&C 42:43). In antebellum America, herbal medicine was a popular and relatively successful alternative to such orthodox medical interventions as bloodletting and administration of calomel. Latter-day Saints participated in the era's growing rebellion against these medical practices and favored faith healing *and* botanic medicine.[38] Joseph Smith is reported to have expressed the view that "doctors should not heal people[,] that medicine would have no effect. The Gentiles studied medicine, and had use for it."[39] Botanic medicine received considerable impetus from the activities of Samuel Thomson, who published the immensely popular *New Guide to Health; or, Botanic Family Physician.* The book sold for two dollars, and a franchise or "right" to apply Thomson's methods within one's own family sold for twenty dollars. By 1835 Thomsonian practitioners in Ohio claimed that half the state's population used botanic medicine. Several prominent early Saints, such as Frederick G. Williams and the Richards brothers, Levi and Willard, were practicing Thomsonian doctors.[40]

In all matters of health and healing, God's will took priority. Despite one's faith, only those "not appointed unto death shall be healed" (D&C 42:48). The inclusion of the biblical phrase "appointed to death" (Psalm 102:20; 1 Corinthians 4:9) is significant. Like other Christians, Latter-day Saints used it to acknowledge the overruling providence of God in all aspects of life. As an example, at some point in Joseph Smith Sr.'s decline due to the disease known as "consumption," his wife, Lucy Mack Smith, "concluded that he was appointed unto death."[41]

Latter-day Saint ministrations to the sick, including the various scenarios set forth in the Law, were later summarized by Wilford Woodruff: "Some times we lay hands upon the sick & they are healed instantly other times with all the faith & medicine they are a long time getting well, & others die."[42] Further, it was stressed that for those who did not have faith to be healed from major ailments such as blindness, deafness, or physical disability, "in asmuch as they break not my Laws thou shalt bear their infirmities" (D&C 42:52).

The Law then returns to a brief discussion of yet another aspect of life in a consecrated community: "Thou shalt not take thy brothers garment thou shalt pay for that which thou <s>shalt receive</s> shall receive of thy Brother" (v. 54). Here the Law explicitly eschews the kind of communal ownership of property found in the various "Family" organizations in which some Ohio converts had been living. John Whitmer, who visited the Morley "Family," wrote, "The disciples had all things common, and were going to destruction very fast as to temporal things for they considered from reading the scripture that what belonged to a brother, belonged to any of the brethren, therefore they would take each others clothes and other property and use it without leave: which brought on confusion and disappointments, for they did not understand the scripture."[43] The Law's correction was reiterated in the instructions given to Bishop Partridge about how to organize the Colesville Saints according to the law of consecration: "Let that which belongeth to this people not be taken & given unto that of another church wherefore if another Church would receive money of this Church let them pay unto this church again according as they shall agree" (D&C 51:10–11). Section 42 made clear that one's stewardship was to be carried out within the ordinary workings of a market economy.[44]

As such, it was expected that in the normal course of "stand[ing] in the place of [one's] stewardship" (D&C 42:53), a surplus would sometimes accrue: "& if thou obtain more than that which would be for thy support thou shalt give it unto my store house" (v. 55). Bishop Partridge endeavored to institutionalize this as an annual requirement. In the printed deeds he prepared, the agreement "binds" the steward "to pay yearly unto the said *Edward Partridge* bishop of said church, or his successor in office, for the benefit of said church, all that I shall make or accumulate more than is needful for the support and comfort of myself and family."[45] Identifying such a surplus, of course, was a subjective judgment, and the Prophet counseled Bishop Partridge that it should be the joint decision of the steward and the bishop:

> Evry m[a]n must be his own judge how much he should receive and how much he should suffer to remain in the hands of the Bishop[.] I speak of those who consecrate more than they need for the support of themselves and their

families[.] The matter of consecration must be done by the mutual consent of both parties for, to give the Bishop power to say how much evry man shall have and he be obliged to comply with the Bishops judgment is giving to the Bishop more power than a king has and upon the other hand to let evry man say how much he needs and the Bishop obliged to comply with his judgment is to throw Zion into confusion and make a slave of the Bishop[.] [T]he fact is there must be a balance or equalibrium of power between the Bishop and the people and thus harmony and good will may be preserved among you.[46]

At this point, the Law abruptly shifts from discussion of the proper handling of surplus to Joseph Smith's "New Translation" of the Bible: "Thou shalt ask & my scriptures shall be given as I have appointed & for thy salvation thou shalt hold thy peace concerning them untill ye have received them" (vv. 56–57). The subsequent redaction of this passage provides a rare view of multiple layers of revision. The first revision appears to have been made in November 1831 in conjunction with the conferences held to plan the publication of the Book of Commandments. At a meeting on November 8, the elders resolved that "Br Joseph Smith Jr. correct those errors or mistakes which he m[ay] discover by the holy Spirit."[47] Among the revisions made at this time was one involving this passage about the New Translation. The unpunctuated original allows for a reading that connects "for thy salvation" to "my scriptures shall be given" rather than to the subsequent phrase "thou shalt hold thy peace concerning them." Joseph, however, revised the passage to make clear that the link was between salvation, understood temporally, and holding their peace about the New Translation: "For thy *safety it is expedient that* thou shalt hold thy peace concerning them."[48]

Apparently not satisfied with this rendition, the Prophet (or those working under his direction) again revised the passage some three years later while preparing the revelation for publication in the Doctrine and Covenants. The later version shifts emphasis from the safety of the Saints to the safety of the scriptures. In its final form, the full passage reads: "My scriptures shall be given as I have appointed, and *they shall be preserved in safety; and it is expedient that* thou shouldst hold thy peace concerning them, *and not teach them* until ye have received them *in full*" (vv. 56–57; emphasis added).

Another example of multiple revisions is found a few lines later, near the close of the long answer to the second question seeking to know "the Law regulating the Church in her present situation till the time of her gathering." At this point, a summary statement is made: "& these Laws which ye have received are sufficient for you both here & in the New Jerusalem but he that lacketh knowledge let him ask of me." In the November 1831 revisions, the door left slightly ajar for future clarifications of, or even additions to, the Law is pushed wide open, and possibility becomes certainty: "These laws which ye have received *& shall hereafter receive shall be* sufficient for you both here & in the New Jerusalem *Therefore* he that lacketh knowledge let him ask of me." In 1835 the text is further edited to clarify that "covenants" rather than "laws" would be forthcoming and that while the laws already received were to be observed, it was these covenants in particular that would "establish" the Saints both in Ohio and Missouri: "*Ye shall observe* the laws which ye have received, *and be faithful. And ye shall hereafter receive church covenants, such as shall be sufficient to establish you* both here, and in the New Jerusalem. *Therefore,* he that lacketh *wisdom,* let him ask of me" (vv. 66–68; emphasis added).

The second unit of text, the core of the Law, concludes with this entreaty: "Lift up your hearts & rejoice for unto you the kingdom has been given, even so, Amen." The passage was edited in 1835 to include the kind of amplificatory insight Joseph sometimes felt inspired to add when redacting the revelations: "Lift up your hearts and rejoice, for unto you the kingdom, *or in other words, the keys of the church,* have been given. Even so. Amen" (v. 69; emphasis added).

D&C 42:70–73

The third unit of text in the Law addresses "how the Elders are to dispose of their families while they are proclaiming repentance or are otherwise engaged in the service of the Church." The answer is that "the Elders are to assist the Bishop in all things & he is to see that their families are supported out of the property which is consecrated to the Lord either a stewardship or otherwise as may be thought best by the Elders & Bishop." By year's end, although the newly called bishop Newel K. Whitney is told to "take an account of the elders as before has been commanded and to administer to their wants," the elders are also encouraged to "pay for that which they receive, inasmuch as they shall have wherewith to pay" (D&C 72:11). In the event that they "have not wherewith to pay, an account shall be taken and handed over to the bishop in Zion, who shall pay the debt out of that which the Lord shall put into his hands. And the labors of the faithful who labor in spiritual things, in administering the gospel and the things of the kingdom unto the church, and unto the world, shall answer the debt unto the bishop in Zion" (D&C 72:13–14).

The following month, the idea of Church support for the elders was broadened from a monetary focus, with its potential for draining the meager resources of the storehouse, to one that relied on the generosity of members at large. Additionally, the elders themselves were to take the initiative in seeking this support. A revelation reminded the Saints that "it is the duty of the church to assist in supporting the families of those, and also to support the families of those who are called and must needs be sent unto the world to proclaim the gospel" (D&C 75:24). Needy elders were to arrange to board their families with willing Church members during their absence (D&C 75:25), but in case an elder was unable to make satisfactory arrangements and was "obliged to provide for his own family," he was told, "Let him provide, and he shall in nowise lose his crown; and let him labor in the church" at home (D&C 75:28). Thus, within a year of the Law's reception, practical considerations compelled modification of the initial declaration that the elders' families were to be "supported out of the property which is consecrated to the Lord."

Not surprisingly, the 1835 revisions reflected these realities. For publication in the Doctrine and Covenants, the text was edited to narrow "support" to only the elders (and later, high priests) appointed as counselors to the bishop: "The elders, *or high priests who* are *appointed* to assist the bishop *as counsellors,* in all things *are to have* their families supported out of the property which is consecrated to the *bishop, for the good of the poor, and for other purposes, as before mentioned; or they are to receive a just remuneration for all their services;* either a stewardship, or otherwise, as may be thought best, *or decided* by the *counsellors* and bishop" (D&C 42:71–72). Without the original prefatory question targeting elders involved in missionary work or "otherwise engaged in the service of the Church," the restriction of support to bishops' counselors was a reasonable interpretation of the original statement that "the Elders are to assist the Bishop in all things." The 1835 revision also added a sentence specifically including the bishop as deserving of temporal assistance: "*And the bishop also, shall receive his support, or a just remuneration for all his services, in the church*" (D&C 42:73).[49]

Text Units 4 and 5 (Not in the Doctrine and Covenants)

The fourth and fifth text units are the shortest of the seven in the Law. Combined, they consist of less than a hundred words, or just over 4 percent of the Law's total. Although they had been included in the Book of Commandments, they were dropped from the revelation when it was published in the Doctrine and Covenants. The fourth question asks, "How far it is the will of the Lord that we Should have dealings with the wo[r]ld & how we Should conduct our dealings with them?" The answer: "Thou shalt contract no debts with them & again the Elders & Bishop shall Council together & they shall do by the directions of the spirit as it must be necessary." Though this brief statement clearly enunciates the basic position of not contracting debts with "the world," it also opens the door, when prompted by the Spirit, to do whatever is "necessary" to advance the cause.[50]

With specific reference to this passage in the Law, the counsel was put more elaborately seven months later: "Behold it is said in my Laws or forbidden to get in debt to thine enemies but Behold it is not said at any time that the Lord should not take when he please & pay as seemeth him good wherefore as ye are agents & ye are on the Lords errand & whatever ye do according to the will of the Lord is the Lords business & it is the Lord's business to provide for his saints" (D&C 64:27–30). Not long after this, the Law was clarified to read, "Contract no debts with *the world except thou art commanded.*" Such a commandment came the following March in response to a question about purchasing paper to print the Book of Commandments: "Let the purchase be made by the Bishop if it must needs <be> by hire[51] let whatsoever is done be done in the name of the Lord."[52] This was followed in April by a decision of the United Firm, the partnership of Church leaders who managed Church properties, to take out a "loan [for] fifteen thousand dollars for five years or longer at six percent anually or semianually as the agreement can be made."[53]

Such "necessary" actions did not come without a cost. By late 1833 the Prophet wrote to refugee Church leaders in Clay County, Missouri, that "it will be impossible for us to render you any assistance in a temporal point of view as our means are already exhausted and are deeply in debt and know no means whereby we shall be able to extricate ourselves."[54] A month later, on January 11, 1834, Joseph and others united in prayer and made several petitions to God, one of which was "that the Lord would provide, in the order of his Providence, the bishop of this Church with means sufficient to discharge every debt that the Firm owes, in due season, that the church may not be braught into disrepute, and the saints be afflicted by the hands of their enemies."[55] Regardless of the occasional need to go into debt, the Prophet's heart on the matter is laid bare in a rare journal entry in his own hand: "My heart is full of desire to day, to <be> blessed of the God, of Abraham; with prosperity, untill I will be able to pay all my depts; for it is <the> delight of my soul to <be> honest. Oh Lord that thou knowes right well!"[56]

It is unclear why this fourth text unit was dropped from the revelation. Certainly in its edited form, it coincided with similar statements made elsewhere in the Doctrine and Covenants. Perhaps it was a casualty of its proximity to the fifth unit, which, as will be seen, was very specific to circumstances in Ohio in 1831 and therefore of limited ongoing relevance to the Church.

The fifth question asks, "What preperations we shall make for our Brethren from the East & when ['where' in the Gilbert manuscript] & how?" The revealed answer was, "There shall be as many appointed as must needs be necessary to assist the Bishop in obtaining places ['houses' in the Gilbert manuscript] that they may be together as much as can be & is directed by the holy Spirit." When revisions were made in

November 1831, the latter part of this statement was clarified to read, "Obtaining places *for the brethren from New York* that they may be together as much as can be, and *as they are* directed by the Holy Spirit." In spring of 1831 it was anticipated that the New York Saints would soon immigrate to Ohio in compliance with previous revelations directing them to gather there (see D&C 37 and 38). Preparing for that event was a matter of importance and the subject of several revelations at the time (see D&C 48 and 51).

The answer to the fifth question included this directive: "Every family shall have places that they may live by themselves & every Church shall be organized in as close bodies as they can be in consequence of the enemy," later adding, "*And this for a wise purpose: even so. Amen.*" The idea of settling the families of the immigrating branches in close proximity to one another, especially since many were kin, made sense for a variety of reasons. Given the Saints' previous experience with persecution, the benefit of protection from the "enemy" is singled out. How close together the immigrants actually settled once they arrived is generally not known. The one outcome that is well documented is that the Colesville Branch was instructed to move together onto Leman Copley's property in Thompson, Ohio (see D&C 51). Living together in "close bodies," however, did not mean living together communally after the fashion of some of the "Family" organizations that the Prophet encountered in Ohio. As the text makes clear, each family was to have a place of its own so that "they may live by themselves."

D&C 42:78–93

This and the text cluster that follows it were recorded two weeks after the first five units of the Law. As explained in the Ryder manuscript, these final segments, "agreed upon by seven Elders Feby 23^d 1831 according to the commandment of God," consisted of the "rules and regulations" for "how the Elders of the church of Christ are to act upon the points of the Law." The first half of unit six specifies actions to be taken in cases of murder, adultery, robbery, theft, and lying, each of which had been proscribed in the Law proper. Murderers were to be "delivered up and dealt with according to the Laws of the land for remember that he hath no forgiveness" (v. 79). Justification for handing the murderer over to civil authorities is explicitly grounded in the Law's earlier declaration that "he that killeth shall not have forgiveness neither in this world neither in the world to come" (v. 18).

Adultery, on the other hand, was to be handled by the Church. The Law decreed that an unrepentant, or repeat, adulterer was to be "cast out" (vv. 24, 26), and this unit articulates the procedures for implementing such a policy. It directs that the accused be tried before two or more elders, with the bishop also present when possible,[57] and it requires the adulterous act to "be established against him" ("*or her*" was added later) by a minimum of two Church-member witnesses. Because at this time the Law stipulated that excommunication required the consenting vote of the Church, "the Elders shall lay the case before the Church and the Church shall lift up their hands against them that they may be dealt with according to <the> Law" (v. 81). This procedure was to serve as the template for Church discipline generally: "Thus ye shall do in all cases which shall come before you" (v. 83). Several sentences later the revelation declares that if the Saints "do any manner of iniquity," they shall "be delivered up unto the Law even that of God" (v. 87). Sandwiched between these two statements are explicit instructions that those who "rob," "steal," or "lie" were to be "delivered up unto the law" (vv. 84–86). Whether this referred to the law of the land or the law of God was unclear until "*of the land*" was added in 1835.

In the same 1835 Doctrine and Covenants, a declaration on "Governments and Laws in General" (now D&C 134) elaborated the Church's position on civil offenses: "We believe that the commission of crime should be punished according to the nature of the offence: that murder, treason, robbery, theft . . . should be punished according to their criminality . . . by the laws of that Government in which the offence is committed." Further, it was affirmed, "We believe that all religious societies have a right to deal with their members for disorderly conduct according to the rules and regulations of such societies, provided that such dealing be for fellowship and good standing; but we do not believe that any religious society has authority to try men on the right of property or life . . . neither to inflict any physical punishment upon them,— they can only excommunicate them from their society and withdraw from them their fellowship" (D&C 134:8, 10).

The Law next elaborates what had only been implicit in the Church's "Articles and Covenants" (D&C 20) regarding Church discipline. "Any member of this Church of Christ," declared the Articles and Covenants, "transgressing or being over taken in a fault[58] shall be dealt with according as the scriptures directs" (D&C 20:80). For some eighteen hundred years, the classic scriptural text on Church discipline had been Matthew 18:15–17.[59] Not surprisingly, the three-step procedure outlined there is here reiterated in the Law. If a member is "offended" by another, he or she is to seek out the offender and present the grievance to them privately. If the trespasser confesses, the two parties are to "be reconciled." If the offender does not acknowledge the impropriety, the offended is instructed to "take another with thee," and if the offender still does not confess, the case is to be turned over to the elders (see D&C 42:88–89).[60] The only variation of significance from Matthew 18:15–17 in the Law is the clarification that to "tell it unto the church" means "not to the members but to the elders" (D&C 42:89).[61] The "Far West Record" and the "Kirtland Council Minute Book" contain many accounts of relatively minor transgressive behavior being aired before the elders of the Church. Latter-day Saint discipline in this era was similar to that practiced by other Christian churches both in terms of its commitment to following Matthew 18:15–17 to resolve interpersonal difficulties as well as serious sin and in its rigorous attempt to maintain the purity and holiness of the body of believers.[62] Today, Church disciplinary councils convene for only the gravest of matters.

The final portion of this textual unit in the Law provides guidelines for public confession and even for public reprimand, aspects of Church discipline that rarely seem appropriate today. While the Bible enjoins, "Them that sin rebuke before all, that others also may fear" (1 Timothy 5:20), this revelation actually restricts public rebuke only to those who "offend many" or who "offend openly" (D&C 42:90–91). In an earlier era, public shaming was felt to facilitate repentance: "If any one offend openly he shall be rebuked openly that he may be ashamed and if he confess not he shall be delivered up unto the law" of God (v. 91).[63] For secret sinners, though, a private chastisement seemed best. Such a practice would enable the errant one "to confess in secret to him whome he has offended and to God that the Brethren may not speak reproachfully of him" (v. 92). "And thus," concludes this text unit, "shall ye conduct in all things" (v. 93).

D&C 42:74–77

Though this segment was positioned ahead of the previous unit when published in the Doctrine and Covenants, it had previously followed it in any source that contained both units (see chart). In two other instances, it alone was appended to the Law proper, and in one case it appeared by itself. In several sources, the unit received its own title—"How to act in case of adultery" or "A Commandment how to act in cases of adultery." Where the unit bears a date, February 23, 1831, is listed.

The segment's title is somewhat misleading because the actual topic is the relationship of adultery to divorce or separation, rather than adultery per se. The text discusses four specific situations and provides instruction on how to act in those cases. The first instance is when a Church member divorces a spouse because the spouse has been sexually immoral: "Whatsoever person among you having put away their companion for the cause of fornication or in otherwords if he shall testify before you in all Lowliness of heart that this is the case ye shall not cast them out" (v. 74). The wording of this statement suggests that divorce put an individual's membership at risk, and only if he or she could establish by satisfactory testimony that the divorce resulted from marital infidelity would the innocent party be able to retain membership in the Church. While attitudes toward divorce and the laws allowing it were beginning to soften in antebellum America,[64] the wording here recalls the rigor of the Sermon on the Mount: "Whosoever shall put away his wife, saving for the cause of fornication, causeth her to commit adultery: and whosoever shall marry her that is divorced committeth adultery" (Matthew 5:32).

The second case is straightforward. The member who leaves a spouse "for the sake of adultery and they themselves are the offender . . . shall be cast out" (D&C 42:75). The third and fourth scenarios are related to the second in that they envision an adulterer who has abandoned his or her faithful companion, but in these cases the adulterer is a nonmember seeking to join the Church. The elders are instructed to "be watchful and careful with all inquiry that ye receive none such among you if [case 3] they are married and if [case 4] they are not married they shall repent of all their sins or ye shall not receive them" (vv. 76–77).

It is noteworthy that in the third scenario, unlike the fourth, no provision is explicitly made for repentance and reception into fellowship. Was this an unimportant oversight because repentance was always understood to be possible in such cases? Or was it an unqualified rejection of the spiritual acceptability of remarriage for a sometime adulterer, along the lines of Matthew 19:9: "Whosoever shall put away his wife, except it be for fornication, and shall marry another, committeth adultery"? Is the seriousness of the case heightened by the fact that "their [aggrieved] companions are living"? The paucity of early sources mentioning divorce makes it difficult to determine with any confidence what the Saints' attitudes actually were. However, a brief report from the diary of Hyrum Smith shows how remarriage after divorce was suspect unless the cause of divorce was unfaithfulness on the part of the former spouse: "Went to Brother Roundays there we met with Brother morse we questioned him on the Subject of his Situation of his life he Being a man that has had two wifes he living with his Seccond wife the first Being yet a live But She was Put away for the Cause of fornication he Being innosent She the offender He testified in all loliness of Heart and Sett free."[65] The wording of this journal entry invokes a number of phrases from the text unit under consideration and demonstrates the seriousness with which the elders followed its guidelines.

Conclusion

The Law was clearly one of the most important documents in the early years of Latter-day Saint history. More prepublication manuscript copies of this revelation have survived than of almost any other revelation. It stands alongside the Articles and Covenants in terms of its utility to early Church leaders. The principal contributions of this study have been to probe significant revisions to the Law's text as well as to provide glimpses into early understandings of its various passages. The quantitative analysis and classification of textual changes have enabled a more precise assessment than previously available of the number and kind of inspired revisions made under prophetic direction. What stands out is that despite the fact that the revelations were given "unto my servants in their weakness, after the manner of their language" (D&C 1:24), the Prophet endeavored to compensate for that linguistic weakness and improve the wording as he felt inspired. He also strove to have the Law reflect current practice, much as the Church today regularly updates its *Handbook of Instructions* used by leaders at all levels to properly administer Church affairs.

Finally, the overall composition of the Law has also been cast in a new light. While a few historians have previously noticed that parts of the Law were received on two different days two weeks apart, this study illuminates the different nature of, and purpose for, the revealed material recorded on those days. What is more, detailed analysis has demonstrated that that material consisted of seven distinct text units, only one of which, albeit the largest of the clusters (58 percent of the entire document), contains the Law proper. More broadly, this close examination of the Law offers insight into the revelatory process that produced the canonical texts of the Doctrine and Covenants and the profound influence they exerted on the early Latter-day Saint community.

NOTES

1. John Whitmer, "Book of John Whitmer," 6, Community of Christ Library-Archives, Independence, Missouri.

2. Whitmer, "Book of John Whitmer," 12.

3. Capitalization conventions were not standard in antebellum America, so there is no consistent capitalization of "the Law" in early manuscripts; however, for clarity the term will be capitalized throughout.

4. Joseph Smith to Martin Harris, February 22, 1831, Joseph Smith Collection, box 2, folder 3, Church History Library, The Church of Jesus Christ of Latter-day Saints, Salt Lake City.

5. The quotation is from a transitional paragraph in the manuscript copy of the Law made by Symonds Ryder (see Revelations Collection, box 1, folder 13, Church History Library).

6. Yet another manuscript copy of the Law is mentioned in a letter Oliver Cowdery wrote to Newel K. Whitney on February 4, 1835: "Bishop Whitney, Will you have the kindness to send us by the bearer the original copy of the Revelation given to 12 elders Feb. 1831 called 'The Law of the Church'? We are preparing the old Star for re-printing, and have no copy from which to correct, and kno[w] of

no other beside yours. Your Ob't Serv't. Oliver Cowdery" (Newel K. Whitney Papers, L. Tom Perry Special Collections, Harold B. Lee Library, Brigham Young University, Provo, Utah). It is uncertain whether Cowdery had firsthand knowledge that the copy in Whitney's possession was the actual dictation copy or whether he was merely assuming that it was the original. In any case, the copy is no longer extant.

7. The current edition provides specific reception dates where they are known, but it lists only February 9, 1831, for section 42.

8. The answers to the first two questions end with "even so amen," thus further setting off those text clusters as distinct units.

9. Verse 73 was not a part of the original answer but was added later when the cluster was revised for publication in the Doctrine and Covenants.

10. It has been suggested that Symonds Ryder illicitly obtained this and the other manuscript copies of the revelations that were in his descendants' possession at the time they were acquired by the Church (see Scott Faulring, "Symonds Ryder," Mormon History Association Newsletter [Fall 1996], 4–5; and Faulring, "An Examination of the 1829 'Articles of the Church of Christ' in Relation to Section 20 of the Doctrine and Covenants," BYU Studies 43, no. 4 [2004]: 75–76). This now appears to be incorrect. It is true that in September 1831, Ryder, along with Ezra Booth, renounced his membership in the Church at a camp meeting in Shalersville, Ohio. It is also true that Ryder loaned his copy (or a copy of his copy) of the Law to the editor of the Western Courier in nearby Ravenna, Ohio, who printed a portion of it in his newspaper, along with a derisive editorial introduction. What is not substantiated by evidence, however, is that Ryder purloined his copies of the revelations while the Prophet was away in Missouri that summer.

The best reading of the evidence is that Ryder made his copies sometime before mid-June 1831, when Joseph Smith left for Missouri, and that he did so, like other early elders, with the permission of the Prophet for his personal use. This seems likely for several reasons. First, such a practice was common and accounts for many of the manuscript copies of the revelations in existence today. Second, there is no reason to believe that Ryder was dishonest. The Prophet never accused him of such behavior, and long after ceasing his association with the Church, Ryder continued as a highly regarded, upstanding member of the Hiram, Ohio, community in which he resided. Third, and most important, he probably made his copy of the Law in May 1831 (see *Painesville Telegraph*, September 13, 1831) when he clearly was in good standing in the Church (he is mentioned positively in D&C 52:37, given in early June 1831). However he acquired his copy, it is clear that he did not tamper with the text. Its wording is very close to that found in other early manuscripts.

11. Original scribal corrections in the various manuscript sources cited throughout this study are indicated by the use of angle brackets to show interlinear insertions and strikethroughs to identify words or letters that were either erased or crossed out.

12. Book of Commandments, 97 (chapter 45, verses 8–9). This wording was later revised for publication in the Doctrine and Covenants (see D&C 43:8–9).

13. Section 42 contains almost the same number of words in the current edition of the Doctrine and Covenants. Although there are dozens of punctuation, grammar, and spelling variations between the two versions, there are no conceptually significant differences. Indeed, textual analysis of the entire Doctrine and Covenants shows that this is true of almost all the revelations. Once they were published in 1835 in the Doctrine and Covenants, their wording seems to have been considered final, and no further updates or other significant revisions appear in subsequent editions.

14. Of similar changes in the Book of Mormon, President Boyd K. Packer remarked years ago, "Of course there have been changes and corrections. Anyone who has done even limited research knows that. When properly reviewed, such corrections become a testimony for, not against, the truth of the books" ("We Believe All That God Has Revealed," *Ensign*, May 1974, 94).

15. Unless it does not agree with the CEW, the Ryder manuscript will be quoted throughout this study.

16. Whitmer, "Book of John Whitmer," 17.

17. John Corrill, *A Brief History of the Church of Christ of Latter Day Saints* (St. Louis: printed for the author, 1839), 17.

18. Book of Commandments, 89 (chapter 44, heading); emphasis added.

19. Jan Shipps and John W. Welch, eds., *The Journals of William E. McLellin, 1831–1836* (Provo, UT: BYU Studies; Urbana: University of Illinois Press, 1994), 41 (September 18, 1831).

20. Richard Bushman, *Joseph Smith: Rough Stone Rolling* (New York: Knopf, 2005), 153.

21. Best known is "the Family," or "Morley's Family," who lived communally on Isaac Morley's farm in the township of Kirtland, Ohio. Of its origin, Family member Lyman Wight wrote, "I went to Kirtland, about twenty miles, to see Bro. I[saac] Morley and [Titus] Billings, after some conversation on the subject we entered into a covenant to make our interests one as anciently. In conformity to this covenant I moved the next February [1830] to Kirtland, into the house with Bro. Morley. We commenced our labors together with great peace and union. We were soon joined by eight other families. Our labors were united both in farming and mechanism, all of which was prosecuted with great vigor. We truly began to feel as if the millennium was close at hand" (*The History of the Reorganized Church of Jesus Christ of Latter Day Saints* [Independence, MO: Herald House, 1977], 1:152–53). Although Isaac Morley's Family lived together on the same property, others, like the smaller Family in Chardon, Ohio, reportedly shared a single house: "One man has torn away all the partitions of the lower part of a good two story house. Here a large number live together" (*The Geauga Gazette* [Painesville, Ohio], February 1, 1831).

22. Leonard J. Arrington, Feramorz Y. Fox, and Dean L. May, *Building the City of God: Community and Cooperation Among the Mormons* (Salt Lake City: Deseret Book, 1976), 15.

23. Noah Webster, *American Dictionary of the English Language* (New York: S. Converse, 1828; reprint, San Francisco: Foundation for American Christian Education, 1989), s.v. "consecrate."

24. See Donald E. Pitzer, ed., *America's Communal Utopias* (Chapel Hill: University of North Carolina Press, 1997).

25. Whitmer, "Book of John Whitmer," 17–18. Church members in Hiram, Ohio, appear to have been among those who "underst[oo]d not the things of the kingdom." A recollection years later by Symonds Ryder seems to refer to section 42 as the source of their disaffection. A long-since-disaffiliated Ryder recalled that several months after recording the Law, when Joseph and others "went to Missouri to lay the foundation of the splendid city of Zion, and also of the temple, they left their papers behind. This gave their new converts an opportunity to become acquainted with the internal arrangement of their church, which revealed to them the horrid fact that a plot was laid to take their property from them and place it under the control of Joseph Smith the prophet. This was too much for the Hiramites, and they left the Mormonites faster than they had ever joined them" (Symonds Ryder to Amos S. Hayden, February 1, 1868, as cited in Hayden, *Early History of the Disciples in the Western Reserve, Ohio* [Cincinnati: Chase & Hall, 1875], 221).

26. See Arrington and others, *Building the City of God*, 15–40.

27. Hereafter, for ease of comparison, textual revisions will be italicized.

28. Levi Jackman, Deed of Stewardship, Edward Partridge Papers, Church History Library.

29. See, for example, incidents reported in *Painesville Telegraph*, April 26, 1833; and *Star*, July 1833, 110.

30. Joseph Smith to Edward Partridge, May 2, 1833, Joseph Smith Collection, box 2, folder 3, Church History Library.

31. *Star*, June 1833, 100. In antebellum America, to be identified as a "common stock" organization or to be said to have "all things common" were characterizations of disparagement. As the editor of the reprinted *Star* remarked, "This assertion is meant, not only to falsify on the subject of property, but to blast the reputation and moral characters of the members of the same." Not that there was something intrinsically wrong with a community of goods, as the editor pointed out by citing the apostolic "church at Jerusalem" or the actions of Book of Mormon peoples "after the appearance of Christ," but the respective "government" under which each lived "was differently organized from ours, and could admit of such a course when ours cannot" (August 1831, reprint [March 1835], 48).

32. That some had gathered to Zion without consecrating is implicit in the strong warning issued in November 1832: "It is conterary to the will and commandment of God that those who receive not their inheritance by consecration agreeable to his law . . . should have there names enrolled with the people of God, neithe[r] is the[ir] geneology to be kept or to be had where it may be found on any of the reccords or hystory of the church there names shall not be found . . . writen in the book of the Law of God saith the Lord of hosts" (Joseph Smith to William W. Phelps, November 27, 1832, Joseph Smith Collection, box 2, folder 1,

Church History Library; compare D&C 85:3–5).

33. "Mormonism.—No. II," *Ohio Star*, October 20, 1831.

34. Morris Phelps, Reminiscence, as quoted in Joseph Smith, *History of the Church of Jesus Christ of Latter-day Saints*, ed. B. H. Roberts, 2nd ed. rev. (Salt Lake City: Deseret Book, 1957), 3:180. This was corroborated by several witnesses at the Richmond Court of Inquiry in November 1838. There John Cleminson testified that "it was frequently observed among the troops, that the time had come when the riches of the Gentiles should be consecrated to the Saints." And George Hinkle averred, "It was taught, that the time had come when the riches of the Gentiles were to be consecrated to the true Israel. This thing of taking property was considered a fulfillment of the above prophecy" (*Document Containing the Correspondence, Orders, &c. in Relation to the Disturbances with the Mormons* [Fayette, MO: Published by Order of the General Assembly, 1841], 115, 128).

35. Whitmer, "Book of John Whitmer," 91.

36. For a sampling of early Latter-day Saint healing accounts and a discussion of the doctrinal ideas that sustained them, see Underwood, "Supernaturalism and Healing in the Church of Jesus Christ of Latter-day Saints," in *Religions of the United States in Practice*, ed. Colleen McDannell (Princeton, NJ: Princeton University Press, 2001), 1:299–309.

37. Milton V. Backman Jr., *The Heavens Resound: A History of the Latter-day Saints in Ohio, 1830–1838* (Salt Lake City: Deseret Book, 1983), 82–83.

38. Lester E. Bush Jr., *Health and Medicine among the Latter-Day Saints: Science, Sense, and Scripture* (New York: Crossroad Publishing, 1993).

39. Kirtland Revelation Book, [138], Church History Library.

40. Robert T. Divett, "Medicine and the Mormons: A Historical Perspective," *Dialogue: A Journal of Mormon Thought* 12 (Fall 1979): 16–25; see also Alex Berman and Michael A. Flannery, *America's Botanico-Medical Movements: Vox Populi* (New York: Haworth Press, 2001); John S. Haller Jr., *The People's Doctors: Samuel Thomson and the American Botanical Movement, 1790–1860* (Carbondale: Southern Illinois University Press, 2000).

41. Lavina Fielding Anderson, ed., *Lucy's Book: A Critical Edition of Lucy Mack Smith's Family Memoir* (Salt Lake City: Signature Books, 2001), 713.

42. "Willford Woodruff's Journal for 1848," February 23, 1848, Church History Library.

43. Whitmer, "Book of John Whitmer," 11. Levi Hancock recorded a similar experience with another Family organization (see Hancock, "Life of Levi Hancock," 28, Church History Library).

44. "Each member was free to work as he pleased within the limitations of his stewardship. The profit system, the forces of supply and demand, and the price system presumably would continue to allocate resources, influence production decisions, and distribute primary or earned income. Some of the institutions of capitalism were thus retained and a considerable amount of economic freedom was permitted. Above all, there was to be no communism of goods" (Arrington and others, *Building the City of God*, 17).

45. Levi Jackman, Deed of Stewardship, Church History Library.

46. Joseph Smith et al. to Brethren [in Zion], June 25, 1833, Joseph Smith Collection, box 2, folder 1, Church History Library.

47. "The Conference Minutes and Record Book of Christ's Church of the Latter Day Saints," 16 (November 8, 1831), Church History Library; hereafter cited as Far West Record.

48. This revision appears in the Whitmer, Coltrin, and Hyde manuscripts, all copied in early 1832 or before, as well as in the excerpt of the Law published later that year in the *Star* and in the Book of Commandments the following year.

49. This merely echoes what had been stated as early as May 1831: "Let all things both in money & in meat which is more then is needful for the want of this People be kept in the hands of the Bishop & let him also reserve unto himself for his own wants & for the wants of his family as he shall be employed in doing this Business" (D&C 51:13–14).

50. That situation-specific guidance from the Spirit always took precedence over general guidelines—"notwithstanding those things which are written it always has been given to the Elders of my Church . . . to conduct all [matters] as they are directed & guided by the Holy spirit" (D&C 46:2)—appears not to have been comprehended initially by some of the Church leaders. Regarding this particular passage in the Law, Ezra Booth reported that in spring of 1831, in order to help settle the emigrating New York Saints, the Prophet felt prompted to direct Bishop Partridge to "secure" a particular land purchase in Thompson by contracting "a debt with the world to the amount of several hundred dollars." When Partridge "hesitated," construing the Law's injunction against debt as an absolute proscription, the Prophet insisted that Partridge "must secure the land" by arranging the loan ("Mormonism VII," *Ohio Star*, November 24, 1831).

51. The phrase "by hire" is an older English expression for "on credit" or "through a loan." The exact financial arrangements whereby the paper was acquired in Wheeling, Virginia, are not known.

52. "Revelation as to Paper," March 20, 1832, Newel K. Whitney Collection, L. Tom Perry Special Collections.

53. Far West Record, 26 (April 30, 1832).

54. Joseph Smith to "Dear Brethren" [in Missouri], December 5, 1833, Joseph Smith Collection, box 2, folder 1, Church History Library.

55. Joseph Smith, Journal (1832–34), 45–46, Joseph Smith Collection, box 1, folder 1, Church History Library; compare D&C 90:22–23.

56. Joseph Smith, Journal (1835–36), 1, Joseph Smith Collection, box 1, folder 2, Church History Library.

57. In the months ahead, the bishop would be "appointed to be a Judge in Israel . . . to Judge his people by the testimony of the Just & by the assistance of his councilors according to the laws of the kingdom" (D&C 58:17–18).

58. Being "overtaken in a fault" is language from Galatians 6:1.

59. See John S. Bowden, *Encyclopedia of Christianity* (New York: Oxford University Press, 2005), s.v. "discipline." For a modern pastoral analysis of the passage, see Jay E. Adams, *Handbook of Church Discipline* (Grand Rapids, MI: Zondervan, 1986).

60. The identical phrase "if he confess not" introduces both steps two and three. When this passage was first published in the *Star* in October 1832, typesetters missed the entire second step—"if he confess not thou shalt take another with thee." Though the error was corrected the following year when the Book of Commandments was published, it was perpetuated in the 1835 reprint of the *Star*. Because the wording in the *Star* reprint was almost always followed in the preparation of the 1835 Doctrine and Covenants, the line was similarly omitted there and was not subsequently restored in any edition of the Doctrine and Covenants.

61. Methodists shared this interpretation. John Wesley, in his "Sermon 49," explained: "It would not answer any valuable end, to tell the faults of every particular member to the church. . . . It remains that you tell it to the elder, or elders of the church, to those who are overseers of that flock of Christ, to which you both belong, who watch over yours and his soul" (John Wesley, *Sermons on Several Occasions* [New York: Lane & Scott, 1852], 1:438).

62. Compare Baptist practice as described in Gregory A. Wills, *Democratic Religion: Freedom, Authority, and Church Discipline in the Baptist South, 1785–1900* (New York: Oxford University Press, 1997), 20–25, 29–31, 37–49.

63. A probing analysis of the widespread social functions of honor and shame in the contemporary South is Bertram Wyatt-Brown, *Southern Honor: Ethics and Behavior in the Old South* (New York: Oxford University Press, 1982). For a particular focus on religious life, see Wyatt-Brown's chapter "Paradox, Shame, and Grace in the Backcountry," in his *The Shaping of Southern Culture: Honor, Grace, and War, 1760s-1890s* (Chapel Hill: University of North Carolina Press, 2001), 106–16.

64. See Norma Basch, *Framing American Divorce* (Berkeley: University of California Press, 1999).

65. Hyrum Smith, Journal (1832–33), April 4, 1833, L. Tom Perry Special Collections.

7

JOSEPH SMITH, EMANUEL SWEDENBORG, AND SECTION 76: IMPORTANCE OF THE BIBLE IN LATTER-DAY REVELATION

J. B. Haws

Influence is a slippery word in the history of ideas. Even when a researcher performs the Herculean task of reading everything that some great thinker read and wrote, contemporary context and conversation are elusive variables complicating every "influence" equation. With that said, this paper might seem inadvisable from the start, because it begins with one of those difficult "influence" puzzles: Was Emanuel Swedenborg the source of Joseph Smith's conception of a three-tiered heaven? Questions like this almost never lend themselves to a clear-cut yes or no; yet some recent observers have firmly pushed in just such a definitive direction in their evaluation of parallels in the writings of the eighteenth-century Swedish visionary and the Prophet Joseph Smith. In contrast to those strong assertions, this paper will argue for caution and tentativeness because the differences between the two revolutionary thinkers are as telling as the possible ties. Though certain similarities are intriguing, they do not necessarily require a

---

J. B. Haws is a seminary teacher in Roy, Utah.

direct connection between Swedenborg's writings and Joseph Smith's revelation. Instead, it might be more reasonable to suggest that both men drew from a common well, the Bible.

Latter-day Saints are generally accustomed to regarding their beliefs about heaven as unique from those of other Christians—and rightly so, many outside observers would say. Craig Blomberg, professor at the Denver Seminary, well represents the feelings of many outside Mormonism when he comments that "Doctrine and Covenants 76 hits [evangelical Christians] like a bolt out of the blue with its elaboration of *four* possible destinies of humanity."[1] But Brigham John Bowen has recently suggested that "the notion of degrees of glory," which today is "often thought of as . . . uniquely Mormon," was "not so in the nineteenth century."[2]

Colleen McDannell and Bernhard Lang, authors of *Heaven: A History*, agree. They detect in the early 1800s a change of religious climate of sorts which drew many thinkers toward a "modern perspective on heaven," one that "[emphasized] the nearness and similarity of the other world to our own and [argued] for the eternal nature of love, family, progress, and work."[3] As part of that theological trend, many religionists posited a multiple-degrees-of-glory conception of the afterlife and speculated about individual and personal differences in intellectual attainment or eternal felicity, based often on the Savior's comment about "many mansions" in His "Father's house" (John 14:2).[4] Bowen, in his review of nineteenth-century religious tracts and treatises, points out that prominent theologians such as Isaac Watts and Thomas Dick (who was a contemporary of Joseph Smith) suggested that heaven consisted of multiple levels and gradations—indeed, "the general consensus" of "numerous . . . visions, sermons, speculative treatises" was "that in some form, different degrees of glory do exist in the heavenly realm."[5] According to McDannell and Lang, "the understanding of life after death in the LDS Church is the clearest example of the continuation of the modern heaven into the twentieth century" because of Latter-day Saint adherence to a theology of heaven that comprises beliefs that once were more widely held—or at least more widely considered—by others.[6] That strain of Christianity seems now mostly forgotten, such that Latter-day Saints today might be surprised to learn that a Swedish nobleman and scientist named Emanuel Swedenborg, writing in the eighteenth century, recorded his visions of a heaven consisting of three regions.[7]

At this point, one might ask, if the notion of heavenly "degrees of glory" was not uncommon in Joseph Smith's day, why focus so much on the question of Swedenborg's influence?[8] Two responses seem relevant. First, the Prophet apparently mentioned Swedenborg by name during an 1839 conversation with Edward Hunter, a student of Swedenborgianism who later became a Latter-day Saint. Hunter had established a seminary dedicated to the free exchange of religious ideas, and when Joseph Smith stopped at this Nantmeal Seminary in Pennsylvania during a return trip from Washington DC, Hunter reported this exchange: "I asked him if he was acquainted with the Sweadenburgers. His answer I verially believe. 'Emanuel Sweadenburg had a view of the world to come but for daily food he perished.'"[9] If accurately remembered, this remark generates a whole range of questions.

Second, because both men described a heaven that consisted of specific and separate realms, there seems to be a greater qualitative correspondence in their respective views than in the more nebulous "many mansions"–type descriptions of heaven found in the writings of other contemporary theologians. McDannell and Lang "trace the roots of the modern heaven, at least in part, to Swedenborg" and see echoes of that "modern heaven" in Mormonism.[10] That correspondence has also been noted by Mary Ann Meyers, Craig Miller, and D. Michael Quinn.[11]

One might then ask, would Latter-day Saints even be troubled if it could be determined that Swedenborgian ideas did influence Joseph Smith? In Mormon thought, revelation is often seen as resulting from specific questions. For example, early revelations addressed the teachings of Ann Lee and the Shakers (see D&C 49) offered correctives to abortive attempts at New Testament–type communal living (D&C 42) and clarified sectarian quandaries over the nature of the Godhead (see D&C 130). Hence, a revelation sparked by questions derived from considering another tradition's doctrinal system would not seem unprecedented to Latter-day Saint observers. Joseph Smith himself said, "We should gather all the good and true principles in the world and treasure them up."[12] If, therefore, it could be determined that Swedenborgian ideas did inspire Joseph Smith's inquiries into the nature of heaven, Latter-day Saints likely would not view that as a threat to their understanding of the development of Mormonism. As Meyers aptly notes, "To stress the parallels between Swedenborgian and Mormon beliefs is neither to deny Smith's vision experiences nor to confirm those of the Swedish baron."[13]

At the same time, however, some who are critical of Joseph Smith skeptically look for the presumed "naturalistic origins" behind his writings to explain away his prophetic work.[14] Therefore, if a proposed connection to Swedenborg is intended to discredit the Prophet Joseph Smith—that is, intended to insinuate that an important doctrinal revelation was instead the wholesale and unacknowledged copy of another's writings—the question of influence bears more weight. The question of influence then gets at issues related to the very historical and religious roots of Mormonism.

What must be conceded is that most of the *historical* connections to be explored here—that is, those moments of opportunity when Joseph Smith might have been introduced to Swedenborgian tenets—are only speculative. The difficulty comes in determining the extent of Swedenborg's influence (if any) on Joseph Smith by the time of his 1839 comment to Edward Hunter (assuming the comment represents an accurate recollection). The *religious* connections that will be discussed afterward—that is, the scriptural ties and doctrinal implications of their respective afterlife theologies—are more substantive because they say important things about the significance of the Bible in understanding Joseph Smith's revelatory work.

Joseph Smith's Possible Encounters with Swedenborgianism

If indeed Joseph Smith was impressed and ultimately influenced by the teachings of Swedenborg, he would have found himself in good company. Swedenborg is not exactly a household name in contemporary American society, but Ralph Waldo Emerson read Swedenborg extensively and devoted one of his "representative men" lectures to him.[15] Henry James Sr. was a convert to Swedenborgianism, as was Helen Keller.[16] John Chapman—the famous "Johnny Appleseed"—was a Swedenborgian missionary.[17] Samuel Taylor Coleridge, William Blake, Thomas Carlyle, and Charles Peirce, among others, were also openly appreciative of Swedenborg's poetic descriptions of his visionary discoveries in the fields of both science and religion.[18]

Swedenborg was born the son of a Swedish bishop but initially pursued an academic career in mathematics and metallurgy. Scientific inquiries basically dominated the first half of his intellectual career, from 1710 to 1744, but recording his spiritual visions occupied the second half of his career, from 1745 to 1772, the year of his death. Over the pages of forty-plus volumes, he touched on subjects as diverse as chemistry, biology, philosophy, mineralogy, marriage, the afterlife, and the nature of God.[19] Considering both the variety and the volume, it is not difficult to see why a century of thinkers would have been drawn to consider Swedenborg's often revolutionary revelations.[20]

After "a spirit . . . spoke with him" in 1745, he "came to believe that God had called him to bring a new revelation to the world," such that he "claimed to have been constantly in touch with the spiritual world for more than a quarter of a century."[21] Based on his understanding of what he witnessed during these interchanges, Swedenborg described heaven as consisting of three divisions. Joseph Smith reported that on February 16, 1832, he and Sidney Rigdon likewise observed in vision that heaven consists of three divisions or kingdoms of glory—a revelation so fundamental to Mormonism that it is often referred to simply as "the Vision."[22]

Joseph Smith's brief but generally complimentary assessment of Swedenborg's visions begs some crucial questions: If Joseph Smith made this comment in 1839, when did he become acquainted with Swedenborg's writings? What was his source of information? Miller raises an intriguing possibility. A Mormon convert, Sarah Cleveland, and her Swedenborgian husband, John Cleveland, moved to Quincy, Illinois, in the mid-1830s, while most Latter-day Saints (including Joseph Smith) were gathering to Kirtland, Ohio, or western Missouri. But in early 1839, the Quincy area became the new gathering place for the exiled Mormons, and the Clevelands became closely associated with the Smith family when "Emma Smith and her children lived with the Clevelands for a short time in 1839 while Joseph was in jail."[23]

Significantly, Joseph Smith was released from jail in Missouri in April 1839 and immediately traveled to the Quincy area, where he began to establish Nauvoo in the spring and summer of 1839. He would certainly have become acquainted with the Clevelands during those months he spent in Illinois before his November 1839 trip to Washington DC. It was during his return from Washington that he met Edward Hunter and reportedly made the remark about Swedenborg's visions.[24]

While the Clevelands thus seem to be a potentially solid, logical source for information on Swedenborg, their informative role could only have been a relatively late one, coming seven years after the publication of Joseph Smith's vision of the degrees of glory. If the Clevelands were his earliest source for Swedenborgian doctrine, the question of influence would be moot, and the puzzle of Joseph Smith's conversation with Edward Hunter would be resolved. Yet this question remains: had Joseph Smith been exposed to information on Swedenborg *before* he and Sidney Rigdon experienced "the Vision"?

Quinn has suggested—and his suggestion has proven very influential—that Joseph Smith could have become acquainted with Swedenborgian ideas through the occasional advertising and sale of Swedenborg's religious tracts in the environs around Joseph Smith's Palmyra home.[25] One author, citing Quinn's work, went so far as to declare that "Mormonism and Spiritualism share a common ancestor in Swedenborgism."[26] Yet there are some problems with this sweeping conclusion, considering both the spottiness of the dates of the newspaper advertisements and the distances between Joseph Smith's home and the places of publication.[27] As Miller also points out, an argument for the likelihood that Joseph Smith gained any type of thorough fluency with Swedenborgian theology through his personal study of those Swedenborgian writings that *might* have been available for perusal would also mean the discounting of this telling observation made by Joseph Smith's mother: "Joseph was less inclined to the study of books than any child we had, but much more given to reflection and deep study," such that when he was "eighteen years of age" he "had never read the Bible through by course in his life."[28] Still, it is possible that local publications made Joseph Smith at least *aware* of Swedenborg's name and reputation.[29]

Meyers presents another possible source for Joseph Smith's introduction to Swedenborgian ideas, and her suggestion seems worthy of additional exploration. Recognizing the importance of Sidney Rigdon in the history of early Mormonism, Meyers notes that Swedenborgian evangelists were active in Rigdon's Pittsburgh as early as 1790.[30] Because Sidney Rigdon participated with Joseph Smith in "the Vision," Meyers's recognition of Rigdon's possible role in transmitting Swedenborgian ideas is intriguing. Such a connection relies on another somewhat tenuous contingency: that Sidney Rigdon was actually exposed to those evangelists and that he engaged them long enough to absorb some of their doctrines about life after death. This circumstantial connection is not without merit, because Rigdon was an avid student of religious ideas. However, an even stronger reason to believe that Sidney Rigdon was at the very least exposed to Swedenborg's ideas comes from the writings of Alexander Campbell.

By 1830, Sidney Rigdon had been a close associate of Campbell's for more than a decade. He had been persuaded by Campbell's preaching in favor of the restoration of Christian primitivism, and he had allied himself with Campbell's movement (now referred to as the "Disciples of Christ" or "Churches of Christ").[31] Rigdon was an active preacher, leading a congregation in Mentor, Ohio. However, in the fall of 1830, his ties with Campbell were strained to the breaking point. Campbell expressed sharp disdain for Rigdon's group's attempts at establishing a type of "New Testament communitarianism," such that the "differences between Rigdon and Campbell boiled over."[32] By late October 1830, Rigdon had been introduced to the newly published Book of Mormon and was soon thereafter baptized a Latter-day Saint. A little over a year later, Sidney Rigdon was with Joseph Smith when "the eyes of [their] understandings ... were opened" (D&C 76:19), and they saw the vision of the three degrees of glory.[33]

Therefore, considering Rigdon's long association with Alexander Campbell before joining with the Mormons, the discovery that Campbell made several references to Swedenborg in the two periodicals that he edited and published seems significant.[34] In fact, in at least two instances, Swedenborg and Rigdon are both mentioned in the same issue of the periodical—once even in the same article. In the October 4,

1830, issue of the *Millennial Harbinger,* an article entitled "Traveller's Reply—Excerpts from the Traveller's Journal" contains this interesting entry: "June 21st. Read two hours in the visions of Swedenborg on Heaven and Hell; and a sketch of his life." Then, after providing a journal entry for June 22, the "traveller," who signs the article "Francis," wrote a summary of his experiences: "I had the privilege of spending several days at [Alexander Campbell's] house, of forming a very pleasing personal acquaintance with him. . . . I was introduced also to Walter Scott, to Sidney Rigdon, to Adamson Bentley; which three ministers have immersed, within three years, at least three thousand persons."[35] While it is impossible to determine the chronological order of the "traveller's" June 21 reading of Swedenborg and his undated introduction to Sidney Rigdon, at least this passage establishes that someone familiar with a specific Swedenborgian text also knew Sidney Rigdon. Because Swedenborg's *Heaven and Hell* is mentioned—a text which discusses the three-tiered heaven—and because of Rigdon's own intellectual curiosity, it seems reasonable to infer that Rigdon could have possessed a basic familiarity with Swedenborg's view of the afterlife before he began his association with Joseph Smith.

Recognizing that any further conclusion beyond this suggestive Swedenborg-Rigdon connection will be speculative, it at least seems appropriate to say something about Rigdon's participation in the vision of the degrees of glory.[36] He had become the principal scribe for Joseph Smith's work on a translation or revision of the Bible. When they came to John 5:29 in the translation work, Joseph Smith records that the verse "caused [them] to marvel," and it was while they "meditated upon these things" that the vision opened (D&C 76:18–19). Could it be possible, then, that in reflecting on the nature of the Resurrection, Sidney Rigdon brought up something he had learned from Swedenborg's idea of a three-tiered heaven or that Joseph Smith may have remembered hearing something of the same? There are other connected possibilities.

Joseph Smith worked extensively on his Bible revision and translation for the first three years after the organization of The Church of Jesus Christ of Latter-day Saints, from 1830 to 1833. Several of his recorded revelations are directly tied to questions that arose during that translation work. It is interesting to note that there is evidence that the translation did not proceed sequentially in all cases. For example, Joseph Smith translated John 5:29, which preceded receiving the revelation now contained in Doctrine and Covenants 76, on February 16, 1832. A month previously Joseph Smith recorded what is now Doctrine and Covenants 74—a revelation directly commenting on 1 Corinthians 7:14.[37] Receipt of Doctrine and Covenants 74 suggests that Joseph Smith had been involved, in January 1832, with a study of at least 1 Corinthians 7. Interestingly, the biblical passage most directly connected to the vision of the three degrees is found in 1 Corinthians 15:40–42. Could it be that Joseph Smith was intrigued by the notion of *three* glories implied in these verses—perhaps even in part because of Swedenborgian doctrine—such that the traditional understanding of John 5:29, which he read a few weeks later, and its resurrection dichotomy seemed incomplete?[38]

As inconclusive as the investigation into the Joseph Smith–Emanuel Swedenborg points of contact seem to be, these questions remain open. Additionally, an examination of the similarities and dissimilarities in the visionary texts speaks even more directly to reasonable limits on the suggested extent of Swedenborg's influence on Joseph Smith, because careful readers of Doctrine and Covenants 76 will notice that Joseph Smith's revelation is built on a framework of direct quotations of biblical passages.

The Visions of Heaven and Their Biblical Ties

There is a sense that the Prophet Joseph Smith's vision is a conscious and careful expansion of pertinent scriptural texts. To be sure, the revelation certainly gives to those texts a significance and meaning that they do not have in traditional Christian understanding, yet the revelation repeatedly grounds itself in the language of the Bible. This point can hardly be overstated, and because it bears on the question of the degree of Swedenborg's influence, it demands a more extensive treatment.

The central New Testament passage that weaves itself throughout Joseph Smith's vision is 1 Corinthians 15:40–42. The Apostle Paul wrote, "There are also celestial bodies, and bodies terrestrial: but the glory of the celestial is one, and the glory of the terrestrial is another.

There is one glory of the sun, and another glory of the moon, and another glory of the stars: for one star differeth from another star in glory. So also is the resurrection of the dead. It is sown in corruption; it is raised in incorruption." Readers familiar with Mormonism's conception of a three-tiered heaven will recognize the points of contact between this passage and the Latter-day Saint description of that heaven. Allusions to this passage from 1 Corinthians 15 abound in Doctrine and Covenants 76: inhabitants of the highest kingdom of glory are "they whose bodies are celestial" (v. 70); the glory of the celestial kingdom is such that "the sun of the firmament is written of as being typical" (v. 70); the difference between the celestial kingdom and the terrestrial kingdom is analogous to the way that "the moon differs from the sun in the firmament" (v. 71); the summary description of the three kingdoms of glory follows—and even adopts—Paul's language: "And the glory of the celestial is one, even as the glory of the sun is one. And the glory of the terrestrial is one, even as the glory of the moon is one. And the glory of the telestial is one, even as the glory of the stars is one; for as one star differs from another star in glory, even so differs one from another in the glory in the telestial world" (vv. 96–98). It seems evident that Joseph Smith understood his visionary experience to be related directly to Paul's description of the Resurrection and thus chose to present his vision as an expansion of that description.

It is therefore surprising to note that Emanuel Swedenborg apparently never quoted from, nor even referred to, 1 Corinthians 15:40–42 in any of his voluminous writings.[39] Swedenborg did call the highest level of heaven the "celestial kingdom," yet because this was a common synonym for heaven in the Christian vernacular, it would seem a serious stretch to see in this shared vocabulary a direct borrowing of Swedenborgian thought in Joseph Smith's writings.[40] Joseph Smith, based on his interpretation of the Pauline passage, called the second kingdom or heavenly level "terrestrial," while Swedenborg called that level "spiritual." The phrase "terrestrial bodies" and the single word *terrestrial* do appear in Swedenborg's translated writings, but never do they describe or even refer to the inhabitants of the second or "spiritual" heaven.[41] The word *telestial*, which Joseph Smith used to describe the lowest degree of heaven, never appears in Swedenborg's works—and indeed seems to be an invented word unique to Joseph Smith.[42]

Quinn, in his review of similarities between Swedenborgianism and Doctrine and Covenants 76, candidly admits that of "the names of the three glories (Celestial, Terrestrial, and Telestial) in Joseph Smith's 1832 vision, . . . only the Celestial corresponded to Swedenborg's theology of three heavens," yet asserts that Swedenborg "stated that the inhabitants of the three heavens corresponded to the sun, moon, and stars."[43] Such an assertion, if true, would seem to imply another Swedenborgian parallel in Joseph Smith's use of 1 Corinthians 15:40–42. However, a review of Swedenborg's writings reveals that Quinn misappropriated or at least overstated the sun-moon-star description in Swedenborg's work, and subsequent writers may have too readily accepted Quinn's conclusions, thus exaggerating the perception of similarity.[44]

The passage that Quinn quotes in support of Swedenborg's sun-moon-star description is from *Arcana Coelestia*. Like so much of Swedenborg's poetic and symbolic writings, the passage is complex and not easily deciphered. However, what seems most clear is that Swedenborg used the sun-moon metaphor to describe the *Lord* rather than the three-tiered heaven (note that the celestial, spiritual, and natural kingdoms or heavens are not even mentioned in this passage). He wrote:

> The sun has a correspondence, and so does the moon; for in heaven the Lord is the Sun, and the Moon too. The fire and heat of the sun, as well as its light, have a correspondence, for it is the Lord's love towards the whole human race that its fire and heat correspond to, and His Divine truth that its light corresponds to. The stars too have a correspondence, the communities of heaven and their dwelling-places being what the stars correspond to. Not that the heavenly communities dwell in the stars, but that they have been set in order in the same kind of way as the stars.[45]

Rather than associating stars with only the third heaven, Swedenborg apparently used the stars as a representative metaphor for *all* the "communities of heaven and their dwelling-places." That analogy could be understood as implying gradations of glory, and Swedenborg does close this passage by noting that "the specific nature of each person's correspondence therefore determines what he looks like in the next life in the light of heaven. This explains why angels have an indescribably bright and beautiful appearance, whereas those in hell have an unspeakably dark and ugly one."[46] Yet nowhere in this passage is there the threefold division of heaven, nor any association with the glory of the sun, moon, and stars.

An interesting line in Swedenborg's *Heaven and Hell* describes the Lord as both sun and moon: "The Lord is seen as a sun by those who are in His celestial kingdom, where love to Him reigns, and as a moon by those who are in His spiritual kingdom, where charity to the neighbor and faith reign."[47] Again, for Swedenborg there is certainly a qualitative difference between those in the highest and second (and, though not mentioned in this passage, the third) heavenly kingdoms, and again he used the sun and moon as metaphors for the Lord, but this is not the explicit "sun/moon/stars" *triad* that Joseph Smith used as an analogy for the glory of the *inhabitants* of the respective kingdoms, "*whose bodies* are celestial" or terrestrial or telestial, "*whose glory* is that of the sun" or moon or stars (D&C 76:70; emphasis added). The strength of this distinction seems to be highlighted by another allusion to the celestial, terrestrial, and telestial glories in a revelation Joseph Smith recorded ten months after section 76. Doctrine and Covenants 88:19–32 makes clear that the kingdoms of glory correspond to the degrees of glory which will "quicken" those resurrected souls who inherit the various kingdoms. On the other hand, the phrases the "glory of the moon" and the "glory of the stars"—Paul's phrases from 1 Corinthians 15:40–42—never appear in Swedenborg's translated writings.

Instead of the sun-moon-star association, it seems that a student of Swedenborg would be naturally led to choose a different analogy for heaven that is more readily apparent in his writings: the divisions among bodily organs. In three of the four passages that Quinn cites in support of the three-tiered heaven, Swedenborg mentions parts of the body in conjunction with heaven, specifically stating that "inhabitants of the Lord's celestial kingdom all belong to the province of the heart, and those of His spiritual kingdom all belong to the province of the lungs. The influx from the celestial kingdom into the spiritual kingdom is similar to the influx of the heart into the lungs, and also to the influx of all things belonging to the heart into those belonging to the lungs."[48] Swedenborg's heart and lung analogy for the two kingdoms of heaven never appears in Joseph Smith's vision. Interestingly, earlier in this same passage Swedenborg writes that "in heaven or the Grand Man there are *two* kingdoms, one called celestial, the other spiritual."[49] This is not to say that he was denying the existence of the third tier, but it perhaps suggests that Swedenborg's view of heaven was not always precisely and consistently described, so that his writings could lead to alternately a three- or two-tiered heaven, depending on which works were consulted.

No evidence therefore suggests that 1 Corinthians 15:40–42 informed Swedenborg's vision of heaven, but this passage directly influenced Joseph Smith. Indeed, the ties to biblical passages in Doctrine and Covenants 76 extend beyond these explicit references to 1 Corinthians 15:40–42.[50] Several chief theological concepts in the revelation are explained with direct scriptural citations. For example, those who inherit hell after final judgment in Latter-day Saint theology are called "sons of perdition," and in describing them in Doctrine and Covenants 76, Joseph Smith used Jesus Christ's description of Judas Iscariot: "It had been better for them never to have been born" (v. 32; compare Matthew 26:24). Their sin, according to Doctrine and Covenants 76:35, is that after "having received [the Holy Spirit]," they have "crucified [the Only Begotten Son of the Father] unto themselves and put him to an open shame," another direct quotation from the New Testament (compare Hebrews 6:6). Swedenborg never referred to Matthew 26:24 or Hebrews 6:6, nor did he ever use the phrase "sons of perdition," verses and terminology that were integral to Joseph Smith's understanding of the inhabitants of hell.

In defining the parameters of the telestial kingdom, and specifically the type of people whose choices would lead to an inheritance in that third kingdom of glory, Joseph Smith again turned to biblical passages, quoting Revelation 22:15 (compare D&C 76:103) and 1 Corinthians

3:22 (compare D&C 76:99). However, those verses are never cited by Swedenborg.

Finally, and perhaps most theologically important for Latter-day Saints, Joseph Smith wrote in Doctrine and Covenants 76:58–59 that those who inherited the celestial kingdom would become "gods, even the sons of God—wherefore, all things are theirs, whether life or death, or things present, or things to come, all are theirs and they are Christ's, and Christ is God's." The language Joseph Smith used to explain this celestial inheritance comes again directly from Paul—1 Corinthians 3:22–23. Neither 1 Corinthians 3 nor the central phrase from Hebrews 12:23, "church of the Firstborn," appear in Swedenborg's works.[51]

To be sure, Swedenborg did quote extensively from the Bible and was a devoted student of the Bible, even in its original languages.[52] What seems telling is that Swedenborg associated his three-tiered heaven with 2 Corinthians 12:2–4, in which Paul reported that he "knew a man in Christ . . . (whether in the body, I cannot tell; or whether out of the body, I cannot tell: God knoweth;) such an one caught up to the third heaven. And I knew such a man, (whether in the body, or out of the body, I cannot tell: God knoweth;) how that he was caught up into paradise, and heard unspeakable words, which it is not lawful for a man to utter."[53] Swedenborg referred to this verse in at least two interconnected ways: first, to describe his own visionary experience of being "caught up" and hearing "unspeakable words";[54] and second, in the context of a specific discussion of the three divisions—celestial, spiritual, and natural.[55]

This extensive list of the real, substantive differences that lie beneath the initial veneer of similarity between the respective Swedenborgian and Latter-day Saint understandings of heaven prompts several observations. First, those writers who have seemed anxious to explain away Joseph Smith's vision as dependent on, or even a wholesale appropriation of, Swedenborgian thought might reconsider the complexity of both revelations. In reality, Meyers's cautious proposal seems wise. She wrote of "the possibility that Joseph Smith's picture of the realms of glory is derived indirectly from Emanuel Swedenborg's *Heaven and Hell*," but the truly distinctive explanations of the two systems underscore the words *possibility* and *indirectly*.[56]

Second, two disaffected, nineteenth-century Mormon writers familiar with both Emanuel Swedenborg and Joseph Smith never hinted at any similarity in their respective conceptions of heaven. At the very least, John Hyde's and William Godbe's conspicuous silence on the Emanuel Swedenborg–Joseph Smith connection recommends caution before making conclusions, perhaps raising the same challenge suggested by the textual comparison of the two descriptions of heaven: the initial similarities seem more superficial after a thorough investigation into the substance of the doctrines.[57]

CONCLUSION

In conclusion, there are parallels, and both Quinn and Miller have noted the uniqueness of the three-tiered heaven when compared with traditional Christian eschatology. How does one account, then, for the similarities found in Joseph Smith's and Emanuel Swedenborg's respective descriptions of the afterlife? Believing Latter-day Saints might answer that question with an explanation that parallels Joseph Smith's reported statement to Edward Hunter: it is possible that Swedenborg saw the heavens. Latter-day Saints readily accept that individuals outside their tradition have been given special, revealed insight into heavenly truths, and thus the points of convergence in Swedenborgianism and Mormonism could reflect accurate, though independent, descriptions of true Christian eschatology. Latter-day Saints could accept that, to a remarkable degree, Emanuel Swedenborg and Joseph Smith both experienced actual visions of *the* afterlife reality.[58]

Observers outside the Latter-day Saint tradition would obviously not be satisfied with this type of shared-vision explanation. Even so, there is another reasonable explanation that can account for the similarities in the two theological systems: both men studied the Bible intensively.

Swedenborg experienced a midlife change following the visionary experience in 1745 that he interpreted as a call "to bring a new revelation to the world," and Sig Synnestvedt notes that "he spent the two years immediately following his 'call' in further close study of the Bible. . . . He perfected his knowledge of Hebrew and Greek in order to study the Bible in the original texts, and, in effect, made a new translation of many of the books of both the Old and New Testaments. In 1747 he began publication of his most extended theological work, *Arcana Coelestia—Heavenly Secrets*. This study of the books of Genesis and Exodus runs to more than 7,000 pages or about three million words."[59] It is significant that while Swedenborg's work is most often described today as mystic or even hermetic, he saw himself as unlocking the Bible.[60] His massive *Arcana Coelestia* commentary represents his immersion into the Bible, and, importantly, it is in this *Arcana Coelestia* that readers find many of the descriptions of the three levels of heaven.

In a similar way, Joseph Smith's most prolific period for recorded revelations corresponded exactly with his translation or revision of the Bible.[61] Like Swedenborg, Joseph Smith systematically worked his way through the Bible, noting changes and doctrinal corrections or clarifications. His vision of the three degrees of glory was reported as a direct outgrowth of that translation endeavor.

Quinn and John Brooke refer to "the seven heavens of Jewish mysticism," "angelology," "magic books," "a wide range of occult influences" as the possible seedbeds for Emanuel Swedenborg's and Joseph Smith's descriptions of heaven.[62] Perhaps their extensive and impressive sifting through this type of esoteric source material is more complicated than it needs to be. Swedenborg could have been prompted to consider a three-tiered heaven simply through reading Paul's intriguing mention of "a third heaven" in 2 Corinthians 12:1–4, verses Swedenborg quoted (and personalized) on several occasions. Joseph Smith could have derived his description of three glories from Paul's description in 1 Corinthians 15:40–42, the very verses that he employed to explain his vision. In fact, the Bible became *the* source by which Joseph Smith verbalized his revelation.

In the end, then, it seems difficult to describe Joseph Smith's recorded vision of heaven as a magical or occult exposition on life after death, if "magical" and "occult" are taken to mean extrabiblical or non-Christian. Instead, Joseph Smith's revelation is thoroughly connected to the Bible, even if his extrapolations from those biblical passages are admittedly unique. And while Swedenborg's writings on heaven have an undeniably distinct feel from Doctrine and Covenants 76, in that Swedenborg rarely adopts direct biblical phraseology, and the poetic freedom of his writing often feels disconnected, it still can be argued that his idea of three heavens could be primarily an expansive interpretation that begins at a biblical starting point.

Therefore, this exercise can lead us finally to consider generally the Bible and the idea of influence as it relates to early Mormonism. Jan Shipps, Richard Bushman, and Philip Barlow, in reviewing Brooke's *The Refiner's Fire,* all settled on a similar observation about his thesis of hermetic influences on Joseph Smith. In the words of Jan Shipps, "Although [Bushman and Barlow] apparently did not compare notes about what they would write, both . . . pointed to Brooke's failure to recognize how much of what he described as hermetic or occult came directly from the New Testament."[63] Shipps then adds, "Brooke concentrates too much on the recondite and radical aspects of this new faith. At no point does he acknowledge that the religious and cultural situation into which Mormonism made its way was one in which . . . authority continued to rest in the Bible—the Bible alone, *sola scriptura.*"[64] The suggestion that Swedenborg appealed to Joseph Smith because of a transmitted hermeticism thus neglects a crucial aspect of Doctrine and Covenants 76: that revelation is more than anything else a blending of literal readings of the Bible into a revolutionary view of heaven. And in that quality of being revolutionary perhaps more than in anything else, Emanuel Swedenborg and Joseph Smith were alike.

NOTES

1. Craig L. Blomberg and Stephen E. Robinson, *How Wide the Divide? A Mormon and an Evangelical in Conversation* (Downers Grove, IL: InterVarsity Press, 1997), 177.

2. Brigham John Bowen, "Present in the World of Glory: Joseph Smith and Early Nineteenth-Century Views of Heaven," in Richard Lyman Bushman, ed., *Archive of Restoration Culture: Summer Fellows' Papers, 2000–2002* (Provo, UT: Joseph Fielding Smith Institute for Latter-day Saint History, Brigham Young University, 2005), 102.

3. Colleen McDannell and Bernhard Lang, *Heaven: A History* (New Haven, CT: Yale University Press, 1988), 313. See McDannell and Lang, *Heaven,* 183, for a fuller description of what they mean by "modern heaven." See Bowen, "Present in the World of Glory," 99–100, for a thoughtful summary of this portion of McDannell and Lang's work.

4. Bowen, "Present in the World of Glory," 103.

5. Bowen, "Present in the World of Glory," 103.
6. McDannell and Lang, *Heaven*, 320.
7. For a summary of Emmanuel Swedenborg's life and influence, as well as an up-to-date report on the activities and organization of one branch of his followers who comprise the New Church denomination of the General Church of the New Jerusalem, see www.newchurch.org. This Web site also has links to the church's "affiliate organizations," including the General Church's Bryn Athyn College in Philadelphia. The General Church of the New Jerusalem split from another New Church organization, the Swedenborgian Church of North America. See their Web site at www.swedenborg.org. Swedenborg himself never organized a church, but the New Church movement was initiated soon after his death by those who were impressed by his writings.
8. It should be noted that Fawn Brodie proposed that Joseph Smith's vision of heaven drew on one of the aforementioned theologians, Thomas Dick (see Bowen, "Present in the World of Glory," 105n11, where he cites both Brodie's *No Man Knows My History* [New York: Vintage Books, 1995], 172–73, as well as Edward T. Jones, "The Theology of Thomas Dick and Its Possible Relationship to That of Joseph Smith" [master's thesis, Brigham Young University, 1969], "for a thorough discussion and refutation of Brodie's claims"; see also Richard Lyman Bushman, *Joseph Smith: Rough Stone Rolling* [New York: Alfred A. Knopf, 2005], 458, 648n81).
9. William E. Hunter, *Edward Hunter: Faithful Steward* (Salt Lake City: Publishers Press, 1970), 316; original spelling retained. The quote comes from the typescript of the "Autobiography of Edward Hunter" included in the final chapter of the book.
10. Bowen, "Present in the World of Glory," 105n2. Chapter 7 of McDannell and Lang's *Heaven* is entitled "Swedenborg and the Emergence of a Modern Heaven."
11. Mary Ann Meyers, "Death in Swedenborgian and Mormon Eschatology," *Dialogue* 14, no. 1 (Spring 1981): 58–64; D. Michael Quinn, *Early Mormonism and the Magic World View*, revised and enlarged edition (Salt Lake City: Signature Books, 1998), 217–19; Craig W. Miller, "Did Emanuel Swedenborg Influence LDS Doctrine?" unpublished paper. Miller has posted his paper at craigwmiller.tripod.com with a note that the page was last updated on June 4, 2000. Miller also gave presentations on Mormon-Swedenborg parallels at the 1998 and 2002 Sunstone symposia in Salt Lake City. His approach is the most extensive and comprehensive, and he deals with remarkable parallels that extend beyond the three-tiered heaven doctrine considered here. His analysis and attention to detail are impressive. I would argue that many of the parallels he discusses (marriage, for example) could be treated in a manner analogous to the treatment of the three heaven parallels we receive here: Emanuel Swedenborg and Joseph Smith both had the Bible as their theological starting point, and their revelations represent expansions of biblical passages.
12. Joseph Smith, *Teachings of the Prophet Joseph Smith*, comp. Joseph Fielding Smith (Salt Lake City: Deseret Book, 1976), 316.

13. Meyers, "Death in Swedenborgian and Mormon Eschatology," 59.

14. Robert D. Anderson, Review of Wayne L. Cowdery, Howard A. Davis, and Arthur Vanick, "Who Really Wrote the Book of Mormon," *Journal of Mormon History* 33, no. 2 (Summer 2007): 244. Though Anderson's comments apply to "the valid quest" for the "skeptic" to seek the "naturalistic origins" of the Book of Mormon, his assertions seem to characterize more general criticism of the Prophet Joseph Smith.

15. Sig Synnestvedt, *The Essential Swedenborg: Basic Teachings of Emanuel Swedenborg, Scientist, Philosopher, and Theologian* (The Swedenborg Foundation and Twayne Publishers, 1970), 5–6; Colin Wilson, "Introduction," in Emanuel Swedenborg, *Heaven and Hell*, trans. George F. Dole (West Chester, PA: The Swedenborg Foundation, 1979), 10; see also Robert D. Richardson Jr., *Emerson: The Mind on Fire* (Berkeley and Los Angeles: University of California Press, 1995), 667, 670, where the number of references to Swedenborg in the book's index exceeds the number of references to Plato by one.

16. Louis Menand, *The Metaphysical Club* (New York: Farrar, Straus, and Giroux, 2001), 82; Wilson, "Introduction," 21; Synnestvedt, *The Essential Swedenborg*, 7.

17. N. J. Paterson, *Johnny Appleseed: A Voice in the Wilderness: The Story of the Pioneer John Chapman* (The Swedenborg Press, 1947).

18. Synnestvedt, *The Essential Swedenborg*, 6; Menand, *The Metaphysical Club*, 275.

19. See Synnestvedt, *The Essential Swedenborg*, 16–35, for both a succinct chronology and biographical sketch of Swedenborg's life.

20. Mary Ann Meyers makes an argument for Swedenborg's appeal to readers who were well educated—especially in the sciences—and affluent, suggesting that Swedenborg's background and career, the complexities of his doctrine, as well as his emphasis on education, contribute to his appeal (Mary Ann Meyers, *A New World Jerusalem: The Swedenborgian Experience in Community Construction* [Westport, CT: Greenwood Press, 1983], 15–16).

21. Synnestvedt, *The Essential Swedenborg*, 25; Meyers, *A New World Jerusalem*, 17 (caption to the illustration). Swedenborg's own description of his visionary experiences comes in his work *Arcana Coelestia*, trans. John E. Elliott, 5; accessed on March 11, 2008, at http://theheavenlydoctrines.org/static/d8086/5.htm: "I have been allowed constantly and without interruption for several years now to share the experiences of spirits and angels, to listen to them speaking and to speak to them myself. I have been allowed therefore to hear and see astounding things in the next life which have never come to any man's knowledge, nor even entered his imagination In that world I have learned about different kinds of spirits, about the state of souls after death, about hell (the miserable state of people who do not have faith), about heaven (the very happy state of those who do have faith), and above all else about the doctrine of the faith that is acknowledged in the whole of heaven. In the Lord's Divine mercy more will be told about these matters in what follows." It should be noted that Swedenborg's works are numbered by passage rather than by page, so that all editions and translations correspond by passage number. Thirty-five of his most important religious texts have been digitized and are provided in a searchable format on the internet at http://theheavenlydoctrines.org. That

resource has proven invaluable to this study. All of Swedenborg's writings cited in this paper come from that digitized collection. Often, more than one translation from Swedenborg's Latin is included on the Web site.

22. On the publication of the vision, see Robert J. Woodford, *Historical Development of the Doctrine and Covenants* (PhD diss., Brigham Young University, 1974), 934, where he notes that "the Vision" was published in the *Evening and Morning Star* five months after the February 1832 receipt of the revelation. Woodford's extensive documentation of textual changes in all editions of this revelation underscores the fact that, minus some spelling and grammar changes and other minor editing, the revelation published today is substantially and doctrinally the same as in its earliest 1832 published form. All references to canonized Latter-day Saint writings (the Book of Mormon, the Doctrine and Covenants, the Pearl of Great Price) will be to the 1981 editions of those scriptures, unless otherwise noted.

23. Miller, "Did Emanuel Swedenborg Influence LDS Doctrine?" 10. Richard Bushman mentions Emma's residency with the Clevelands, but he does not mention Judge Cleveland's religious background (Bushman, *Rough Stone Rolling*, 376).

24. Hunter, *Edward Hunter*, 51.

25. Quinn, *Early Mormonism*, 217–18; see also John L. Brooke, *The Refiner's Fire: The Making of Mormon Cosmology, 1644–1844* (New York and Cambridge: Cambridge University Press, 1994), 205: "Michael Quinn has noted that the idea of three heavens, or degrees of glory, was available in Emmanuel Swedenborg's cosmic system, in which three heavens—topped by a 'celestial kingdom'—were associated with the sun, the moon, and the stars. . . . Swedenborg's cosmos was summarized in various short texts available in Palmyra, and translations of his original texts would not have been too difficult to locate in the 1830s." Brooke's book received wide acclaim as a winner of the Bancroft Prize.

26. Michael W. Homer, "Spiritualism and Mormonism: Some Thoughts on Similarities and Differences," *Dialogue* 27, no. 1 (Spring 1994): 174n16.

27. Quinn, *Early Mormonism*, 217–18. He mentions a summary of those beliefs published in an 1808 Canandaigua, New York, newspaper (although Joseph Smith's family did not move to New York from Vermont until 1816) and a summary "in a book owned by Smith's hometown library since 1817." Finally, "in 1826 the Canandaigua newspaper also advertised Swedenborg's *A Treatise Concerning Heaven and Hell* for sale." Canandaigua is about twelve miles from Palmyra.

28. Lucy Mack Smith, *The Revised and Enhanced History of Joseph Smith by His Mother*, ed. Scot Facer Proctor and Maurine Jensen Proctor (Salt Lake City: Bookcraft, 1996), 111; see also Miller, "Did Emanuel Swedenborg Influence LDS Doctrine?" 11.

29. Michael Quinn added a new reference to an 1830 Palmyra publication mentioning Swedenborg in his 1998 revised edition of *Early Mormonism and the Magic World View*, 176, that did not appear in his original 1987 edition. Interestingly, though, Quinn does not refer to this 1830 account in his notes related to Swedenborg's vision of heaven (Quinn, *Early Mormonism and the Magic World View*, rev. ed., 520nn319–29). Because of its geographic and temporal proximity to Joseph Smith, this new discovery seems the most promising in support of Quinn's

suggestion that Joseph Smith at least could have been aware of Swedenborg through local newspapers.

30. Meyers, "Death in Swedenborgian and Mormon Eschatology," 64. Compare also Miller, "Did Emanuel Swedenborg Influence LDS Doctrine?" 9–10, where he explores the possibility that other Swedenborgian evangelists may have been active in cities seventy-five miles from Palmyra. One Swedenborgian apparently lived in Rochester, twenty-four miles from Palmyra, but Miller notes that he could find no evidence of contact between this Mr. Harford—or between other Swedenborgian evangelists, for that matter—and any in the Palmyra Latter-day Saint community.

31. See Richard S. Van Wagoner, *Sidney Rigdon: A Portrait of Religious Excess* (Salt Lake City: Signature Books, 1994), 26. See pages 18–23 for a summary of Rigdon's decision to join Alexander Campbell.

32. Van Wagoner, *Sidney Rigdon*, 53–54.

33. The most detailed account of the actual receipt of this revelation was given sixty years later by Philo Dibble, who reported that he was present when the vision was given, although he himself did not see the vision. His recollection was published in the Salt Lake City periodical *The Juvenile Instructor*, May 15, 1892, 303–4.

34. The two periodicals are the *Christian Baptist* (published from 1823 until 1830) and its successor, the *Millennial Harbinger* (first published in 1830). Both periodicals are part of the digitized collection of restoration movement religious texts provided by the Memorial University of Newfoundland at www.mun.ca/rels/restmov/people/acampbell.html.

35. *Millennial Harbinger*, October 7, 1830, 447–48; http://www.mun.ca/rels/restmov/texts/acampbell/tmh/MH0110.HTM.

36. Sidney Rigdon had a falling out with Joseph Smith in the 1840s but did not officially break with the Church until after Joseph Smith's death. He was subjected to repeated accusations that he had been the primary writer of the Book of Mormon, yet even though he had broken with the Church, and even though he "never showed an inclination to relinquish his due, [he] vigorously maintained throughout his life that he had no part in the production of *The Book of Mormon* and never saw it until it was published" (Donna Hill, *Joseph Smith: The First Mormon*, reprint [Salt Lake City: Signature Books, 1999], 104). Significantly, and in a similar way, even after his trouble with Joseph Smith, and soon after Joseph Smith's death, Rigdon still witnessed of his participation in the vision of the degrees of glory (Van Wagoner, *Sidney Rigdon*, 337).

37. Robert J. Matthews, "A Plainer Translation," *Joseph Smith's Translation of the Bible: A History and Commentary* (Provo, UT: Brigham Young University Press, 1975), 34–35.

38. See Bushman, *Rough Stone Rolling*, 196, about the Prophet's encounter with John 5:29: "The scripture raised the question of how God could divide people into stark categories of saved and damned when individuals were so obviously a mix in ordinary life. 'It appeared self-evident,' Joseph wrote, 'that if God rewarded every one according to the deeds done in the body, the term "heaven," as intended for the Saints eternal home, must include more kingdoms than one.' The question

Joseph posed was a classic post-Calvinistic puzzle. For over a century Anglo-American culture had struggled to explain the arbitrary judgments of the Calvinist God who saved and damned according to his own good pleasure with little regard for human effort."

39. This assertion, and subsequent assertions about the use of certain words, phrases, and scriptural passages in Swedenborg's writings, are based on the searchable database of Swedenborg's religious works at theheavenlydoctrines.org. Although Craig Miller, in the body of his paper, seems to imply that Swedenborg *did* draw on 1 Corinthians 15:40–42, in an endnote Miller provides the important clarification that Swedenborg never referenced 1 Corinthians 15:40–42 and that "his followers generally don't see the three heavens in the words of these scriptures" (Miller, "Did Emanuel Swedenborg Influence LDS Doctrine?" 14n8).

40. For example, the searchable database Early English Books Online lists seventy-three seventeenth-century works—including the writings of John Foxe, Richard Baxter, and early translations of Augustine, Jerome, Eusebius, and John Calvin—that contain the phrase "celestial kingdom," all of which predate Emanuel Swedenborg's writings (http://eebo.chadwyck.com).

41. In all seventy-six passages containing the word *terrestrial*, Swedenborg uses it interchangeably with the associated (and most often listed) synonyms worldly, corporeal, or material—in other words, *terrestrial* always refers to the present life, and never the afterlife.

42. Bushman, *Rough Stone Rolling*, 602n11: "'Telestial' was not a known word. It has the ring of telos, meaning 'end' or 'uttermost,' a Greek word that appears in the New Testament in 1 Corinthians 15:24, a few verses before a passage on bodies celestial and terrestrial in verse 40."

43. Quinn, *Early Mormonism*, 217, 219.

44. See, for example, Brooke, *The Refiner's Fire*, 205: "Michael Quinn has noted that the idea of three heavens, or degrees of glory, was available in Emmanuel Swedenborg's cosmic system, in which three heavens—topped by a 'celestial kingdom'—were associated with the sun, the moon, and the stars." See also Richard Bushman, *Rough Stone Rolling*, 198: "Building on Paul, 'The Vision' [of Joseph Smith] made the three resurrected glories of sun, moon, and stars into three heavenly realms. The *same scripture* inspired eighteenth-century Swedish scientist and visionary Emanuel Swedenborg to divide the heavens into three parts, 'celestial,' 'spiritual,' and 'natural,' *equivalent to sun, moon, and stars*" (emphasis added). Bushman cites Quinn's work in his notes (*Rough Stone Rolling*, 602n16), but he then adds this important caveat, which parallels the argument of this paper: "Since Swedenborg attracted the attention of New England intellectuals . . . his ideas may conceivably have drifted into Joseph Smith's environment, but it was more likely the passage from Paul sparked the revelations of both men" (*Rough Stone Rolling*, 198–99).

45. Swedenborg, *Arcana Coelestia*, trans. Elliott, 5377; http://theheavenly doctrines.org/static/d8086/5377.htm.

46. Swedenborg, *Arcana Coelestia*, 5377.

47. Swedenborg, *Heaven and Hell*, trans. John C. Ager, 118; http://the heavenlydoctrines.org/static/d5399/118.htm.

48. Swedenborg, *Arcana Coelestia*, 3887; http://theheavenlydoctrines.org/static/d8086/3887.htm. See again Swedenborg, *Arcana Coelestia*, 5377: "The subject at the end of the previous chapter was the correspondence of certain internal organs of the body with the Grand Man, that is to say, the correspondence of the liver, pancreas, stomach, and certain other organs with it. In this present section the same subject moves on to the correspondence of the peritoneum, kidneys, ureters, bladder, and also the intestines with it. Whatever exists in the human being, both in the external man and in the internal man, has a correspondence with the Grand Man. Without that correspondence with the Grand Man—that is, with heaven, or what amounts to the same, with the spiritual world—nothing can ever come into being and remain in being." See also Swedenborg, *Heaven and Hell*, 60.

49. Swedenborg, *Arcana Coelestia*, 3887; emphasis added.

50. For a thoughtful (and more thorough) discussion of the biblical passages outlined here, and their continued expansion into the doctrinally important revelations which soon followed "the Vision," see Bushman, *Rough Stone Rolling*, 195–214.

51. I am indebted to Greg Simpson for pointing out the repeated connection between Doctrine and Covenants 76 and Hebrews 12:22–24. On the doctrinal importance of Doctrine and Covenants 76:58, see also Joseph Fielding McConkie and Craig J. Ostler, *Revelations of the Restoration* (Salt Lake City: Deseret Book, 2000), 531: "This verse stands at the heart of Mormonism." While Joseph Smith did not explicitly teach the doctrine of deification—the potential for humans to become gods—for another decade, it is significant that he would thus expand upon early revelations (D&C 76:58–59, 95, for example, and related passages like D&C 88:107 and 93:19–20) and carry the implications of those passages in this doctrinal direction, a direction in which Swedenborg did not go. I appreciate Lori Nelson for providing the perspective of a Swedenborgian on this point (e-mail from Lori Nelson, October 3, 2007). Importantly, McDannell and Lang make this comment about Latter-day Saint distinctiveness: "While even nineteenth-century spiritualists were reluctant to predict that spiritual growth in the other world could eventually end with human deification, LDS theology took spiritual progress after death to its logical conclusion. The possibility of people evolving into gods is a Latter-day Saint tenet" (*Heaven*, 321–22). On this question of human deification, see Richard Bushman's review of John L. Brooke's *The Refining Fire*, "Mysteries of Mormonism," *Journal of the Early Republic* 15, no. 3 (1995): 503. Bushman notes that since, for John Brooke, "the goal of hermeticism was to recover divine power and perfection; 'divinization,' is Brooke's word for it," and since "Mormonism promised that the faithful would become gods," these "parallels lead Brooke to argue that Mormonism should be understood as more of an hermetic restoration than a return to primitive Christianity." For a differing view of parallels in the Mormon doctrine of exaltation and the early Christian (and contemporary Eastern Orthodox Christian) belief in human deification, see Jordan Vajda, *"Partakers of the Divine Nature": A Comparative Analysis of Patristic and Mormon Doctrines of Divinization* (Berkeley, CA: master's thesis, Graduate Theological Union, 1998); see also

Stephen E. Robinson, *Are Mormons Christians?* (Salt Lake City: Bookcraft, 1991), 60–65, 68, 70.

52. Michael Stanley, *Emanuel Swedenborg: Essential Readings* (Wellingsborough, England: Crucible, 1988), 23.

53. In later sermons, Joseph Smith also referred to this "third heaven" passage from 2 Corinthians 12 and connected it with "the Vision" and the three degrees of glory (see, for example, *Teachings of the Prophet Joseph Smith*, 304–5, 311). Although the "caught up to the third heaven" (2 Corinthians 12:2) passage does not appear in the language of Doctrine and Covenants 76, the Prophet does use a phrase from 2 Corinthians 12:4 in Doctrine and Covenants 76:115 ("not lawful for a man to utter"). Compare also Doctrine and Covenants 137:1, where the phrase, "whether in the body or out I cannot tell," from 2 Corinthians 12:2 is used in a description of the Prophet's later (1836) vision of the celestial kingdom. It seems apparent that, like Swedenborg, Joseph Smith saw 2 Corinthians 12:2–4 as implying that heaven consisted of multiple kingdoms or glories.

54. See, for example, Emanuel Swedenborg, *De Verbo*, 3.

55. See, for example, Emanuel Swedenborg, *Conjugial Love*, 328.

56. Meyers, "Death in Swedenborgian and Mormon Eschatology," 59.

57. John Hyde Jr. was a teenager when he joined The Church of Jesus Christ of Latter-day Saints in England in the early 1850s. He served a mission in France, immigrated to Utah, left for a mission to Hawaii, and there, at age 23, became disaffected and separated himself from Mormonism. In fact, for several months thereafter, he launched some vicious attacks on the Church. He published in 1857 a stinging exposé entitled, *Mormonism: Its Leaders and Designs*, in which he portrayed Joseph Smith a charlatan and the Book of Mormon a sham. The exposé was published while Hyde was living in New York. He soon returned to England and there, in 1858, wrote a novel (never published) about Mormon conspiracies and crimes. But soon thereafter he became a follower of Swedenborg and eventually a well-known exponent of his teachings (Lynne Watkins Jorgensen, "John Hyde, Jr., Mormon Renegade," *Journal of Mormon History* 17 [1991]: 134–36). Even today he is renowned among Swedenborgians for his groundbreaking bibliography of Swedenborg's works. Hyde himself also wrote several books and pamphlets and articles on the tradition's theology. Grateful acknowledgement is given to Carroll Odhner, head librarian at the Swedenborg Library of Bryn Athyn College, Pennsylvania. I am indebted to Ms. Odhner for the insight about John Hyde's current reputation and notoriety among Swedenborgians (conversation with Carroll Odhner, May 4, 2005). It might seem natural, therefore, that a man in Hyde's position—one who had already criticized Joseph Smith for his unoriginality and deceit—could use his familiarity with Swedenborgian theology to bolster his accusations against Mormons by suggesting that they deceptively co-opted Swedenborg's teachings on heaven. Yet Hyde apparently never mentioned Mormon doctrines in connection with any of his writings on Swedenborg, even though one of his extensive pamphlets dealt specifically with the afterlife. He did criticize Mormons in 1868 for what he saw as their political attempts to establish an Old Testament–type theocracy, yet he never mentioned the doctrine of the

degrees of glory (see John Hyde, "Adaptation," *The New Jerusalem Magazine* [Boston], August 1868, 89). Carroll Odhner brought this reference to my attention.

Likewise, William Godbe was a Mormon who was drawn to Spiritualism, and eventually he left the Church to pursue his spiritualist interests. In doing so, he actively persuaded other Church members to join him. Before his final break with the Church, however, Godbe published *Utah Magazine*. During its three-year run, the periodical featured a smattering of articles related to spiritualism and the occult. Two of those dealt with Swedenborg. The first, "Swedenborg's Curious Powers," was an excerpt from a biography of Swedenborg that chronicled his most famous manifestations of spiritual communication: directing a widow to find the secret drawer of her deceased husband; and describing a fire in Stockholm, as it happened, while he was in a city three hundred miles away (see "Swedenborg's Curious Powers," *Utah Magazine*, March 7, 1868, 104–5). But the second article, "Emanuel Swedenborg," not only provided a glowing biographical sketch but also an excerpt from his teachings (see *Utah Magazine*, October 16, 1869, 380). Copies of *Utah Magazine* are housed in Special Collections, Marriott Library, University of Utah. If Godbe wanted to win followers to his spiritualist cause, and his reading audience consisted mostly of Latter-day Saints, one might expect that he would want to impress them with Swedenborg's prefiguring of Joseph Smith's vision of heaven. But as with John Hyde, Godbe is apparently silent about those suggested similarities.

58. See this representative passage in Spencer J. Palmer, Roger R. Keller, Dong Sull Choi, and James A. Toronto, eds., *Religions of the World: A Latter-day Saint View* (Provo, UT: Brigham Young University, 1997), 249: "Latter-day Saints believe that the spiritual influence which emanates from God is not confined to selected nations, races, or groups. All people share an inheritance of divine light. Christ himself if the light of the world. . . . If people act according to this inspiration, they progress from grace to grace, learning precept upon precept, until they receive full enlightenment" (see D&C 93:19–20; 98:11–12).

59. Synnestvedt, *The Essential Swedenborg*, 25–26; see also Stanley, *Emanuel Swedenborg*, 23.

60. See, for example, Brooke, *The Refiner's Fire*, 205: "Swedenborgian theology . . . provided one direct connection to the high hermetic tradition, and its system of a triad of heavens reflected a wide range of occult influences."

61. See Robert J. Matthews, "A Plainer Translation," 256: "The Prophet [Joseph Smith] was actively engaged in making the translation of the Bible from June 1830 until July 1833. Examination of the chronological table in the forepart of the Doctrine and Covenants will quickly show that most of the doctrinal revelations were received during this period. I believe this is not a coincidence but a consequence. It was Joseph Smith's study and translation of the Bible that set the stage for the reception of many revelations on the doctrines of the gospel. There is an inseparable connection between the New Translation of the Bible and many of the revelations that constitute the book of Doctrine and Covenants."

62. Quinn, *Early Mormonism*, 217, 219; Brooke, *The Refiner's Fire*, 205.

63. Jan Shipps, *Sojourner in the Promised Land: Forty Years Among the Mormons* (Urbana: University of Illinois Press, 2000), 205. Compare also Richard Bushman, "The Mysteries of Mormonism," *Journal of the Early Republic* 15, no. 3 (1995): 501–5, and Philip Barlow, "Decoding Mormonism," *Christian Century*, January 17, 1996, 52–53.

64. Shipps, *Sojourner in the Promised Land*, 210–11; see also Philip L. Barlow, *Mormons and the Bible: The Place of the Latter-day Saints in American Religion* (New York and Oxford: Oxford University Press, 1991), especially his introduction, "The Bible in Antebellum America."

8

UNIVERSALISM AND THE REVELATIONS OF JOSEPH SMITH

Casey Paul Griffiths

The revelations of Joseph Smith cast a startling ray of light into the theological world. Foreordained in the eternities, raised in a spiritual environment, and schooled by divine messengers, the Prophet set the religious world on fire. Yet no fire begins in a vacuum. The intellectual climate of the time, influence of his immediate family, and spiritual background of his ancestors all nurtured the divine spark of the Restoration. This study intends to answer three questions. First, what was the religious background of the Prophet's family? Next, how did it prepare him for his labors? Finally, how did this background frame the work of his prophetic career?

While the truths of the Restoration can only be explained in the context of eternity, it is useful for us to understand the background of those who received the revelations. The Lord comments in the first section of the Doctrine and Covenants that He taught His disciples "after the manner of their language, that they might come to understanding"

Casey Paul Griffiths is a seminary teacher in Sandy, Utah.

(D&C 1:24). The language the Lord mentions refers not only to the vernacular of the day but also to the language of ideas in which the Prophet and his contemporaries were fluent. From this perspective, the Lord prepared the mind of the Prophet not only through the teaching of heavenly messengers but also in the religious philosophies of the day. In all things, Joseph was prepared not only to receive revelation but to accept it. This in turn helped him to assist others in making the transition from their own theological backgrounds to the restored doctrines of the true Church. A simple case study might best illustrate the value of the Prophet's religious background in his labors.

Early Reactions to Doctrine and Covenants 76

Doctrine and Covenants section 76, commonly called "The Vision," was a milestone in the revelations of the Prophet Joseph Smith. Today there is rarely a course taught in the Church without at least one discussion showing the familiar circles representing the three degrees of glory. This profound outline, presented with such grace in the descriptions given by the Prophet and Sidney Rigdon, provides eternal perspective and a convenient roadmap for Latter-day Saints. However, while the vision is accepted today as one of the crowning jewels of our theology, it initially received a mixed reception by the early Saints. The reaction to this stunning revelation says more about the diverse religious backgrounds of the early adherents of the Church than about the revelation itself. How one reacted to the vision was a kind of litmus test, acting as a measure of the hearer's ability to comprehend and incorporate new ideas into their perception of God and salvation. Many wrestled to reconcile these concepts with their theological backgrounds. Others, however, sprang from backgrounds that allowed them to see the power of this new revelation and gave them the will to nurse these profound truths until they became fully integrated into Latter-day Saint thought.

Foremost among those who embraced the revelation was the Prophet himself. Joseph was jubilant upon the reception of the vision. Looking back on the experience, he wrote:

> Nothing could be more pleasing to the Saints upon the order of the kingdom of the Lord, than the light which burst upon the world through the foregoing vision. Every law, every commandment, every promise, every truth, and every point touching the destiny of man, from Genesis to Revelation, where the purity of the scriptures remains unsullied by the folly of men, go to show the perfection of the theory [of different degrees of glory in the future life] and witnesses the fact that that document is a transcript from the records of the eternal world. The sublimity of the ideas; the purity of the language; the scope for action; the continued duration for completion, in order that the heirs of salvation may confess the Lord and bow the knee; the rewards for faithfulness, and the punishment for sins, are so much beyond the narrow-mindedness of men, that every honest man is constrained to exclaim: "*It came from God.*"[1]

While Joseph marveled at the "sublimity of the ideas," others in the Church struggled to accept the new revelation. Brigham Young gave a summary of the general feeling in the Church toward the vision:

> When God revealed to Joseph Smith and Sidney Rigdon that there was a place prepared for all, according to the light they had received and their rejection of evil and practice of good, it was a great trial to many, and some apostatized because God was not going to send to everlasting punishment heathens and infants, but had a place of salvation, in due time, for all, and would bless the honest and virtuous and truthful, whether they ever belonged to any church or not. It was a new doctrine to this generation, and many stumbled at it.[2]

Records of the time verify the truth of Brigham Young's observations. Orson Pratt and John Murdock both recorded several incidents where members of local branches rebelled against the teachings contained in the vision. In one branch a certain brother rose up and declared that the revelation was from Satan, and he "believed it no more than he believed the devil was crucified" and "would not have the vision taught in the church for $1000."[3] Elders Pratt and Murdock worked patiently to help the man accept the doctrine but were ultimately unsuccessful.

Realizing new converts may not be ready for the profound message of the vision, the Prophet counseled missionaries traveling to England not to mention it before the proper foundation could be built. He wrote: "My instructions to the brethren were, when they arrived in England, to adhere closely to the first principles of the Gospel, and remain silent concerning the gathering, the vision, and the Book of Doctrine and Covenants, until such time as the work was fully established, and it should be clearly made manifest by the Spirit to do otherwise."[4]

Why did so many stumble to accept what today is taken for granted as one of the most appealing parts of Latter-day Saint theology? It must be remembered that when the vision was received there was no one in the Church who had been a member for more than three years. The most devoted followers struggled with the dramatic new ideas of the vision. Even a stalwart such as Brigham Young could not conceal his difficulties in understanding the revelation. He recalled, "My traditions were such, that when the Vision came first to me, it was so directly contrary and opposed to my former education, I said, wait a little; I did not reject it, but I could not understand it."[5] Though he would later be one of its greatest proponents, at the time he first heard of the vision, Brigham was a new and tender convert wrestling to grasp concepts diametrically opposed to everything he had known. Like Brigham, most of the converts of early Mormonism came from a background of what might be called "heaven and hell" Protestantism. Taught so long of the firm dividing line between the saved and the damned, they struggled to comprehend the largesse of God's plan of salvation, where even a murderer could inherit a kingdom glorious enough to surpass all understanding (see D&C 76:89). Brigham Young's brother Joseph perhaps best captures the spirit of the mood: "When I came to read the visions of the different glories of the eternal world, and of the sufferings of the wicked, I could not believe it at the first. Why the Lord was going to save every body."[6]

If so many members recoiled at the liberal nature of salvation as revealed in the vision, why did Joseph Smith seem to immediately embrace the revelation? No single answer may suffice, but the reason may be traced in part to his religious upbringing and the religious heritage of his ancestors.[7] Many streams of religious thought seemed to flow into the Smith household, but in the writings of family members and those who knew them, the theology of Universalism appears more prominently than the others. Starting with Asael Smith, the Prophet's grandfather, and continuing down to Joseph and his family, the spiritual tenets of Universalism provided fertile soil in which the Prophet's religious feelings began to grow and bloom.

What Is Universalism?

Before the connection between Universalism and the Smith family can be explored, it may first be helpful to explain, in a general sense, what Universalism is. By the time Joseph entered the Sacred Grove and began his prophetic career, the Universalist movement was already widespread in New England. Its popularity may have stemmed from its optimistic appraisal of the human nature and the loving kindness of God. In layman's terms, Universalism was the belief that all men will eventually be saved. A Universalist declaration of faith adopted in 1803 read, "We believe that there is one God, whose nature is Love, revealed in one Lord Jesus Christ, by one Holy Spirit of Grace, who will finally restore the whole family of mankind to holiness and happiness."[8]

Universalism in America was a diverse movement, but its principal founder in the United States was John Murray. In England, Murray was initially one of its harshest critics. Encountering a Universalist preacher and seeking to rebuke him, Murray was in turn confounded by the logic and power of the preacher's scriptural arguments. He then launched into an intense regimen of study designed to disprove the Universalists but found his antagonism waning into tolerance and blossomed into full acceptance. He soon became an influential leader in the new faith in England. After a series of financial and personal setbacks, Murray departed from England in 1770 to start fresh in America. He did not come to the New World intending to spread the teachings of Universalism, but a series of fortunate events led him to begin preaching, and soon he developed a sizable number of disciples.[9]

Murray embraced America as a new homeland, becoming a passionate advocate for American independence, even serving as a chaplain in the Continental army. He counted among his closest connections prominent figures such as George Washington, John and Abigail Adams, John Hancock, and Benjamin Rush, who was also a Universalist. For Murray, Rush, and other followers of the faith, Universalism captured the millennial promise of the revolution. They felt it would transform the religious world, while the spread of democracy would transfigure the secular. After the American Revolution, Murray and his followers continued to prosper. Their ideals seemed to fit particularly well with the ideals of the Founding Fathers. As the new republic championed the equality of men in this life, Universalists trumpeted the equality of men in the salvation of God's plan.

The Smith Family and Universalism

Murray preached for many years in Gloucester, Massachusetts. Only fifteen miles away was Topsfield, where Joseph's grandfather Asael lived. Latter-day Saint historians Richard L. Bushman and Richard Lloyd Anderson have pointed out the philosophical similarities and geographical proximity of Asael Smith and John Murray.[10] Like Murray, Asael had served during the revolution, sacrificing to ensure the birth of the new nation, and both were deeply enmeshed in the ideals of the revolutionary generation. Whether because of direct contact or filtering through the local community, Asael came to accept a conception of universal salvation very similar to Murray's.

Asael eventually came to settle in Vermont, one of the Universalist strongholds in New England. In 1797, Asael and his two oldest sons, Jesse and Joseph Sr., the father of the future prophet, organized a Universalist society in Tunbridge, Vermont.[11] The society itself was short-lived, but for the rest of his life, Asael adhered to the principles of Universalism. His grandson George A. Smith recalled that "not long before his death he wrote many quires of paper on the doctrine of universal salvation."[12] In an address written to his family, Asael devoted the larger part of his letter toward his views on religion. He wrote, "And if you can believe that Christ [came] to save sinners, and not the righteous, Pharisees, or self righteous; that sinners must be saved by the righteousness of Christ alone, without mixing any of their own righteousness with his; then you will see that he can as well save all, as any, and there is no respect of persons with God, who will have all mankind to be saved and come to the knowledge of the truth."[13]

How successful was Asael in passing his beliefs on to his children? The two sons who joined Asael in founding the Universalist society followed divergent spiritual paths.[14] Jesse Smith rejected it outright and instead became a devoted Calvinist, while Joseph Sr. seems to have maintained a philosophical, though not an institutional, tie to the faith. George A. Smith recalled his grandfather as "too liberal in his views to please his children, who were covenanters, Congregationalists and Presbyterians, *with I think the single exception of his son Joseph* [Sr.]."[15] William Smith, brother of the Prophet, also believed Father Smith's convictions leaned toward Universalism. He wrote, "My father's religious habits were strictly pious and moral, his faith [was] in the Universal restoration doctrine [which] often brought him in contact with the advocates of the doctrine of endless misery."[16] Father Smith was not a formal member of any particular religious sect until the Restoration, and Universalism may have been a good fit for those put off by the religious contentions of the time. Lucy Mack Smith recalled that "he would not subscribe to any particular system of faith, but contended for the ancient order, as established by our Lord and Saviour Jesus Christ, and his Apostles."[17]

Another significant factor in the Prophet's religious background was the impact of his mother. Lucy's father, Solomon Mack, showed no inclination toward any particular religion for much of his life. He underwent a remarkable conversion of faith later in his life, well after Lucy had married and begun her own family. He experienced and knew of Universalist doctrine early on, but he later denounced it as "building on sand."[18] Lucy's leanings when it came to religion seem to have been inherited from her mother, who taught her piety but established no formal church connections.[19] Though she affiliated with several churches before her son's ministry, for the most part she remained aloof from close affiliation with any single group. Lucy and several of her children did begin attending a Presbyterian church in 1820, but Joseph was not among the children joining her.[20] In religious matters, he seems to have been more inclined to follow his father.[21]

Though the Smiths were not part of any Universalist organizations during the Prophet's formative years, the doctrine may have formed a rough outline for Joseph's religious thinking. There were many aspects of Universalist beliefs which may have helped prepare the Prophet and his family for the times they faced ahead. First, Universalism emphasized the loving nature of God's personality more than most of the religions of the day. The doctrine of universal salvation brought its followers to see God as a loving father figure, not an arbitrary sovereign or an angry God bent on the punishment of mankind. One of Murray's followers, Hosea Ballou, summarized the Universalist concept of God in homely language: "Your child has fallen into the mire, and its body and its garments are defiled. You cleanse it, and array it in clean robes. The query is, Do you love your child because you have washed it? Or, Did you wash it because you loved it?"[22]

At best, Universalists may have erred on the side of mercy; at worst, such an argument could be used to deprive men of their agency. But such a simple analogy helps capture the appeal of this faith—their concept of God was that of an approachable, loving father. Raised in an environment where these teachings were present, it is not surprising that a passage like James 1:5 would have stood out to the young Joseph. The Prophet had this kind of being in mind when he concluded that God answers prayers "liberally, and upbraideth not" (James 1:5). Walking into the Sacred Grove, the Prophet expected an answer from a concerned parent, not a rebuke from a distant ruler.

Second, the Prophet grew up in a home outside the realm of religious orthodoxy. Universalism was a radical departure from the creeds and sects of the day, and partly because of Father Smith's affiliations with it, his family found itself outside of mainstream Christianity. Universalists were outspoken critics of the priestcraft and pretense found in many religions. They saw their system of belief as tied into the rights of the individual, and many felt the growing power in sectarianism in America was leading to the submission of individual rights. Many

Universalists were concerned with the shameless emotional and psychological manipulation that took place in the revivals of the day,[23] a concern shared by the young Joseph as he attended revivals and noted that "the seemingly good feelings of both the priests and the converts were more pretended than real" (Joseph Smith—History 1:6). The generous nature of salvation in Universalist thought was well suited to many, like Father Smith, who continued to search for the true faith amidst the sectarian strife surrounding them. The broadness of the ideas of the movement allowed a great degree of theological flexibility and openness to new views. While Jesse Smith became so entrenched in his belief in Calvinism that he rejected the gospel and ordered his brother "not to talk 'about the Bible at all in his home unless it was upon Limited Election,'"[24] Joseph Sr. remained open to new ideas and revelations. Lucy Mack Smith recognized the blessings of this attitude. She once described a dream in which she saw two trees, one gracefully and gently moving with the wind, and another standing stiff and unmoving. When she sought an interpretation of the dream, it was revealed to her "that the stubborn and unyielding tree was like Jesse; that the other, more pliant and flexible, was like Joseph, my husband; that the breath of heaven, which passed over them, was the pure and undefiled Gospel of the Son of God, which Gospel Jesse would always resist, but which Joseph, when he was more advanced in life, would hear and receive with his whole heart."[25] The Lord also recognized the malleable nature of the father of the Prophet. After the first visitation of Moroni, the first person the young prophet was directed to confide in was his father (see Joseph Smith—History 1:49–50).

The influence of Universalism was not confined solely to the Prophet's family either. The pliancy of Universalist doctrine and its emphasis on God's love made it an ideal philosophical home for many who were religiously minded but concerned with the failings of the churches of the day. Many of the small circle of believers which formed around the Prophet in the infant days of the Church were adherents of Universalism, most notably Martin Harris, the Joseph Knight family, and the Hezekiah Peck family.[26]

Last, Universalism had prepared the Smiths to live in the face of religious persecution. As would be imagined, the doctrine of universal salvation was such a departure from conventional Christian thinking that it often raised the ire of the sectarians of the day. Universalism was spurned as a destroyer of morals, an insult to common piety, and the first cousin of atheism.[27] One minister wrote, "What has a Universalist, who really and sincerely believes that doctrine, to fear? . . . Just nothing at all; for this flesh-pleasing, conscience soothing doctrine will not only justify him in his neglect of God and man, but gives fallen nature an unlimited license to serve the devil with greediness in any and every possible way."[28] When most of their contemporaries referred to Father Smith, Martin Harris, the Knights or any other member of the early Church as Universalist, it was intended as an slander on their character.[29] Asael Smith, who apparently possessed a deformation of the neck, was derided by one member of the community who said "some regarded his sentiments as more distorted than his neck." A more sympathetic recollection of him called him "a man of very liberal views . . . which he would not yield to bigotry nor opposition."[30]

As the only son of his father to remain close to the tenets of Universalism, Joseph Smith Sr. seems to have inherited the persecution Asael had dealt with. William Smith recalled that Father Smith often faced persecution because of his Universalist beliefs: "The belief in the ultimate and final redemption of all mankind to heaven and happiness, brought down upon my father the approbrium or slur of Old Jo Smith."[31] The Prophet's courage in the face of persecution, even at a young age, is not surprising since both his grandfather and father before him had chosen a less popular road. When he wrote that experiencing persecution was second nature to him and that "deep water is what I am wont to swim in" (D&C 127:2), he was upholding family tradition. The Prophet's progenitors had been treading water in a sea of persecution for years before his first revelations came.

Was Universalism the Smith family religion? In the strictest sense, it was, as one historian has called it, an important overlay of the family's spiritual values. Early in the Prophet's life, his family's beliefs provided Joseph with a conception of God as an approachable, loving, and concerned father. The open nature of Father Smith's beliefs, combined with his suspicion of feigned religion, gave the young Joseph the freedom to explore religious beliefs and a critical eye toward hypocrisy. Not only was Universalism important in the Prophet's early life, it also played an important role during his work as the head of the Church. The debates raging over the implications of Universalist doctrine and its rapid spread through the new republic also influenced Joseph's later prophetic career.

Universalism and the Restoration

The peak period of Joseph Smith's revelations coincided with the apex of Universalist activity in America. By 1833 the movement had grown to include three hundred official preachers, six hundred societies, and membership numbered at three hundred thousand. Adherents to the faith could be found in locations as distant as Georgia and Michigan, though it remained the strongest in the northeast United States, the area in which the Latter-day Saints were geographically centered at the time.[32] The discussion on Universalism was also growing. The period from 1820 to 1850 saw an explosion in the number of books and articles produced on the movement. These publications peaked in the 1830s, the same period in which the majority of Joseph's revelations were received.[33] Whether followers or detractors of the movement, most Americans in the Restoration period found themselves caught up in the discussion about the movement, and the Saints were no exception. The theological questions raised by the Universalists provide the context for many of the most crucial revelations of the Restoration. A comparison of the spiritual system constructed from the revelations retained the true elements of Universalism while highlighting and eliminating many of the movement's shortcomings.

While the teachings of Universalism may have provided questions leading to many of the revelations given to the Prophet, the power and authority with which the revelations were received highlighted many of the problems of the Universalist movement. The revelation found in section 19 of the Doctrine and Covenants is a good example of this. Given to Martin Harris, a former Universalist, the revelation quickly settled an argument that had rent the unity of the Universalist movement in America nearly from the beginning. Even while John Murray was alive, a vigorous debate erupted among the Universalists concerning the punishment for sinners. Some, including Murray, taught that souls would be saved through a mystical union with Christ, while others taught that souls would be saved after a long period of suffering for sin, and some taught that suffering for sin would be confined solely to earthly life. The division caused by this one doctrine was such that most churches could not ratify any type of unified profession of belief without filling it with numerous concessions to make all parties happy. One such creedal statement reads, "We regard all as Universalists who believe in the final salvation of all men through divine grace, however they may differ in opinion as to punishment or discipline extending into the future state and as to progressive improvement and different degrees of happiness in the future world."[34] Such wide-ranging and vague statements led to the unraveling of any sense of doctrinal unity, and social cohesion of the Universalist movement suffered because of it.

In section 19 the conflict rending the Universalist movement was settled for good. The Lord simply declares, "It is not written that there shall be no end to this torment, but it is written *endless torment*. . . . I am endless, and the punishment which is given at my hand is endless punishment, for Endless is my name. Wherefore—Eternal punishment is God's punishment. Endless punishment is God's punishment" (D&C 19:6, 10–12). This episode serves to indicate how Universalism, which was originally intended to simplify the gospel, found itself caught in the endless theological wrangling of the day. This incongruence was partly because its doctrine, however well intended, was produced by scriptural reasoning and debate, not revelation.

The main source of contention concerning Universalism stemmed from the fact that it offered a broad form of salvation without giving accountability for sin. Universalists frequently cited such scriptures as Romans 5:18–19, which speaks of the Savior's sacrifice as bringing salvation unconditionally, but they had a difficult time squaring this notion with such scriptures as Mark 16:16, where the Savior declared that "he that believeth and is baptized shall be saved; but he that believeth not shall be damned." While universal salvation fit the picture of loving God, it did not fit well with the concept of a just God. While some decried its Universalist overtones, the revelation declaring the three degrees of glory did not align well with universal salvation when it was carefully analyzed. Salvation was still graded, devotion was still required, and ordinances of the gospel still provided the gateway to the kingdom of God. Later revelations, such as the vision that became section 137, offered a liberal view of salvation but not without acknowledging commitment on the part of the followers. Later revelations offered salvation to all men while still acknowledging the necessity of the ordinances and covenants of the gospel.

The debate over Universalism was also used by the critics of the Church as a framework for attacking the authenticity of the Prophet's work. For example, the Book of Mormon has frequently been denounced as an attack on Universalism in the Prophet's day and into our time as well.[35] Even recently these arguments have been revived and cited as evidence for a modern origin for the book. Critics cite such passages as 2 Nephi 28:7, which criticize those who say "eat, drink, and be merry, for tomorrow we die; and it shall be well with us" as an implicit indictment of the Universalist doctrine. Other frequently cited examples include the story of Nehor in the first chapter of Alma with his teaching that "all mankind should be saved at the last day" (Alma 1:4). Such criticisms reveal ignorance of the book's themes. It would be just as easy to pick out certain other passages such as 2 Nephi 2:4, which reads that "salvation is free" and argue that the Book of Mormon is a *pro*-Universalist tract! Moreover, it is curious that the critics of the Book of Mormon have always criticized it for doing exactly what it claims to do. Alexander Campbell, one of the earliest critics of the book, lambasted the book and Joseph Smith for deciding "all the great controversies" of his time when the book claims it was meant to do exactly that.[36] Nearly all the major writers of the Book of Mormon stated that they were writing for generations yet to come (see 2 Nephi 25:21; Jacob 1:3; Enos 1:15–16; Jarom 1:2; Mormon 7:1; 8:34–35). If Mormon and Moroni saw our day, as they claimed, wouldn't we have expected them to write on topics related not only to us but to those of Joseph Smith's day? As one of the burning issues of the day, if the book did not deal with Universalism, it wouldn't be fulfilling its promises.

Not only were Joseph's revelations designed to deal with the religious culture of the time, but they provided a firm organizational structure for the Church also. This allowed the movement to form an institutional home, something the Universalists struggled to accomplish. While Universalism may have provided fertile philosophical ground for the Prophet to grow up in, its open theology tended to lead its followers away from unified organizations and toward private devotion. Most converts to the movement were interested in the propagation and defense of a rational faith, not in the organization and administration of an ecclesiastical body.[37] To become a viable and lasting organization, an ideal needs to provide institutions, and the free nature of Universalism did not easily lend itself to organization. Asael Smith and the father of the Prophet are prime examples of this difficulty. Both moved to form a Universalist society in 1797, but within two years it had been disbanded. Asael remained devoted to the doctrines of the movement long beyond this period, though his feelings seemed to remain private, without any further attempts at public unity with fellow believers. Joseph Sr. may have been less devoted to the movement, but it still provided the theological framework for his search for the true faith. In spite of his devotion, Asael's writings indicate that he felt a desire for something more. One of his grandsons recalled a prophecy by Asael that "God was going to raise up some branch of his family to be a great benefit to mankind."[38] Shortly after the publication of the Book of Mormon in 1830, Joseph Sr. took a copy to Asael. Asael received it gladly and read it through, declaring that the prophet he had predicted would come had at last arrived. Unfortunately, Asael passed on before he could receive the ordinance of baptism.[39]

While Universalism may have played an important role in the development of the Prophet and his family, it did not provide the answers that could only be found in revelation from God. What it did do was give the Smiths a spiritual foundation, encourage them in their study of the scriptures, and cultivate in them a belief in a merciful God who would be willing to answer their questions.

Are Mormons Universalists?

While the teachings of his fathers concerning universal salvation may have prepared Joseph Smith for the radical concepts of the vision of the degrees of glory, it took time for the rest of the Church to accept this new concept of the afterlife. The revelation was published five months after it was received in the *Evening and Morning Star*. Most of the controversy surrounding it seems to have come during the first two years after it was made known to the Church. Throughout the rest of the 1830s and into the early 1840s, it was rarely mentioned in the publications of the Church or the private writings of Church members during the time.[40] The first substantive discussion on the vision is found in Joseph Smith's 1843 poetic version. Written to W.W. Phelps, the entire revelation was rewritten as an epic poem, a work that may have caused him to ponder the doctrinal significance of the revelation. During the last eighteen months of his life, the Prophet issued a number of revelatory statements concerning the doctrine of the afterlife. The King Follett discourse delivered in 1844 contains a number of points relating to a different concept of the afterlife. During this landmark speech, the Prophet announced, "I have no fear of hell fire, that doesn't exist, but the torment and disappointment of the mind of man is as exquisite as a lake burning with fire and brimstone."[41] Several other important sermons from this time mention the degrees of glory, providing doctrine which would later form part of Doctrine and Covenants 131.[42]

The revelations of the Nauvoo period represent the pinnacle of Joseph Smith's labors. During this time, the Lord completed the bridge between the expansive view of salvation that Joseph's grandfather held and the concept of a just God taught in the scriptures. He wrote, "But while one portion of the human race is judging and condemning the other without mercy, the Great Parent of the universe looks upon the whole of the human family with a fatherly care and paternal regard; He views them as His offspring, and without any of those contracted feelings that influence the children of men, causes, 'His sun to rise on the evil and on the good, and sendeth rain on the just and on the unjust.'"[43] Views like this line up surprisingly well with Asael Smith's, who warned his children not to conclude that God loved them more than "the worst heathen in the darkest corner of the deserts of Arabia" but that "there is no respect of persons with God, who will have all mankind to be saved."[44] Further visions and revelations confirmed the Prophet's teachings of a kind and generous God. The January 1836 vision contained in Doctrine and Covenants 137 gave the Prophet the knowledge that God would "judge all men according to their works, according to the desire of their hearts" (D&C 137:9).

The final great phase of the Prophet's work consisted of bringing about a successful marriage of the munificent view of salvation given in the vision with the system of covenants and ordinances found in the ancient scriptures and revealed anew to the Prophet in our dispensation. When he learned that proxy work for the dead could be performed, a view of salvation was opened up that would allow all men who so desired to be saved, even if they had never heard the gospel or received the ordinances in this life. In essence, the revelations of the Restoration allowed for a merciful God, while not taking away from the need for order and justice. Joseph came to know God as a kind, fair being. His views may be best summed up in his own words: "Our heavenly Father is more liberal in His views, and boundless in His mercies and blessings, than we are ready to believe or receive; and, at the same time, is more terrible to the workers of iniquity, more awful in the executions of His punishments, and more ready to detect every false way, than we are apt to suppose Him to be."[45]

In time the vision was recognized as one of the greatest revelations received by the Prophet. Brigham Young, who had initially struggled to accept it, became one of the most fervent teachers and admirers of its doctrine. Speaking in 1860 he said,

> I can truly say that, in my estimation, no other revelation so glorious was ever given. You may read the character of the Deity as portrayed in all that has ever been revealed, until you come to this vision [D&C 76], in relation to his justice, his judgment, his power, his life, his glory, his excellence, his goodness, his mercy, and the fulness of every gift, of every trait, of every principle inherent in the character of the Supreme Being, and it is not equal in magnitude, in my reflections, to that which God revealed to Joseph Smith and Sydney Rigdon.[46]

Any hesitation which may have come from the doctrines of the vision being associated with Universalism seems to have abated as well. Rather than seeking to distance themselves from Universalists, Latter-day Saints began to recognize the similarities in belief. Speaking on the doctrine of universal resurrection, Parley P. Pratt said, "This salvation being universal, I am a universalist in this respect,—this salvation being a universal restoration from the fall." While pointing out similarities, Elder Pratt also recognized that universal doctrine did not paint a complete picture of salvation.[47] What remained from the Universalist background of the Restoration was an emphasis on the goodness of God. On another occasion President Young read the revelation in its entirety then summarized its lessons by saying, "He is compassionate to all the works of His hands, the plan of His redemption, and salvation, and mercy, is stretched out over all; and His plans are to gather up, and bring together, and save all the inhabitants of the earth, with the exception of those who have received the Holy Ghost, and sinned against it. With this exception, all the world besides shall be saved.—*Is not this Universalism? It borders very close upon it.*"[48] Within one generation the Saints had not only come to accept the vision but also to rejoice in its meaning and beauty.

Religious Yearnings Fulfilled

In truth, disillusionment with the churches of the day kept most of Joseph Smith and his progenitors from fully embracing any system until the true Church could be restored again to the earth. But it is clear that the ideals and doctrines of Universalism played an important role in the development of the Prophet's spirituality. If Brigham Young's upbringing made it difficult to understand the great generosity of God's plan, something in the Prophet's background made him embrace and rejoice in it. We are fortunate that Joseph was taught upon his father's knee of a generous and kind God, one that would give liberally if asked. Recognizing this, it must also be acknowledged that Universalism only provided a temporary shelter for the Smiths, while they sought the true Church of Christ. For all the comfort Universalism's doctrines may have given members of the family, only the true gospel could bring everlasting joy. No event better exemplifies this than the baptism of the Prophet's own father, on April 6, 1830, the day of the organization of the Church. Lucy Mack Smith records this touching event: "Joseph stood on the shore when his father came out of the water he cried out Oh! my God I have lived to see my father baptized into the true church of Jesus Christ and he covered his face in his father's bosom and wept aloud for joy as did Joseph of old when he beheld his father coming into the land of Egypt."[49] This moment was the culmination of the religious yearnings long felt by both father and son. The work of John Murray, the beliefs of Asael Smith, and the heritage of Joseph Smith Sr. were all important events leading to this moment. Just as the Prophet was led by the hand of the Lord, it is clear that his ancestors were also led into the right paths. As Brigham Young taught, "The Lord had his eye upon him, and upon his father, and upon his father's father, and upon their progenitors clear back to Abraham, and from Abraham to the flood, and from the flood to Enoch, and from Enoch to Adam."[50]

NOTES

1. Joseph Smith, *History of the Church of Jesus Christ of Latter-day Saints*, ed. B. H. Roberts, 2nd ed. rev. (Salt Lake City: Deseret Book, 1957), 1:252–53; brackets and emphasis in original.

2. Brigham Young, in *Journal of Discourses* (London: Latter-day Saints' Book Depot, 1874–86), 16:42.

3. John Murdock Diary (1830–59), 27–29, Orson Pratt Journal (1833–34), cited in Robert J. Woodford, "The Historical Development of the Doctrine and Covenants" (PhD diss., Brigham Young University, 1974), 2:930–31.

4. Smith, *History of the Church*, 2:492.

5. *Deseret News*, September 14, 1852, 24, cited in Woodford, "Historical Development," 2:929.

6. *Deseret News*, March 18, 1857, 11.

7. Richard L. Bushman, *Joseph Smith: Rough Stone Rolling* (New York: Alfred A. Knopf, 2005), 199–200.

8. Profession of Faith of the General Convention of Universalists, 1803, Winchester, New Hampshire, Article II, citing Rev. A. B. Grosh, "Universalists" and I. Daniel Rupp, *An Original History of the Religious Denominations* (Philadelphia, 1844), 727, cited in Milton V. Backman Jr., *American Religions and the Rise of Mormonism*, rev. ed. (Salt Lake City: Deseret Book, 1965), 219.

9. Russell E. Miller, *The Larger Hope: The First Century of the Universalist Church in America, 1770–1870* (Boston: Unitarian Universalist Association, 1979), 8–12.

10. Richard Lloyd Anderson, *Joseph Smith's New England Heritage*, rev. ed. (Salt Lake City: Deseret Book, 2003), 136; see also Richard L. Bushman, *Joseph Smith and the Beginnings of Mormonism* (Urbana: University of Illinois Press, 1984), 27–28.

11. Dan Vogel, ed., *Early Mormon Documents* (Salt Lake City: Signature Books, 1996), 1:633–34.

12. Anderson, *New England Heritage*, 133.

13. Anderson, *New England Heritage*, 161–62; punctuation modernized.

14. A Tunbridge, Vermont, declaration of membership in the Tunbridge Universalist Society contains the signatures of Asael Smith, Joseph Smith Sr., Jesse Smith, and thirteen others (Vogel, *Early Mormon Documents*, 1:633). Jesse's later devotion to Calvinism and the doctrine of election suggests that he may have only joined the Universalist Society for tax purposes.

15. Anderson, *New England Heritage*, 68; emphasis added.

16. Vogel, *Early Mormon Documents*, 1:487; punctuation modernized.

17. Anderson, *New England Heritage*, 279n203.

18. Anderson, *New England Heritage*, 62.

19. Bushman, *Joseph Smith and the Beginnings of Mormonism*, 5.

20. Bushman, *Joseph Smith and the Beginnings of Mormonism*, 140.

21. An excellent summary of Joseph Smith Sr. and Lucy Mack Smith's background may be found in Richard L. Bushman and H. Rodney Sharp, "Joseph Smith's Family Background," in *Prophet Joseph: Essays on the Life and Mission of Joseph Smith*, ed. Susan Easton Black and Larry C. Porter (Salt Lake City: Deseret Book, 1988), 1–16.

22. Ernest Cassara, *Hosea Ballou: The Challenge to Orthodoxy* (Boston: Universalist Historical Society, 1961), 150.

23. Ann Lee Bressler, *The Universalist Movement in America, 1770–1880* (Oxford: Oxford University Press, 2001), 62.

24. Jesse Smith, as quoted in Anderson, *New England Heritage*, 141. "Limited Election" refers to the Calvinist doctrine of predestination, or the notion that God had already selected the saved, and thus salvation was unconditional and the Atonement of Christ applied only to that group.

25. Lavina Fielding Anderson, ed., *Lucy's Book: A Critical Edition of Lucy Mack Smith's Family Memoir* (Salt Lake City: Signature Books, 2001), 293–94.

26. Vogel, *Early Mormon Documents*, 3:29–30, 4:21, 110.

27. Bressler, *The Universalist Movement*, 40.

28. Miller, *The Larger Hope*, xv. For a good summary of the arguments against Universalists during the early years of the Restoration, see Bressler, *The Universalist Movement*, 37–40.

29. See Vogel, *Early Mormon Documents*, 2:29, 4:110.

30. Donna Hill, *Joseph Smith: The First Mormon* (New York: Doubleday, 1977), 17; see also Anderson, *New England Heritage*, 267–68.

31. Vogel, *Early Mormon Documents*, 1:487; spelling and grammar modernized.

32. Bressler, *The Universalist Movement*, 32.

33. The number of American publications relating to Universalism rose dramatically from 54 during the 1800–9 decade, to 134 in 1810–19, 304 in 1820–29, peaked at 378 in 1830–39, fell slightly to 351 during 1840–49, and then dropped off generally for the rest of the nineteenth century (Bressler, *The Universalist Movement*, 55).

34. Miller, *The Larger Hope*, 49.

35. Critics advocating this view can be found as early as 1835. Most recently Dan Vogel has taken up this view and written about it extensively in an essay

entitled "Anti-Universalist Rhetoric in the Book of Mormon," in Brent L. Metcalfe, ed., *New Approaches to the Book of Mormon* (Salt Lake City: Signature Books, 1993), 47. A good summary and response to these arguments may be found in Terryl L. Givens, *By the Hand of Mormon* (Oxford: Oxford University Press, 2002), 164–66.

36. For Campbell's arguments, see Milton V. Backman Jr., *The Heavens Resound* (Salt Lake City: Deseret Book, 1983), 54–55.

37. Bressler, *The Universalist Movement*, 58.

38. Anderson, *New England Heritage*, 148.

39. Anderson, *New England Heritage*, 149. Further details surrounding Asael's feelings about his grandson's works may be found in Anderson, *New England Heritage*, 288. One account reads, "Father Asael Smith . . . on his deathbed declared his full and firm belief in the everlasting gospel and also regretted that he was not baptized when Joseph his son was there and acknowledged that the doctrine of universalism, which he had so long advocated, was not true. For although he had lived by this religion 50 years, yet he now renounced it as insufficient to comfort him in death."

40. A more detailed history of the movement of Doctrine and Covenants 76 toward acceptance in Latter-day Saint thought may be found in Grant Underwood, "'Saved or Damned': Tracing a Persistent Protestantism in Early Mormon Thought," *BYU Studies* 3 (Summer 1985): 95–100.

41. Stan Larson, "The King Follett Discourse: A Newly Amalgamated Text," *BYU Studies* 18 (Winter 1978): 205.

42. See Smith, *History of the Church*, 5:392–93, 6:363–67, 6:473–79.

43. Smith, *History of the Church*, 4:595.

44. Anderson, *New England Heritage*, 161–62; spelling and capitalization modernized.

45. Smith, *History of the Church*, 5:136.

46. Young, in *Journal of Discourses*, 8:153.

47. Parley P. Pratt, *The Essential Parley P. Pratt* (Salt Lake City: Signature Books, 1990), 57.

48. Young, in *Journal of Discourses*, 3:92; emphasis added.

49. Anderson, *Lucy's Book*, 477; capitalization modernized.

50. Young, in *Journal of Discourses*, 7:289.

9

REDEMPTION'S GRAND DESIGN FOR BOTH THE LIVING AND THE DEAD

Jennifer C. Lane

Redemption is a golden thread running through the tapestry of scripture. If we follow it back, we find its origins in the ancient world. Today we often use the terms *save* and *redeem* interchangeably, and understandably so, because they both testify of Christ's role as Savior and Redeemer. But when we look more closely at the terms themselves and their Old Testament background, we find that redemption is a subset of salvation. Salvation can imply help and deliverance through any means. Redemption, however, is a particular kind of salvation.[1] It specifically means deliverance from bondage through the payment of a ransom price.[2] Redemption emphasizes both captivity and payment—that individuals would remain in bondage or captivity without the intervention of a redeemer and also that deliverance comes through payment of a ransom price. In the ancient Near East, people became enslaved by selling themselves because of debt or by becoming prisoners of war.

Jennifer C. Lane is an assistant professor of religion at Brigham Young University–Hawaii.

It was a widespread practice to be redeemed from captivity through the payment of a ransom price.

This ancient meaning of redemption becomes even more illuminating from a gospel perspective with the unique practice of redemption in Israel. While the ancient Israelites shared the general Semitic root term for "redeem" (*padah*) with their neighbors, they had another term for "redemption" (*ga'al*) that was unique to them. In Israelite practice, the *go'el,* or "kinsman-redeemer," was a family member, specifically the oldest male member in an extended family.[3] This background enlivens the description of the Lord as the Redeemer of Israel. Because of the covenants we make, He becomes our collective Father, seeking to rescue us and buy us out of bondage.

In the Old Testament world, covenants with the Lord were not sterile business formalities but adoptions.[4] Entering into a covenant was not making a contract; it was becoming part of a family and even involved receiving a new name.[5] This practice can be seen both in individuals receiving new names and also in the people collectively taking on the Lord's name and becoming His: "O Israel, fear not: for I have redeemed thee, I have called thee by thy name; thou art mine" (Isaiah 43:1).

The golden thread of redemption is woven throughout the Doctrine and Covenants, and, connected to this ancient background, the deeper significance of "Redeemer" and "redemption" comes to life. First, the Saints are clearly understood as covenant Israel, the Lord's adopted people. The Lord speaks to them as He did to His ancient covenant people: "I am the Lord your God, even the God of your fathers, the God of Abraham and of Isaac and of Jacob. I am he who led the children of Israel out of the land of Egypt; and my arm is stretched out in the last days, to save my people Israel" (D&C 136:21–22). The covenant-family relationship provides the assurance of redemption. The understanding that the Lord redeemed the children of Israel *because of* the covenants is a central gospel theme (see Exodus 6:2–8; Deuteronomy 7:8; 1 Nephi 17:40).[6]

In addition, the concept of the "redemption of Zion" found repeatedly in the Doctrine and Covenants is tied to the understanding of the Lord as the Redeemer of Israel, who restores things to their proper state. Both land that had been lost as well as people who were in captivity would be restored by this "kinsman-redeemer."

Redemption of the Land: Redemption of Zion

One prominent theme of redemption in the Doctrine and Covenants is the redemption of Zion. The loss and recovery of the "promised land" is both a biblical and latter-day concern. As the Saints were driven from Jackson County, Missouri, and as we go through our own times of extreme hardship and discouragement, it was, and is, important for the Saints to remember that because of the covenant relationship that has been established, the Lord is bound to act as our Redeemer just as He redeemed the children of Israel.

In Deuteronomy the Lord's redemption of Israel is directly tied to the covenants made by the patriarchs: "The Lord did not set his love upon you, nor choose you, because ye were more in number than any people; for ye were the fewest of all people: but because the Lord loved you, and *because he would keep the oath which he had sworn unto your fathers, hath the Lord brought you out with a mighty hand, and redeemed you out of the house of bondmen,* from the hand of Pharaoh king of Egypt" (Deuteronomy 7:7–8; emphasis added). In Leviticus this covenant memory had a specific tie to the promise of land: "Then will I remember my covenant with Jacob, and also my covenant with Isaac, and also my covenant with Abraham will I remember; and I will remember the land" (Leviticus 26:42).

In the Doctrine and Covenants, we first see the Redeemer's responsibility for the restoration of land discussed in sections 100–105. The redemption of Zion is initially used to mean that Jackson County, Missouri, will be returned to the Saints. This idea of the land being returned to its proper state is one of the functions of the kinsman-redeemer in the Old Testament and among the Israelites. In these sections the Saints are gradually told that the Lord will redeem Zion, but it will be in His time and will require the Saints to receive an endowment from on high. In these revelations the physical sense of the kinsman-redeemer redeeming the land and restoring it to its proper owners is gradually developed into a long-term vision of the redemption of Zion as the Lord sanctifying and preparing His people. This spiritual vision of the redemption of Zion will also include a return of the land, but it is no longer the central feature of the message. The Lord still promises to redeem because of His covenant relationship with His people, but the developing vision of what is involved in redemption becomes more profound and personal.

The development of this doctrine begins during the troubles in October 1833 when the Saints are told, "Zion shall be redeemed, although she is chastened for a little season" (D&C 100:13). How long this "little season" would be or what the chastening would include is not specified. In December of the same year, after the Saints were driven from their homes, the Lord explained that He would not forget His covenant promises. He promised that He would act to "redeem my vineyard; for it is mine" (D&C 101:56). The Lord gave this parable of the nobleman and the vineyard with olive trees "that you may know my will concerning the redemption of Zion" (D&C 101:43).

In this parable the Jackson County Saints are told that they have a responsibility to do their part to reclaim the land. The servants are to be gathered and to go "straightway unto the land of my vineyard, and redeem my vineyard; for it is mine" (D&C 101:56). This command foreshadows the role of Zion's Camp, initially understood by the participants to be about the physical redemption of the land. The Saints were told that their responsibility to participate in the redemption of the land also included legal petitions: "It is my will that they should continue to importune for redress, and redemption, by the hands of those who are placed as rulers and are in authority over you" (D&C 101:76).

It is clear that the redemption of Zion is contingent not on the Lord's willingness to fulfill His covenant role but on the obedience of Israel to its covenants. The Lord explains, "There is even now already in store sufficient, yea, even an abundance, to redeem Zion, and establish her waste places, no more to be thrown down, *were* the churches, who call themselves after my name, *willing* to hearken to my voice" (D&C 101:75; emphasis added). This potential for redemption was not realized at this time because the covenant people who "call themselves after my name," as part of the new family relationship of the covenant, were not "willing to hearken to my voice."

The relationship of covenant faithfulness and the redeeming of the land is emphasized in section 103. In February 1834 the Lord tells them "how to act in the discharge of your duties concerning the salvation and redemption of your brethren, who have been scattered on the land of Zion" (v. 1). He explains that the blessings of redemption He offered would come after tribulations and would result in "your redemption, and the redemption of your brethren, even their restoration to the land of Zion, to be established, no more to be thrown down" (v. 13). Again He stresses that His redemption is contingent on their covenant faithfulness: "Nevertheless, if they pollute their inheritances they shall be thrown down; for I will not spare them if they pollute their inheritances" (v. 14).

The Lord's voice as the Redeemer of Israel to His modern covenant people is that of assurance that redemption is in His hands. By referring to His acts as the Redeemer of Israel in biblical times, the Lord reinforces that His people need not fear they will be abandoned if they are faithful to their covenant relationships: "Behold, I say unto you, the redemption of Zion must needs come by power; therefore, I will raise up unto my people a man, who shall lead them like as Moses led the children of Israel. For ye are the children of Israel, and of the seed of Abraham, and ye must needs be led out of bondage by power, and with a stretched-out arm. And as your fathers were led at the first, even so shall the redemption of Zion be" (D&C 103:15–18). The direct parallels to the redemption of the covenant people in ancient times could not be more clear.

The spiritual dimension of redemption in the Lord's latter-day work can be seen in the context of the winter of 1833–34. Here, in sections 103 and 105, this pattern can be found in the Lord's specific directions for the gathering of Zion's Camp, which was to march to Jackson County. Those who participated, as was mentioned earlier, envisioned their actions as leading to the short-term physical redemption of the land. In section 103 Sidney Rigdon was told to "lift up his voice in the congregations in the eastern countries, in preparing the churches to keep the commandments which I have given unto them concerning the restoration and redemption of Zion" (D&C 103:29). Some of the Saints in the East, but not as many as were hoped for, gathered for this effort for the redemption of Zion.

Once Zion's Camp finally arrived in Missouri, they were taught that the redemption of Zion was not going to be what they had expected. Section 105 gives this further insight into the Lord's plans. First, the Lord expressed displeasure with the Saints collectively and explained that their own choices were keeping them from seeing the redemption of Zion: "Verily I say unto you who have assembled yourselves together that you may learn my will concerning the redemption of mine afflicted people—Behold, I say unto you, were it not for the transgressions of my people, speaking concerning the church and not individuals, they might have been redeemed even now" (vv. 1–2). He specifically explains that their lack of obedience, unity, and consecration prevents the redemption of Zion.

This is one of the most significant revelatory moments in early Church history because the Lord explains here that redemption is not simply to return to a place of God but to a state of being like God. Zion could not be redeemed by people who were not themselves redeemed from the natural man. The redemption of Zion required the redemption of people: "Zion cannot be built up unless it is by the principles of the law of the celestial kingdom; otherwise I cannot receive her unto myself" (D&C 105:5). Zion is a people as much as a place. This principle had recently been reinforced in section 97, given in August 1833 where the Lord clearly explained: "This is Zion—THE PURE IN HEART" (v. 21). We are in bondage to our sins and weaknesses until we allow the Lord to redeem us through our faith, repentance, and covenant faithfulness. In Christ's atoning sacrifice, His ransom payment has been offered, but we experience redemption only when we choose to make and keep covenants. As we choose redemption, His sanctifying power brings us out of bondage to the natural man and makes us Zion, the pure in heart.[7]

Given this more expansive, spiritual vision of the redemption of Zion, it is clear why the process of sanctifying the Church is ongoing. Section 105 also clarifies the role of the temple and temple covenants in allowing redemption from our fallen state to take place:

> Therefore, in consequence of the transgressions of my people, it is expedient in me that mine elders should wait for a little season for the redemption of Zion—
>
> That they themselves may be prepared, and that my people may be taught more perfectly, and have experience, and know more perfectly concerning their duty, and the things which I require at their hands.
>
> And this cannot be brought to pass until mine elders are endowed with power from on high.
>
> For behold, I have prepared a great endowment and blessing to be poured out upon them, inasmuch as they are faithful and continue in humility before me.
>
> Therefore it is expedient in me that mine elders should wait for a little season, for the redemption of Zion. (D&C 105:9–13)

This section clearly connects our spiritual redemption as individuals and as a people with the endowment of "power from on high." As we become the Lord's covenant people even more and take His name upon us more fully, we experience a greater degree of redemption.

This is precisely the message of the parable given in section 101, and the Lord returns to the imagery here in section 105. He explains that His command to gather "the strength of my house" for "the redemption of my people" was not accomplished as it should have been because so many Church members were not obedient to the call to sacrifice and unite with Zion's Camp: "the strength of mine house have not hearkened unto my words" (vv. 16–17). However, despite the opportunity for collective redemption that was forfeited, the Lord recognizes those faithful members who did obey: "But inasmuch as there are those who have hearkened unto my words, I have prepared a blessing and an endowment for them, if they continue faithful" (v. 18). These blessings were richly poured out as the Quorum of the Twelve Apostles and the Seventy were soon selected from those who were choosing spiritual redemption through their faithfulness and obedience. From among these leaders, those who stayed faithful went on to receive their endowment in the Nauvoo Temple.

Section 105 emphasizes again how this revelation serves to shift an understanding of redemption from the focus on redeeming the land. In verse 34 the Lord commands: "And let those commandments which I have given concerning Zion and her law be executed and fulfilled, after her redemption." This has been taken to mean the temporary suspension of requirements for the Church to live the law of consecration the way it was earlier explained. The Lord's desire for us to live the law of consecration as explained in the Doctrine and Covenants is clearly ongoing, but until we as a people are redeemed from our selfishness and jealousy through deeper conversion and sanctification, the specific institutional implementation of something like the law of consecration and stewardship or of a "United Order" serves little use.

The promise of the physical redemption of the land is real, and requests for its fulfillment can be seen in the dedicatory prayer of the Kirtland Temple, in which Joseph pleads that the Lord will "redeem that which thou didst appoint a Zion unto thy people" (D&C 109:51). There is also a prayer for the redemption of Jerusalem and the Jews (see D&C 109:62–63). These prayers can, perhaps, be seen as both temporal and spiritual in compass. It is clear that the discussion of redemption can be found in many other contexts in the Doctrine and Covenants, and this shared physical and spiritual dimension is an ongoing theme.

Redemption of the Body and Spirit

Returning to the world of the ancient Near East, kinsman-redeemers in ancient Israel were responsible not only to redeem land but also to buy individuals out of bondage. People in this ancient world could find themselves in bondage as slaves either because they were prisoners of war or because they had sold themselves, or been sold, to pay off a debt. The kinsman-redeemer would then repay that debt or ransom money and restore the one in bondage to his or her previous state. This social practice was then used by the prophets to explain the relationship between the covenant family of Israel and their adoptive Father and Redeemer, the Lord. Because of the covenant relationship with the house of Israel, Jehovah had become the *go'el,* or Redeemer of Israel. Isaiah expresses this, saying: "Doubtless thou art our father, though Abraham be ignorant of us, and Israel [Jacob] acknowledge us not: thou, O Lord, art our father, our redeemer; thy name is from everlasting" (Isaiah 63:16). Because of their covenant relationship, Israel could rely on the Lord to act as their kinsman-redeemer, even when blood relations failed.

The imagery of physical and spiritual death as forms of bondage from which we are redeemed through the payment of Christ's atoning sacrifice is the central message of the gospel (see 3 Nephi 27:13–21; 2 Nephi 9:5–27). The Apostle Paul taught that "ye are not your own; . . . ye are bought with a price" (1 Corinthians 6:19–20). The Book of Mormon prophets repeatedly emphasize that we have been redeemed from the captivity of the devil, "the bands of death," and "the chains of hell" through the redemption of the Savior (see 1 Nephi 14:4–7; 2 Nephi 1:18; 2 Nephi 2:27; Alma 5:7–10; Alma 12:11; Alma 13:30; Alma 40:13; 3 Nephi 18:15). This emphasis on both bondage and payment are essential points that make the doctrine of redemption a particularly important witness of our captivity due to the Fall and the role of Christ's atoning sacrifice to pay the price of our deliverance. If we were to see the terms *salvation* and *redemption* as simply interchangeable, we would miss this vital spiritual truth.

Both the physical and spiritual aspects of Christ's redemption addressed in other books of scripture can be found in revelations contained in the Doctrine and Covenants. Resurrection is explained as redemption of the body, and we also see how through covenant relationships Christ can act as our Redeemer from spiritual death. This spiritual redemption can be seen in regard to both the living and the dead. The Doctrine and Covenants' unique message is that the redemption of Christ can be extended to those in the spirit world through their repentance and forming covenant relationships with Christ. This additional insight into redemption is essential in understanding the work of temples and family history in the latter days.

Resurrection as redemption of the body. The redemption of all who have lived from the bondage of physical death is a key component of the good news of the gospel. Paul testified that "for as in Adam all die, even so in Christ shall all be made alive" (1 Corinthians 15:22). Moroni taught that "because of the redemption of man, which came by Jesus

Christ, they are brought back into the presence of the Lord; yea, *this is wherein all men are redeemed,* because the death of Christ bringeth to pass the resurrection, which bringeth to pass a redemption from an endless sleep" (Mormon 9:13; emphasis added). Unlike spiritual redemption, this universal aspect of Christ's redemption does not require any personal covenant relationship with Christ. People do not have to choose to be redeemed physically.[8]

While the doctrine of the resurrection of the body is also found in the Bible, the further witness found in the Doctrine and Covenants and the Book of Mormon is particularly important in our day because people are increasingly inclined not to believe in physical resurrection and not to see death as bondage. The Doctrine and Covenants reaffirms the doctrine of resurrection as physical redemption and further explains how it relates to our true nature and God's nature. In section 45, clarifying the revelation Christ gave to His disciples on the Mount of Olives, the Savior tells them they had "looked upon the long absence of your spirits from your bodies to be a bondage" (D&C 45:17). Christ then promises that "day of redemption shall come" (v. 17). This same understanding of the separation of body and spirit as bondage can be found in section 93 where we learn about God's nature and our own: "The elements are eternal, and spirit and element, inseparably connected, receive a fulness of joy; and when separated, man cannot receive a fulness of joy" (vv. 33–34). The Restoration teaching of an embodied God helps us to appreciate the importance of physical redemption to allow us to receive the joy that He experiences.

This emphasis on the bondage of physical death is particularly important in the vision of the spirit world in section 138. Here the faithful covenant Saints who lived before Christ's birth "were assembled awaiting the advent of the Son of God into the spirit world, to declare their redemption from the bands of death" (D&C 138:16), and we find the same clear doctrine revealed in section 93 about the need for body and spirit to be united. The Redeemer brings things to their proper state: "Their sleeping dust was to be restored unto its perfect frame, bone to his bone, and the sinews and the flesh upon them, the spirit and the body to be united never again to be divided, that they might receive a fulness of joy" (D&C 138:17). The separation of our spirits and bodies is a bondage that prevents us from enjoying the kind of life that God enjoys.

Yet it is not simply redemption from the bondage of physical death that will bring us this fullness of joy. In speaking to His disciples on the Mount of Olives, the Savior explains what full redemption will mean: "If ye have slept in peace blessed are you; for as you now behold me and know that I am, even so shall ye come unto me and your souls shall live, and your redemption shall be perfected" (D&C 45:46). Having our souls live and our redemption perfected will require both physical and spiritual redemption. We will need to come unto Christ both as we stand before Him at Judgment Day and also as we are perfected through our covenant relationship with Him.

The Doctrine and Covenants clarifies that "the day of redemption" will be different for each individual to the extent they allowed Christ to redeem them spiritually. As Moroni explained, resurrection is redemption from the bondage of physical death, but it also brings us to the presence of God for judgment: "They shall come forth, both small and great, and all shall stand before his bar, being redeemed and loosed from this eternal band of death, which death is a temporal death. And then cometh the judgment of the Holy One upon them; and then cometh the time that he that is filthy shall be filthy still; and he that is righteous shall be righteous still; he that is happy shall be happy still; and he that is unhappy shall be unhappy still" (Mormon 9:13–14). We become what we have chosen to become. The Doctrine and Covenants clarifies that our resurrected bodies will literally embody the choices that we have made in this life in response to Christ's offer of spiritual redemption (see D&C 88:21–31). Those who have chosen to be redeemed through making and keeping covenants will be free from all that keeps them away from being with and like God. Those who have refused to receive the redemption offered them through covenant relationships with the Redeemer will be left "to enjoy that which they are willing to receive" (D&C 88:32).

Covenants, sanctification, and spiritual redemption. In teaching the people of Zarahemla, Alma explained that without Christ's redemption people are "encircled about by the bands of death, and the chains of hell, and an everlasting destruction did await them" (Alma 5:7). This metaphor of captivity is central to the ancient meaning of redemption. We are in bondage, and through the payment of a price we can be loosed from our chains and restored to our original status. The Doctrine and Covenants not only teaches about the redemption from the bands of death but also serves as a second witness of how Christ's Atonement becomes the payment to loose us from the chains of hell.

In these explanations, covenants and repentance allow us to choose spiritual redemption. Christ's redemption price is universal: "He suffereth the pains of all men, yea, the pains of every living creature, both men, women, and children, who belong to the family of Adam" (2 Nephi 9:21). He has already paid this price, but the application of it is individual. The revelations in the Doctrine and Covenants clarify that it is through our repentance and covenant faithfulness that He can act to redeem us from our spiritual bondage.

The Doctrine and Covenants emphasizes the universal scope of spiritual redemption through Christ; it witnesses that this message was taught in all dispensations. Adam and his family were kept from physical death "until I, the Lord God, should send forth angels to declare unto them repentance and redemption, through faith on the name of mine Only Begotten Son" (D&C 29:42). The gift of full redemption, being "raised in immortality unto eternal life," was designed to be given to "even as many as would believe" (D&C 29:43). The choice of faith, repentance, baptism, and the gift of the Holy Ghost allows spiritual redemption to become active. Those who are not redeemed are not abandoned by the Redeemer, but they simply "cannot be redeemed from their spiritual fall, because they repent not" (D&C 29:44). When we understand spiritual redemption as the conversion and sanctification that come from faith in Christ, we understand that He cannot redeem us *in* our sins, but only *from* them (see Helaman 5:10).

The Doctrine and Covenants' accompanying message of the expansive redemption is that all those who are not capable of choosing spiritual redemption through Christ are not damned by their inability. The principle "that little children are redeemed from the foundation of the world through mine Only Begotten" (D&C 29:46) helps us understand the great mercy of God in redeeming those who cannot choose to make and keep covenants, such as little children before the age of accountability and those with mental impairments. The Atonement of Christ allows all of us to be redeemed, but most of us are able and required to choose to make Christ our spiritual Father and Redeemer through covenant.

This message that we are free to choose Christ's redemption is a stark contrast to the notion of total depravity, in which the Fall makes it impossible for individuals to choose good of their own accord. The Doctrine and Covenants confirms the important teaching of the Book of Mormon that it is actually the Atonement of Christ that redeems us from the bondage that we would have been in and makes it possible for us to choose between captivity and liberty (see 2 Nephi 2:26–27). In section 93 the Lord reaffirms this expansive vision of the Redemption, declaring that "every spirit of man was innocent in the beginning; and God having redeemed man from the fall, men became again, in their infant state, innocent before God" (v. 38). This redemption from the first death along with the physical redemption from the bonds of death are universal gifts that make right that which was lost in the Fall—our immortality and freedom from original sin.

In the Pearl of Great Price, the Lord teaches Adam: "I have forgiven thee thy transgression in the Garden of Eden. Hence came the saying abroad among the people, that the Son of God hath atoned for original guilt, wherein the sins of the parents cannot be answered upon the heads of the children, for they are whole from the foundation of the world" (Moses 6:53–54). Given this freedom to choose, made possible by Christ's redemption, we are then accountable for our choices: "Thus saith the Lord; for I am God, and have sent mine Only Begotten Son into the world for the redemption of the world, and have decreed that he that receiveth him shall be saved, and he that receiveth him not shall be damned" (D&C 49:5).

As Christ's covenant people, the knowledge of how to receive spiritual redemption is a priceless gift to enjoy and to share. The purpose of the Church to perfect the Saints, proclaim the gospel, and redeem the dead is a mission of redemption. As members, we are redeemed as we deepen our conversion and sanctification through faith and repentance. Through missionary work, we invite others to enter covenant relationships with Christ so they too may experience the spiritual redemption of forgiveness and sanctification. This prayer that others may enjoy redemption is echoed in the dedicatory prayer of the Kirtland Temple. Joseph pleads with the Lord that "all the scattered remnants of Israel, who have been driven to the ends of the earth, come to a knowledge of the truth, believe in the Messiah, and be redeemed from oppression, and rejoice before thee" (D&C 109:67).

We see in this prayer how Joseph's covenant faithfulness gives him confidence to call on his Redeemer: "O Lord, remember thy servant, Joseph Smith, Jun., and all his afflictions and persecutions—how he has covenanted with Jehovah, and vowed to thee, O Mighty God of Jacob—and the commandments which thou hast given unto him, and that he hath sincerely striven to do thy will" (D&C 109:68). He prays that the Lord will convert those in opposition to the truth: "Have mercy upon all their immediate connections, that their prejudices may be broken up and swept away as with a flood; that they may be converted and redeemed with Israel, and know that thou art God" (D&C 109:70). Joseph Smith is asking in confidence that the Lord will remember His faithful covenant people with redemption. Like him, we can also know that the Lord is faithful to His covenant relationship with us. We can have faith in the faithfulness of our Redeemer (see Hebrews 11:11–19). Because of the covenants that we have made, we are Christ's spiritual children and are called by His name (see Mosiah 5:7–12), and the Lord has promised that He will redeem His people (see, for example, 2 Samuel 7:22–24).

This promise of redemption seen throughout the Old Testament and other books of scripture is reaffirmed in the Doctrine of Covenants. The Lord answered a question posed by Elias Higbee in section 113 about whom Isaiah was referring to when he said, "Put on thy strength, O Zion" (v. 7). The Lord responded with a message that should give heart and courage to all who seek to make and keep covenants with Him: "He [Isaiah] had reference to those whom God should call in the last days, who should hold the power of priesthood to bring again Zion, and the redemption of Israel; and to put on her strength is to put on the authority of the priesthood, which she, Zion, has a right to by lineage; also to return to that power which she had lost" (D&C 113:8). The redemption of Israel is ongoing as individuals choose to "come unto Christ, who is the Holy One of Israel, and partake of his salvation, and the power of his redemption" (Omni 1:26).

The Day of Redemption and the Redemption of the Dead

The Doctrine and Covenants provides a radically new perspective on the reach of Christ's redemption. While Christianity has long given assent to the idea of the resurrection of the body, the good news of this universal redemption from physical death has at times been clouded by fears that few would enjoy God's presence in the next life. It has sometimes been feared that many, if not most, would be resurrected to suffer eternally. Those who had not heard of Christ and not received baptism were presumed to be lost. Many who were basically good were not good enough and thus in danger of hellfire. The message of the Restoration contained in the Doctrine and Covenants is a joyful answer with an expansive vision of redemption.

We are taught in sections 76 and 88 that almost all will be redeemed by Christ from the hell of being separated from God and be able to enjoy the presence of God in some degree. We are also taught that these gradations of redemption are not due to any lack of power or desire on the part of the Redeemer, but only on the desire of individuals to be redeemed. The spiritual blessings of full redemption, being restored to the presence of God the Father in eternal life, will not be limited by earthly opportunities. The power of Christ to rescue each individual from spiritual bondage is not limited by when or where they were born. The covenants needed to allow Christ to be our spiritual Redeemer are available to all through the work done in the temples.

Resurrection as the day of redemption. The gradations of redemption and resurrection become clear in the Doctrine and Covenants' teachings on the degrees of glory. The expansive vision in section 76 extends redemption to more than those in "heaven" because in some sense He redeems all who will be in any of the degrees of glory. However, the fullness of the redemption that Christ offers is available only to those who enter into covenant relationships with Him and are faithful to those covenants. Section 88 clarifies how the redemption of resurrection is for all, but also how it literally differs in degrees of light and glory depending on how we respond to Christ's offer of spiritual redemption.

The foundation of the doctrine taught in section 88 is the explanation that Christ is our hope of redemption, "that through the redemption which is made for you is brought to pass the resurrection from the dead" (v. 14). This is tied to the basic principle that "the spirit and the body are the soul of man" (v. 15) and a corresponding explanation that Christ as the Redeemer restores things to their proper order: "And the resurrection from the dead is the redemption of the soul. And the redemption of the soul is through him that quickeneth all things" (vv. 16–17). It is essential to remember that without the redemption of resurrection all would be eternally lost and in bondage to Satan, never to be restored to the presence of God (see 2 Nephi 9:6–9). It is sobering and humbling to remember that "the redemption of the soul is through him that quickeneth all things" (D&C 88:17). Christ's ransom price was sufficient to compensate for the eternal suffering and banishment of all God's children. Because of Christ's redemption, all will be brought back into God's presence for judgment, and all but the sons of perdition will be able to remain in the light of one of the members of the Godhead.

In the Doctrine and Covenants' description of resurrection as the "day of redemption," we see several important and interrelated points. Not all will be resurrected at the same time, and not all will be resurrected to dwell in the same degree of God's glory. Here are found the interwoven strands of human agency and the power of redemption. While the ransom price of Christ's Atonement was paid for the souls of all, body and spirit, not all will choose to receive and apply that payment. This is most tragically so with those sons of perdition who have received all and then completely turn away from that relationship.[9] Speaking of these, Christ explains that they are "the only ones on whom the second death shall have any power; yea, verily, the only ones who shall not be redeemed in the due time of the Lord, after the sufferings of his wrath. For all the rest shall be brought forth by the resurrection of the dead, through the triumph and the glory of the Lamb, who was slain" (D&C 76:37–39). This might be mistakenly understood as saying that the sons of perdition are not resurrected, but we do know that "the death of Christ shall loose the bands of this temporal death, that all shall be raised from this temporal death" (Alma 11:42). All will be resurrected and brought to stand before Christ at Judgment Day. However, in this very small group of individuals, physical immortality is coupled with the second death, meaning that they have chosen banishment from any degree of light and life that come from God.

The positive corollary of this sorrowful vision is Christ's glorious proclamation that He "shall redeem all things, except that which he hath not put into his power" (D&C 77:12). This means that the day of resurrection will be a day of redemption for all others, essentially all that have ever lived. As mentioned earlier, the "day of redemption" will be staggered, beginning with the righteous. We learn that those who will be raised to telestial glory "shall not be redeemed from the devil until the last resurrection, until the Lord, even Christ the Lamb, shall have finished his work" (D&C 76:85). They will be redeemed from hell at the end of the Millennium and will be able to enjoy the presence of the Holy Ghost, but they will not have been willing to receive the fullness of redemption offered them through the messengers in the spirit world (see D&C 138:30–34).

Section 88 also gives an outline of the sequence of the "day of redemption," and in it we see degrees of spiritual redemption from captivity to darkness and spiritual death. The last group mentioned are the sons of perdition, "who shall remain filthy still" (v. 102). They are preceded by those "found under condemnation" who "live not again until the thousand years are ended" (vv. 100–101). The Resurrection begins with the covenant Saints from previous and current dispensations (see vv. 97–98). Preceding this "cometh the redemption of those who are Christ's at his coming; who have received their part in that prison which is prepared for them, that they might receive the gospel, and be judged according to men in the flesh" (v. 99). Some may have taken this statement along with D&C 76:71–74 to mean that those who do not receive the gospel during mortality will not be resurrected to celestial glory and eternal life. But we must remember that the Second Coming of Christ will take place at the beginning of the Millennium, and in some ways the work for the dead will still just be starting. The "first fruits" (D&C 88:98) of those who are Christ's covenant people will be able to receive their full redemption of a glorious resurrection at the time of His arrival. The resurrection and judgment of those who have not yet had a chance to become His covenant people must be delayed until they are ready.

The redemption of the dead. The Doctrine and Covenants' expansive vision of redemption can be seen in the Lord's explanation that after His Second Coming, the Millennium will be the time when "the heathen nations be redeemed, and they that knew no law shall have part in the first resurrection; and it shall be tolerable for them" (D&C 45:54). The vexing problem of "what of those who have not heard?" is answered in the additional revelation of the Restoration. Christ is the Redeemer of Israel. Both ancient and modern Saints have taken Him to be their spiritual Father and have become His spiritual children through covenant. Because of this covenant relationship, the spiritual redemption of conversion and sanctification can bring us out of bondage to sin and our fallen natures. The percentage of people who have had access to the message of redemption and also the priesthood authority to make covenant relationships is, however, miniscule.

The plan of redemption was not designed for a tiny fraction of God's children. Well does the language of section 128 break into effusive praise at God's merciful and expansive plan to offer the power of Christ's redemption to all who have ever lived: "Brethren, shall we not go on in so great a cause? Go forward and not backward. Courage, brethren; and on, on to the victory! Let your hearts rejoice, and be exceedingly glad. Let the earth break forth into singing. Let the dead speak forth anthems of eternal praise to the King Immanuel, who hath ordained, before the world was, that which would enable us to redeem them out of their prison; for the prisoners shall go free" (v. 22). The covenants made available in the holy temples allow everyone who has ever lived the opportunity to receive the fullness of Christ's redeeming power.

The full scope of this wondrous love and mercy is revealed in section 138. President Joseph F. Smith was "reflecting upon the great atoning sacrifice that was made by the Son of God, for the redemption of the world; and the great and wonderful love made manifest by the Father and the Son in the coming of the Redeemer into the world; that through his atonement, and by obedience to the principles of the gospel, mankind might be saved" (vv. 2–4). President Smith knew the great ransom price that had been paid for the redemption of the world. He also knew that it was only by making and keeping covenants, "obedience to the principles of the gospel," that individuals could receive spiritual redemption in their lives.

The vision recorded in section 138 clarifies the universal message of scripture, the golden thread of redemption, and extends it to all who have ever lived. In the spirit world, Christ taught the Saints "the everlasting gospel, the doctrine of the resurrection and the redemption of mankind from the fall, and from individual sins on conditions of repentance" (v. 19). These Saints had already made and kept their covenants, and they "rejoiced in their redemption, and bowed the knee and acknowledged the Son of God as their Redeemer and Deliverer from death and the chains of hell" (v. 23).

The vision did not end with this joyous encounter but with a commission for those Saints in the spirit world and for us in mortality to share the blessings of redemption that we enjoy. They were to "carry the message of redemption unto all the dead" (v. 37). This message is shared with all, no matter how they had lived their lives: "Thus was the gospel preached to those who had died in their sins, without a knowledge of the truth, or in transgression, having rejected the prophets" (v. 32). By teaching the covenant Saints directly and then organizing them to share this message, the Lord "made known among the dead, both small and great, the unrighteous as well as the faithful, that redemption had been wrought through the sacrifice of the Son of God upon the cross" (v. 35). Through this teaching and the accompanying temple work, Christ's redemption is made available to all. The Saints in the spirit world teach "faith in God, repentance from sin, vicarious baptism for the remission of sins, the gift of the Holy Ghost by the laying on of hands, and all other principles of the gospel that were necessary for them to know in order to qualify themselves that they might be judged according to men in the flesh, but live according to God in the spirit" (vv. 33–34). The Redeemer paid the ransom price for all and stands ready to redeem all who will choose Him as their Redeemer.

This work of redemption, while "wrought through the sacrifice of the Son of God upon the cross" (D&C 138:35), requires that we choose to make and keep covenant relationships to allow Christ to act as our Redeemer. Those in the spirit world can exercise faith in the message of Christ's Redemption and begin to repent from their sins, but that is not enough: "They without us cannot be made perfect" (D&C 128:15). As spirits they can be taught about baptism, the gift of the Holy Ghost, and temple covenants, but they cannot perform these ordinances. It is requisite that we who have become the Lord's family, His covenant people, extend these redemptive blessings to others. So much is this vicarious work a part of our own process of spiritual redemption that the Lord taught that "they without us cannot be made perfect—neither can we without our dead be made perfect" (D&C 128:15). This teaching has even further implications in the binding together of family ties which becomes part of exaltation as the fullness of redemption. Not only are we restored to God's presence through Christ's merciful redemption, but His redeeming power binds us together as husbands and wives, parents and children, throughout the generations (see D&C 138:47–48). So this perfecting dimension of temple work includes being made whole as families forever but also becoming whole and spiritually refined now in mortality. The very act of temple service has a sanctifying and spiritually redeeming power.

As we become His covenant people, Christ gives us His name. This is an essential feature of a covenant in the ancient world and reflects the new nature and relationship that covenant creates. The ancient themes of a name conveying one's nature and of a covenant as the creation of family relationships are both well illustrated in Mosiah 5:7–8: "Because of the covenant which ye have made ye shall be called the children of Christ. . . . There is no other name given whereby salvation cometh; therefore, I would that ye should take upon you the name of Christ." We are Christ's covenant family. He is our spiritual Father, and He is inviting us to take His name and His nature upon us. As we accept that invitation through our repentance and conversion, we receive His redemption. Only to the extent that we leave behind the natural man and become Saints through the Atonement of Christ is the redemption working in our lives (see Mosiah 3:19). By asking us to dedicate ourselves to the redemption of all around us—members, nonmembers, and those who are dead—Christ is asking us to become as He is.

The Doctrine and Covenants' revelations about the redemption of the dead clarify how these ancient concepts of covenant, name, and redemption have direct meaning in living the gospel today. We can see from this understanding of Christ as the covenant Redeemer of Israel that our work in the temples allows us to become saviors on Mount Zion (see Obadiah 1:17, 21). In saying this, it is essential that we remember that "redemption [has] been wrought through the sacrifice of the Son of God upon the cross" (D&C 138:35). Our role in redeeming the dead helps us receive His name as a "savior on Mount Zion" because we are becoming like Him in vicariously working for the redemption of others. The sacrifice, mercy, and love manifest in the transcendent redemption wrought on our behalf calls us to lives of greater sacrifice and mercy to others. As we respond to His redeeming love with mercy toward others, we become redeemed. As we become instruments in His hands, we more fully take on Christ's name and nature as a kinsman-redeemer.

Conclusion: The Lord Will Redeem His People

The Doctrine and Covenants testifies of Christ's role as our Redeemer and of our place in His expansive plan of redemption. As the Redeemer of Israel, the Lord spoke through His prophets in ancient days. With a more profound understanding of the ancient context of the biblical imagery used in modern scripture, we can more fully hear the Lord's voice in the Doctrine and Covenants. Once we grasp the doctrine of redemption, our appreciation of this golden thread enriches our vision of the latter-day work. Isolated from its ancient meaning, the expression "redeeming of the dead" can easily become a tired platitude. Connected to the ancient biblical meaning, the message of the redemption of the dead, which is so central to the Restoration and the work of our dispensation, comes to life. We more deeply appreciate the privilege of making covenants and vicariously performing this work for our ancestors.

The collective redemption of the covenant people can be seen in their singing the song of redeeming love as a people. We see this response to redemption in Alma 5: "And again I ask, were the bands of death broken, and the chains of hell which encircled them about, were they loosed? I say unto you, Yea, they were loosed, and their souls did expand, and they did sing redeeming love. And I say unto you that they are saved" (v. 9). The Doctrine and Covenants stands as a second witness to the Book of Mormon's teaching about redeemed souls singing the song of redeeming love.

The Doctrine and Covenants explains that this joyous response to the experience of spiritual redemption will be found in the promises connected with the Millennium. We can see how the process of sanctification preceded this time when "my people shall be redeemed and shall reign with me on earth" (D&C 43:29) because His elect "shall abide the day of my coming; for they shall be purified, even as I am pure" (D&C 35:21). With the return of the Savior and the resurrection of the just, the Saints will experience both spiritual and physical redemption.

Understanding the ancient relationship of covenant and redemption allows us to more fully appreciate the content of this millennial hymn. We are told that at this day:

> All shall know me, who remain, even from the least unto the greatest, and shall be filled with the knowledge of the Lord, and shall see eye to eye, and shall lift up their voice, and with the voice together sing this new song, saying:
> The Lord hath brought again Zion;
> The Lord hath redeemed his people, Israel,
> According to the election of grace,
> Which was brought to pass by the faith
> And covenant of their fathers.
> The Lord hath redeemed his people;
> And Satan is bound and time is no longer.
> The Lord hath gathered all things in one.
> The Lord hath brought down Zion from above.
> The Lord hath brought up Zion from beneath. (D&C 84:98–100)

The promised redemption and sanctification of Zion will be fully accomplished because the Lord remembers "the faith and covenant of their fathers." The Doctrine and Covenants testifies of Christ's role as our Redeemer and of our place in His expansive plan of redemption. As the Redeemer of Israel, the Lord spoke through His prophets in ancient days. With a more profound understanding of the ancient context of the biblical imagery used in modern scripture, we can more fully hear the Lord's voice in the Doctrine and Covenants. Once we grasp the doctrine of redemption, our appreciation of this golden thread enriches our vision of the latter-day work. Deracinated from its ancient meaning, the expression "redeeming of the dead" can easily become a tired platitude. Connected to the ancient biblical meaning, the message of the redemption of the dead which is so central to the Restoration and the work of our dispensation comes to life. We more deeply appreciate the privilege of making covenants and vicariously performing this work for our ancestors. These covenants make us part of the family of Christ and allow Him to act on our behalf as the kinsman-redeemer of Israel.

Notes

1. In the following section, I summarize my previous research on the Lord as the Redeemer of Israel. For a more in-depth discussion of these issues and a summary of the scholarship on renaming, covenants as family relationships, the role of the kinsman-redeemer, and Jehovah as the Redeemer of Israel in the Old Testament, see Jennifer C. Lane, "The Lord Will Redeem His People: Adoptive Covenant and Redemption in the Old Testament," in *Sperry Symposium Classics: The Old Testament*, ed. Paul Y. Hoskisson (Provo, UT: Religious Studies Center; Salt Lake City: Deseret Book, 2005), 298–310. I have written elsewhere about the adoptive covenant and redemption in the New Testament, the Book of Mormon, and the Book of Abraham.

2. A brief overview of redemption in the Old Testament is provided by Helmer Ringgren, "Ga'al" in *Theological Dictionary of the Old Testament* (Grand Rapids, MI: Eerdmans, 1975), 2:354; Jeremiah Unterman, "Redemption (OT)," in *The Anchor Bible Dictionary*, ed. David Noel Freedman (New York: Doubleday, 1992), 5:650–54; J. Murray, "Redeemer; Redemption," in *The International Standard Bible Encyclopedia*, ed. Geoffry W. Bromiley (Grand Rapids, MI: Eerdmans, 1979), 4:61–63.

3. While we may be most familiar with the *go'el's* responsibilities as seen in the book of Ruth, the kinsman-redeemer was also responsible to buy back sold property; buy back a man who had sold himself to a foreigner as a slave; avenge blood

and kill a relative's murderer; receive atonement money; and, figuratively, to be a helper in a lawsuit (Ringgren, "Ga'al," 351–52). An excellent discussion of the role of the kinsman-redeemer can be found in Robert L. Hubbard, "The Go'el in Ancient Israel: Theological Reflections on an Israelite Institution," *Bulletin for Biblical Research* 1 (1991): 3–19.

4. On creating family relationships in covenants, see, for example, Dennis J. McCarthy, *Treaty and Covenant: A Study in the Ancient Oriental Documents and in the Old Testament* (Rome: Biblical Institute Press, 1978), 266. He comments: "To see a great chief and eat in his place is to join his family . . . the whole group related by blood or not which stood under the authority and protection of the father. One is united to him as a client to his patron who protects him and whom he serves. . . . *Covenant is something one makes by a rite, not something one is born to or forced into, and it can be described in family terms.* God is patron and father, Israel servant and son" (McCarthy, *Treaty and Covenant*, 266; emphasis added).

5. The Hebrew word *šem*, usually translated "name," can also be rendered "remembrance" or "memorial," indicating that the name acts as a reminder to its bearers and others. The name shows both the true nature of its bearer and indicates his relationship to others. Central background on the role of names and renaming in showing new family relationships can be found in G. F. Hawthorne, "Name," *International Standard Bible Encyclopedia* (Grand Rapids, MI: Eerdmans, 1979), 3:481–83; Bruce H. Porter and Stephen D. Ricks, "Names in Antiquity: Old, New, and Hidden," in *By Study and Also by Faith*, ed. John M. Lundquist and Stephen D. Ricks (Salt Lake City: Deseret Book, 1990), 1:501–22.

6. While this concept is particularly clear and relevant in light of the additional truths of the Restoration, the biblical connections between covenant and redemption have been noticed by only a few scholars. See my discussion in "The Redemption of Abraham," in *The Book of Abraham: Astronomy, Papyrus, and Covenant*, ed. John Gee and Brian M. Hauglid, Studies in the Book of Abraham (Provo, UT: Institute for the Study and Preservation of Ancient Religious Texts, 2005), 3:167–68.

7. I discuss the theme of sanctification as redemption in more depth in "Choosing Redemption," in *Living the Book of Mormon: Abiding by Its Precepts*, ed. Charles Swift and Gaye Strathearn (Provo, UT: Religious Studies Center; Salt Lake City: Deseret Book, 2007), 163–75.

8. They do not even need to want to be redeemed. Redemption from physical death requires no choice on our part, perhaps because our being in its bondage was not our choice. We are all in bondage to death because of the Fall, and we have all been redeemed through Christ's death and Resurrection (see 1 Corinthians 15:21–23).

9. Joseph Smith, *Teachings of the Prophet Joseph Smith*, comp. Joseph Fielding Smith (Salt Lake City: Deseret Book, 1976), 358.

10

"ALL THINGS ARE THE LORD'S": THE LAW OF CONSECRATION IN THE DOCTRINE AND COVENANTS

Steven C. Harper

The law of consecration contained in the Doctrine and Covenants is not the law many Latter-day Saints believe it to be. The intervening history between when and why the revelations were given and the present day has resulted in what some historians have called a "folk memory" among Latter-day Saints. This version of the past recalls that early Saints could not live the law of consecration, so the Lord rescinded the higher law and gave the lower law of tithing instead. Someday we will live the higher law again.[1] No matter how widely believed it is, that is not the law of consecration contained in the Doctrine and Covenants.

Elder Neal A. Maxwell taught that "many ignore consecration because it seems too abstract or too daunting. The conscientious among us, however, experience divine discontent."[2] Conscientious covenant keepers need to know the law of consecration contained in the Doctrine and Covenants. This chapter works to meet that need, though

Steven C. Harper is an associate professor of Church history and doctrine at Brigham Young University and an editor of the Joseph Smith Papers.

it must do so summarily rather than exhaustively. The purpose of this chapter is to help conscientious Saints understand and live the law of consecration as it is embodied in present-day Church practices.

The first premise of this chapter is, as President Gordon B. Hinckley taught, that "the law of sacrifice and the law of consecration were not done away with and are still in effect."[3] No revelations in the Doctrine and Covenants rescind, suspend, or revoke the law of consecration. The Doctrine and Covenants never refers to a *higher* or a *lower* law, only *the* law. Indeed, the revelations do not speak of the laws of God as we do of bills before the legislature, as subject to passage, veto, or amendment. Rather, they speak of the laws of God as eternal. The law, in other words, was revealed to Joseph Smith in February 1831, but the law itself simply has been, is, and ever will be. Consecration is the law of the celestial kingdom, and section 78 teaches that no one will receive an inheritance there who has not obeyed the law (see D&C 78:7).

The Law of Consecration

The law itself is stated plainly enough in each of the standard works and most explicitly in the Doctrine and Covenants. It is, wrote Hugh Nibley, "explained there not once but many times, so that there is no excuse for not understanding it."[4] It was first revealed in this dispensation at a conference of a dozen elders gathered in Kirtland, Ohio, on February 9, 1831. The Lord had promised to reveal the law on the condition that the New York Saints would gather to Ohio (see D&C 38:32). Days after Joseph and Emma arrived in Kirtland, the Lord fulfilled His word. He said:

> And behold, thou wilt remember the poor, and consecrate of thy properties for their support that which thou hast to impart unto them, with a covenant and a deed which cannot be broken.
>
> And inasmuch as ye impart of your substance unto the poor, ye will do it unto me; and they shall be laid before the bishop of my church and his counselors, two of the elders, or high priests, such as he shall appoint or has appointed and set apart for that purpose.

And it shall come to pass, that after they are laid before the bishop of my church, and after that he has received these testimonies concerning the consecration of the properties of my church, that they cannot be taken from the church, agreeable to my commandments, every man shall be made accountable unto me, a steward over his own property, or that which he has received by consecration, as much as is sufficient for himself and family.

And again, if there shall be properties in the hands of the church, or any individuals of it, more than is necessary for their support after this first consecration, which is a residue to be consecrated unto the bishop, it shall be kept to administer to those who have not, from time to time, that every man who has need may be amply supplied and receive according to his wants.

Therefore, the residue shall be kept in my storehouse, to administer to the poor and the needy, as shall be appointed by the high council of the church, and the bishop and his council;

And for the purpose of purchasing lands for the public benefit of the church, and building houses of worship, and building up of the New Jerusalem which is hereafter to be revealed—

That my covenant people may be gathered in one in that day when I shall come to my temple. And this I do for the salvation of my people. (D&C 42:30–36)

The law of consecration found in the Doctrine and Covenants is both simple and sublime. Summed in a single short verse, it says, "If thou obtainest more than that which would be for thy support, thou shalt give it into my storehouse" (D&C 42:55).

But consecration is more than the act of giving. It is the sanctification that comes of giving willingly, for the right reasons, which section 82 describes as "every man seeking the interest of his neighbor, and doing all things with an eye single to the glory of God" (v. 19). To consecrate is not to give away; it is to sanctify or make sacred or holy.

Possessions, time, and spiritual gifts can be made sacred by offering them, but philanthropy is not consecration, nor is making a token offering of one's abundance, as illustrated by the Gospel of Luke's account of the Savior distinguishing between the rich men who cast gifts into the treasury and the widow who offered all (see Luke 21:1–4).

Consecration is keeping the two great commandments, where the key words are *love* and *all*. "Thou shalt love the Lord thy God with *all* thy heart, and with *all* thy soul, and with *all* thy strength, and with *all* thy mind; and thy neighbour as thyself" (Luke 10:27; emphasis added). This command to consecrate all is reiterated in the Doctrine and Covenants: "Thou shalt love the Lord thy God with *all* thy heart, with *all* thy might, mind, and strength; and in the name of Jesus Christ thou shalt serve him" (D&C 59:5). The outward manifestation of *all* of one's *love* has been identified by one scholar as "giving all we can" as compared to obligatory donations of what is required.[5] Amounts of money and time may be the same in both scenarios, but one who gives all is consecrated. One who keeps back part is not yet consecrated (see Acts 5:1–11).

Our money-conscious culture conditions us to think of consecration in monetary terms. The Lord asks for offerings of money to build the kingdom and to assess the desires of our hearts, "for where your treasure is, there will your heart be also" (Matthew 6:21). If consecration must be thought of in terms of exchange, then it is the exchange of *all* we have for *all* the Father has, or what the revelations call "the riches of eternity" (D&C 38:39), in clear contrast to the trifling "things of this world" (D&C 121:35), or what the Lord elsewhere in the Doctrine and Covenants called "all their detestable things" (D&C 98:20; see also 67:2; 68:31; 78:18). "What an exchange rate!" declared Elder Neal A. Maxwell.[6] Only the shortsighted would refuse it (see Luke 12:16–21).

Agency, Stewardship, and Accountability

The law of consecration found in the Doctrine and Covenants can be envisioned as a three-legged stool, where the legs are agency, stewardship, and accountability. Agency is the power we have to act independently on the law, regardless of what anyone else thinks, says, or does. Once we know the law, we can keep or reject it, procrastinate or obey, ignore or observe, offer all or keep back part. No one will ever be forced to comply with the law of consecration. Note how this worked in the early 1830s: "Thou wilt remember the poor, and consecrate of thy properties for their support that which thou hast to impart unto them, with a covenant and a deed which cannot be broken. And inasmuch as ye impart of your substance unto the poor, ye will do it unto me; and they shall be laid before the bishop of my church and his counselors, two of the elders, or high priests, such as he shall appoint or has appointed and set apart for that purpose" (D&C 42:30–31).

A few early Saints consecrated their property to the poor with both a covenant and a deed, according to details explained in a May 1831 revelation to Joseph Smith (see D&C 51). Bishop Edward Partridge, as the revelation said, was to

> appoint unto this people their portions, every man equal according to his family, according to his circumstances and his wants and needs.
>
> And let my servant Edward Partridge, when he shall appoint a man his portion, give unto him a writing that shall secure unto him his portion, that he shall hold it, even this right and this inheritance in the church, until he transgresses and is not accounted worthy by the voice of the church, according to the laws and covenants of the church, to belong to the church.
>
> And if he shall transgress and is not accounted worthy to belong to the church, he shall not have power to claim that portion which he has consecrated unto the bishop for the poor and the needy of my church; therefore, he shall not retain the gift, but shall only have claim on that portion that is deeded unto him.
>
> And thus all things shall be made sure, according to the laws of the land. (D&C 51:3–6)

Joseph wrote Bishop Partridge his "views concerning consecration, property, [and] giving inheritances," highlighting the fundamental principle of agency:

The law of the Lord, binds you to receive, whatsoever property is consecrated, by deed, The consecrated property, is considered the residue kept for the Lords store house, and it is given for this consideration, for to purchase inheritaces for the poor, this, any man has a right to do, agreeable to the laws of our country, to donate, give or consecrate all that he feels disposed to give, and it is your duty, to see that whatsoever is given, is given legally, therefore, it must be given for the consideration of the poor saints.[7]

The Prophet continued to teach Bishop Partridge the law of consecration, reminding him always to preserve agency in individuals: "Concerning inheritances, you are bound by the law of the Lord to give a deed, secureing to him who receives inheritances, his inheritance for an everlasting inheritance, or in other words, to be his individual property, his private stewardship."[8]

The deeds Bishop Partridge used in the early 1830s to receive consecrations and give inheritances illustrate the principles of agency, stewardship, and accountability. Less than a dozen of these deeds are known to exist. One that does exist belongs to Levi Jackman, a carpenter who lived in Portage County, Ohio. In 1831, Levi Jackman met Joseph Smith, read the Book of Mormon, and converted. He and other converts gathered to Zion in Jackson County, Missouri. There he deeded his property to Bishop Partridge, on behalf of the Church, "of [his] own free will." It was not much—"sundry articles of furniture valued thirty seven dollars, also two beds, bedding, and feathers valued forty four dollars fifty cents, also three axes and other tools valued eleven dollars and twenty five cents"—but it was *all* he possessed. In return, Brother Jackman received a parcel of land in present-day Kansas City and "sundry articles of furniture . . . two beds bedding and feathers . . . also three axes and other tools."[9] Brother Jackman offered the Lord all he had. The Lord returned his meager offering and added a handsome farm. For Levi Jackman, obedience to the law of consecration was no vow of poverty; it was a wise investment both spiritually and temporally—a willing exchange based on obedience to the first great commandment to love God with all he had and to receive in return all of God's love.

Though the personal property Jackman received from the bishop was exactly what he consecrated, the exchange represents more than a technicality. By consecrating his possessions to the Lord, Jackman had placed himself in the capacity of a steward rather than an owner. Note how the Lord highlights stewardship in this passage from the law:

> And it shall come to pass, that after they [properties] are laid before the bishop of my church, and after that he has received these testimonies concerning the consecration of the properties of my church, that they cannot be taken from the church, agreeable to my commandments, every man shall be made accountable unto me, a steward over his own property, or that which he has received by consecration, as much as is sufficient for himself and family.
>
> And again, if there shall be properties in the hands of the church, or any individuals of it, more than is necessary for their support after this first consecration, which is a residue to be consecrated unto the bishop, it shall be kept to administer to those who have not, from time to time, that every man who has need may be amply supplied and receive according to his wants. (D&C 42:32–33)

An owner is accountable to no one. A steward is a free agent empowered to act independently but accountable to the actual owner for all actions. For this reason, the law is often and accurately referred to as both consecration and stewardship. It commands: "Thou shalt stand in the place of thy stewardship" (D&C 42:53), and further revelations elaborate: "An account of this stewardship will I require of them in the day of judgment" (D&C 70:4), "and he that is a faithful and wise steward shall inherit all things" (D&C 78:22).

In July 1831, the Lord made William Phelps a free agent. He had power to act independently, and in Doctrine and Covenants section 55, the Lord gave him a commandment to act upon. He was to assist Oliver Cowdery as a steward over the Church's printing press and publication efforts, tasks he carried out with a paper and a press purchased with consecrated resources (see D&C 55:4). With the power to act, talents and property to act upon, and a commandment from the Lord, Phelps was accountable to the Lord for what he did with what the Lord had given him: agency, talent, time, a printing press, ink, and paper. In March 1834, Joseph wrote to William Phelps from Kirtland to correct an errant sense of ownership: "Bro. William—You say 'my press, my types, &c.' W[h]ere, our brethren ask, did you get them, & how came they to be '*yours?*' No hardness, but a caution, for you know that it is, *We, not I,* and all things are the Lord's, and he opened the hearts of his Church to furnish these things, or *we* should not have been privileged with using them."[10]

Moses had to issue the same reminder to the wandering Israelites, who seemed to forget as easily as we do: "Thou shalt remember the Lord thy God: for it is he that giveth thee power to get wealth" (Deuteronomy 8:18). How easy it is to remember what we have earned or are owed. How easy to forget or fail to recognize how much we take, literally, for granted. Hugh Nibley worked hard to debunk the notion that there is no free lunch. Lunch is free in the sense that matters most. So, said Father Lehi, is salvation (see 2 Nephi 2:4). As King Benjamin profoundly taught, we neither earn nor own anything except in terms of earthly agreements that evaporate "when men are dead" (D&C 132:7; see also Mosiah 2:21–25). When we see things as they really are and will be, we see ourselves as stewards of the Lord's bounty.

The law of consecration and stewardship makes free agents of stewards by appointing them their "own property" without giving a false sense of ownership (D&C 42:32). The underlying doctrines here are agency and accountability. The false doctrine is ownership, which implies unaccountability.[11] Perhaps because our culture of ownership so deeply conditions us to the concept of "mine," actually acting as if we were simply accountable stewards is difficult, even countercultural. President Brigham Young taught that "no revelation that was ever given is more easy of comprehension than that on the law of consecration. . . . Yet, when the Lord spoke to Joseph, instructing him to counsel the people to consecrate their possessions, and deed them over to the Church in a covenant that cannot be broken, would the people listen to it? No, but they began to find out they were mistaken, and had only acknowledged with their mouths that the things which they possessed were the Lord's." President Young continued, "What have you to consecrate that is actually your own? Nothing."[12]

The Lord is adamant about the connections between agency, stewardship, and accountability. Because He has empowered us to act independently with His property, we will be held accountable. He repeats this point clearly throughout the Doctrine and Covenants, including in section 104: "Organize yourselves and appoint every man his stewardship; that every man may give an account unto me of the stewardship which is appointed unto him. For it is expedient that I, the Lord, should make every man accountable, as a steward over earthly blessings, which I have made and prepared for my creatures" (vv. 11–13). As if to emphasize that last point about the real ownership of the earth and its contents, the Lord continues emphatically: "I, the Lord, stretched out the heavens, and built the earth, my very handiwork; and all things therein are mine. And it is my purpose to provide for my saints, for all things are mine. . . . I prepared all things, and have given unto the children of men to be agents unto themselves." The implication? "Therefore, if any man shall take of the abundance which I have made, and impart not his portion according to the law of my gospel, unto the poor and the needy, he shall, with the wicked, lift up his eyes in hell, being in torment" (D&C 104:14–15, 17–18).

This potent passage draws on the New Testament story of Lazarus and the rich man in Luke 16. The earliest manuscripts of section 104 link the Lord's point even more closely with that passage in the gospel of Luke. The Kirtland Revelation Book, for example, says that if one does not share according to the Lord's law "he shall *with Dives* lift up his eyes <in hell> being in torment."[13] *Dives* is the Latin word for *rich* and, drawing on Latin translations of the Bible, was adopted as the name of the rich man in Christ's story of the rich man and Lazarus in Luke 16:19–31. In the account recorded in Luke, the rich man "fared sumptuously" (v. 19) in life while a "beggar named Lazarus" (v. 20) waited in vain for some of his table scraps. When the two men died, angels carried Lazarus into Abraham's bosom while the rich man went to hell. "And in hell he lift up his eyes, being in torments" (v. 23), ironically begging Lazarus to relieve his suffering. Doctrine and Covenants 104:18 evokes that story and applies it to Latter-day Saints. When the Church published this revelation as section 98 in the 1835 Doctrine and Covenants, the name *Dives* was changed to "the wicked," perhaps because the name is not found in the New Testament but comes from later lore, or perhaps because the meaning of *Dives* may not have been well known among Latter-day Saints. Even so, the presence of *Dives* in the earliest manuscripts makes the essential meaning of this passage unmistakable, namely that stewards of the Lord's abundance who do not impart to the poor of the substance they possess will, like the rich man in Christ's story, someday regret that use of their agency.

This is one of the Lord's main points in section 104. He emphasizes, "Again, a commandment I give unto you concerning your stewardship which I have appointed unto you. Behold, all these properties are *mine,* or else your faith is vain, and ye are found hypocrites, and the covenants which ye have made unto me are broken" (D&C 104:54–55).

The Lord claims ownership of "the earth" and "all things therein," including "all these properties" and compels us to choose. Either He is the omnipotent Creator and owner of the earth and everything in it or else He is something less and therefore incapable of rewarding our faith. If we acknowledge Him as Lord of all and yet fail to consecrate per His command, we are hypocrites. To acknowledge God is to grant that He is well within His divine prerogative to redistribute His own wealth according to His own will. Thus the revelations do not apologize for such radical notions as one of the law's stated purposes: "I will consecrate of the riches of those who embrace my gospel among the Gentiles unto the poor of my people who are of the house of Israel" (D&C 42:39), or the Lord's decree "that the poor shall be exalted, in that the rich are made low" (D&C 104:16; see also 58:8–12). Indeed, the revelations give stewards no right to keep or use the Lord's things for any other purposes than His. "It is not given that one man should possess that which is above another," the Lord told Joseph in May 1831, "wherefore the world lieth in sin" (D&C 49:20).

Consecration Today

When the Saints were driven from the Jackson County land Bishop Partridge had legally purchased and deeded to the Saints, Joseph Smith prayed to the Lord in July 1838 and asked, "O! Lord, show unto thy servents how much thou requirest of the properties of thy people for a Tithing?"¹⁴ Modern Saints may be puzzled that he had to ask the question. Didn't he know that tithing is 10 percent? The answer is no for two reasons. First, though the Hebrew roots for the word *tithes* in Malachi 3:8, 10 refer to a tenth, tithing was not associated with one-tenth in this dispensation until the Lord answered Joseph's prayer with Doctrine and Covenants section 119. Second, that revelation uses the word *tithing* once and *tithed* twice. In all three cases the words refer to the revelation's first commandment: "Thus saith the Lord, I require all their surplus property to be put into the hands of the bishop of my church in Zion" (D&C 119:1). That is the beginning of tithing, which is not a lower or temporary law according to section 119, but rather "a standing law unto them forever" (D&C 119:4), given for the same purposes as the law of consecration in section 42 and several others. Though some of the tactics for implementation are different, there is no great discrepancy between what the Lord expects of the Saints today and what He originally commanded in section 42 or the later amendment in section 119. In other words, section 119 is not given instead of the law of consecration; it is a restatement of the law of consecration and sets the terms by which we can live the law today.

Brigham Young was present when the Lord revealed section 119. He was assigned to go among the Saints "and find out what surplus property the people had, with which to forward the building of the Temple we were commencing at Far West." Before setting out he asked Joseph, "'Who shall be the judge of what is surplus property?' Said he, 'Let them be the judge themselves.'"¹⁵ As a result, some Latter-day Saints offered their surplus property. Some offered some of it. Some offered none. None were coerced. And so it remains. Individuals decide to obey or not of their own free will. Sometimes we say that we should be ready to live the law of consecration when we are asked to do so. Sometimes we use the word *required,* essentially putting the responsibility on the Church or its leaders. I'm often asked by students, why don't Church leaders require us to live the law of consecration today? I wonder what they mean by *require.* Do we anticipate that the deacons quorum will be sent to inspect our pantries or audit our bank accounts? If so, we do not understand the law of consecration or the way God works. And we definitely do not understand the law of consecration as contained in the Doctrine and Covenants. Put another way, we have been commanded to keep the law of consecration. And many have covenanted to do so. We are, in that sense, required to do so if we hope to claim the promised blessings, including celestial glory. The Lord may not send the deacons to confiscate our surplus now, but, as Doctrine and Covenants 104:13–18 declares, covenant breakers will end up tormented in hell later on.

What, then, the conscientious covenant keeper wants to know, does the Lord expect? What does it mean in the twenty-first century to comply with the law of consecration? What is meant by ambiguous terms in the law, like *residue, sufficient, more than is necessary, wants,* and *amply supplied?* The carefully worded law clearly teaches principles, not dogma. It gives knowledge of the Lord's will without coercion or compulsion. It enables anyone to become "anxiously engaged in a good cause, and do many things of their own free will, and bring to pass much righteousness; for the power is in them, wherein they are agents unto themselves. And inasmuch as men do good they shall in nowise lose their reward. But he that doeth not anything until he is commanded, and receiveth a commandment with doubtful heart, and keepeth it with slothfulness, the same is damned" (D&C 58:27–29). Put another way, words like *sufficient* leave stewardship and therefore accountability where it belongs. Ironically, they compel us to exercise our agency and act for ourselves. We decide what they mean in terms of amounts of time or money, because we are the empowered stewards accountable to the Lord for our use or abuse of what is rightfully His. Joseph understood and taught this principle. He counseled Bishop Partridge, who was sometimes officious, not to "condescend to very great particulars in taking inventories." As Joseph put it, "A man is bound by the law of the Church, to consecrate to the bishop before he can be considered a legal heir to the kingdom of Zion and this too without constraint and unless he does this he cannot be acknowledged before the Lord on the Church book. . . . Evry man must be his own Judge how much he should receive and how much he should suffer to remain in the hands of the Bishop."[16]

After the Saints were driven from Jackson County in 1833, Bishop Partridge no longer received offerings and gave stewardships by deed.

The Fishing River revelation that ended Zion's Camp in the summer of 1834, now section 105, has a verse that some commentators believe postpones compliance with the law of consecration: "Let those commandments which I have given concerning Zion and her law be executed and fulfilled, after her redemption" (v. 34). It says nothing about revoking the law. It says that the specific commands to purchase land and build a temple in Jackson County, and perhaps even the deeding of specific stewardships, are to be executed after Jackson County is returned to the Saints. How will that ever happen unless the law is obeyed beforehand? Hugh Nibley wrote with some frustration that "the express purpose of the law of consecration is the building up of Zion. . . . We do not wait until Zion is here to observe it; it is rather the means of bringing us nearer to Zion."[17] Lorenzo Snow taught that the Saints were "not justified in anticipating the privilege of returning to build up the center stake of Zion, until we shall have shown obedience to the law of consecration." He was certain the Saints would "not be permitted to enter the land from whence we were expelled, till our hearts are prepared to honor this law, and we become sanctified through the practice of the truth."[18]

Empowered with correct knowledge of the law, we are free agents—accountable stewards of the Lord's possessions, including ourselves. We must act right now either in obedience or disobedience to the law of consecration. To ignore it is to disobey. But the bishop neither asks me for a deed nor gives me an inheritance. How can I obey? Elder Orson Pratt wisely observed that there is nothing "laid down in the revelations, requiring us to take [a] particular method."[19] So what does the Lord expect? C. S. Lewis believed that "the only safe rule is to give more than we can spare. In other words, if our expenditure on comforts, luxuries, and amusements, etc., is up to the standard common among those with the same income as our own, we are probably giving away too little. If our charities do not at all pinch or hamper us, I should say they are too small. There ought to be things we should like to do and cannot do because our charities expenditure excludes them."[20] Beside the Lord's open invitation to do much good of our own free will, priesthood leaders extend specific opportunities to offer time, talent, and property to relieve poverty and build the kingdom. One offered this guide (consistent with D&C 42:54; 104:18; and section 119) to exercising agency: "In addition to paying an honest tithing, we should be generous in assisting the poor."[21] President Marion G. Romney asked, "What prohibits us from giving as much in fast offerings as we would have given in surpluses [in the 1830s]? Nothing but our own limitations."[22] President Spencer W. Kimball commanded, "Give, instead of the amount we saved by our two meals of fasting, perhaps much, much more—ten times more where we are in a position to do it."[23] Parents live the law when they "lay aside the things of this world" in favor of raising God's children (D&C 25:10). Couples live the law when they forego leisure to venture into places far and near where they can "bring to pass much righteousness" (D&C 58:27). Professionals live the law when they offer their skills to the needy without concern for compensation or acclaim. We can live the law by becoming "the common property of the whole church," and "seeking the interest of [our] neighbor, and doing all things with an eye single to the glory of God" (D&C 82:18–19). Often the only necessary paperwork is the familiar tithing and offering slip available wherever Latter-day Saints gather. The only limitations, said President Romney, are self-imposed.

Wilford Woodruff, one of the valiant soldiers of Zion's Camp, did not believe that the revelation that ended the camp (see D&C 105) either rescinded or postponed the law of consecration. At the end of 1834, six months after that revelation was given, Wilford wrote Bishop Partridge a paper with these words inscribed on it: "Be it known that I Willford Woodruff do freely covenant with my God that I freely consecrate and dedicate myself together with all my properties and affects unto the Lord for the purpose of assisting in building up his kingdom even Zion on the earth that I may keep his law and lay all things before the bishop of his Church that I may be a lawful heir to the Kingdom of God even the Celestial Kingdom," and then he listed his property.[24]

Wilford perfectly understood the doctrines of the law of consecration. He was a free agent. Twice he says that he acted *freely,* without coercion or even any other invitation than the original revelation. He was a steward of "properties and affects," and he was accountable to the Lord and His servant Bishop Partridge. Wilford Woodruff seized his agency and became anxiously engaged in the only cause that ultimately matters. Neither the disobedience of brothers and sisters, the viciousness of mobs, nor an oppressive, materialistic culture preoccupied with consumption for its own sake deterred him from the path of consecration. It would have been hard to persuade him that the Lord had revoked the law. Joseph realized as the Saints were driven destitute from Missouri in 1839 that they would be unable to build New Jerusalem then or live the law as a group. He did not say the Lord had revoked it, only that the Saints had little subsistence, to say nothing of surplus. But Joseph was hardly out of Liberty Jail before he began to build Nauvoo, crowning it with its consecrated temple, whose powerful ordinances climaxed in the covenant to consecrate one's life to the kingdom of God. Having been endowed with power under Joseph's hands in Nauvoo, Wilford left his front door open and went west to build more temples. His home and property had served their purpose as a temporary means to a sacred end. Levi Jackman joined with him and the others who were led by President Young and inspired by these words in Doctrine and Covenants section 136, a revelation that reaffirms every principle of the law of consecration: "This shall be our covenant—that we will walk in all the ordinances of the Lord" (v. 4).

"In pondering and pursuing consecration," said Elder Neal A. Maxwell, "understandably we tremble inwardly at what may be required. Yet the Lord has said consolingly, 'My grace is sufficient for you' (D&C 17:8). Do we really believe Him? He has also promised to make weak things strong (Ether 12:27). Are we really willing to submit to that process? Yet if we desire fulness, we cannot hold back part!"[25]

NOTES

1. Leonard J. Arrington, Feramorz Y. Fox, and Dean L. May, *Building the City of God: Community and Cooperation among the Mormons* (Urbana: University of Illinois Press, 1992), 426.
2. Neal A. Maxwell, in Conference Report, April 2002, 41.
3. Gordon B. Hinckley, *Teachings of Gordon B. Hinckley* (Salt Lake City: Deseret Book, 1997), 639.
4. Hugh W. Nibley, *Approaching Zion*, ed. Don E. Norton (Salt Lake City: Deseret Book, 1989), 167.

5. Clark V. Johnson, "The Law of Consecration: The Covenant That Requires All and Gives Everything," in *Doctrines for Exaltation: The 1989 Sperry Symposium on the Doctrine and Covenants* (Salt Lake City: Deseret Book, 1989), 112.

6. Maxwell, in Conference Report, April 2002, 43.

7. Joseph Smith to Edward Partridge, May 2, 1833, Church History Library, Salt Lake City.

8. Joseph Smith to Edward Partridge, June 25, 1833, *Joseph Smith Letter Book 1829–35*, 44–50, Church History Library.

9. Levi Jackman, Deed of Consecration, Church History Library, is reproduced in Arrington, Fox, and May, *Building the City of God*, 28–29. As originally commanded, Bishop Partridge leased the property he bought to the Saints. Legal controversy, Joseph's counsel, and his prophetic revision of section 51 altered the technical procedure, resulting in Bishop Partridge's being instructed to deed land to the Saints in fee simple. Under this way of implementing the law, the Saints rather than Bishop Partridge were to "own" their stewardships in the proximate, legal sense. But subsequent revelations (section 104 especially) continued to stress that ultimate ownership rests with God and that we are still stewards.

10. Postscript, Joseph Smith to Edward Partridge and Others, March 30, 1834, in Joseph Smith, *Personal Writings of Joseph Smith*, ed. Dean C. Jessee, rev. ed. (Salt Lake City: Deseret Book, 2002), 338–39.

11. Orson Pratt, in *Journal of Discourses* (Liverpool: Latter-day Saints' Book Depot, 1881), 21:148.

12. Brigham Young, in *Journal of Discourses* (Liverpool: Latter-day Saints' Book Depot, 1855), 2:305, 307.

13. Kirtland Revelation Book, 102, Church History Library, forthcoming in Steven C. Harper, Robin Scott Jensen, and Robert J. Woodford, eds., *The Joseph Smith Papers: Revelations and Translations Series, vol. 1* (Salt Lake City: Church Historian's Press).

14. Joseph Smith, journal, July 8, 1838, in Dean C. Jessee, ed., *The Papers of Joseph Smith* (Salt Lake City: Deseret Book, 1992), 2:257.

15. Brigham Young, in *Journal of Discourses*, 2:306.

16. Joseph Smith Jr., Sidney Rigdon, and Frederick Williams to William Phelps and Others, June 25, 1833, *Joseph Smith Letter Book 1829–35*, 44–50, Church History Library.

17. Nibley, *Approaching Zion*, 390.

18. Lorenzo Snow, in *Journal of Discourses* (Liverpool: Latter-Day Saints' Book Depot, 1874), 16:276.

19. Orson Pratt, in *Journal of Discourses*, 21:148.

20. C. S. Lewis, *Mere Christianity* (San Francisco: HarperCollins, 2001), 86.

21. Joe J. Christensen, in Conference Report, April 1999, 11.

22. Marion G. Romney, in Conference Report, April 1966, 100.

23. Spencer W. Kimball, in Conference Report, April 1974, 184.

24. Wilford Woodruff, journal, December 31, 1834, Church History Library.

25. Maxwell, in Conference Report, April 2002, 44.

INDEX

Aaronic Priesthood, 93, 96
Acceptance, 3–4, 6–7, 12, 14–15, 21–22; qualities for obtaining, 8–10; conditional, 17–18, 21; guarantee of, 19
Adam and Eve, 43, 49–51, 199–200
Agency, 50–51, 200, 203; in law of consecration, 215–17, 219, 222–25
Alma the Younger, 93
America the Beautiful, 3
Atonement, 199–200, 203, 206–7

Baptism, 4–5, 13, 31, 93, 206–7; covenant of, 22, 199–200
Baptist faith, 4
Bennett, John C., 15
Bible, 158; New Translation, 4; interpretations of, 82–83; revelations relating to, 92
Blake, William, 146
Blomberg, Craig, 143
Book of Commandments, 27, 109; compilation of, 24; witnesses of, 31
Book of Mormon, 14; lost 116 pages, 16; 1830 edition, 25–26; in Canada and United Kingdom, 38
Booth, Ezra, 121
Bowen, Brigham John, 143

Brooke, John, 157–58
Bushman, Richard, 70, 117, 158

Calling and election, 18–19
Campbell, Alexander, 33, 74, 148–49, 180
Celestial kingdom, 151, 155, 193, 213, 223–25
Chapman, John (Johnny Appleseed), 145
Christ, Jesus. *See* Savior; *see also* Lord
Church: offices of, 32; First Presidency of, 34, 36–37, 109; organization of, 42, 117–18; distinguishing features of, 68; Law of the, 108
Clarke, Adam, 99
Cleveland, John and Sarah, 146–47
Colesville, 119, 124, 130
Commandments, keeping, 7
Consecration, 214–15, 218
Copley, Leman, 130
Corrill, John, 67, 74–75, 116
Covenants, 8, 190–92, 205, 224; in temple, 194, 202, 208, 210
Covill, James, 4–6, 29
Cowdery, Oliver, 38, 218; commanded to study scriptures, 43, 49; commanded to establish Zion, 53; scribe for Joseph Smith, 91–92, 96–97, 99

Creation, 49–50
Criticism, 9

Diligence, 14–15
Discipleship, 6
Doctrine and Covenants: truths in, 3; 1835 edition, 31–32, 128; sequence of revelations, 47

Enoch, 52–53, 55, 59–62; translation of, 100; city of, 118
Emerson, Ralph Waldo, 145
Enthusiasm, 71–72
Eternal life, 20–21; unconditional promise of, 19, 21
Eternal principles, 4

Failure, 2–4, 12, 14; because of disobeying eternal principles, 4; in keeping covenants, 5–6
Fall, the, 49, 51
Fayette, New York, 108
First Vision, 84–85, 175
French Prophets, 72, 78
Foreordination, 168
Forgiveness, 8
Formalism, 71–72

Garden of Eden, 43
Gause, Jesse, 36
Genesis, translation of, 46, 61
Gift of tongues, 73–78; purpose of, 77
Glossolalia. *See* Gift of tongues

Hancock County, Illinois, 122
Harmonists, 54, 118
Harris, Martin, 108, 176–78
Hayden, Amos S., 33
Healing: by faith, 79, 122; through conversion, 80
Heaven, 157–58; three-tiered, 142, 154, 156–58, 169; modern concept of, 143; nineteenth-century concept of, 143; scriptural ties to LDS concept of, 143, 145, 153; terminology and symbolism for, 151–54
Heaven: A History, 143
Hinckley, Gordon B., 9, 213
Hubble, Ann, 17

Humility, 8
Hunter, Edward, 147, 156

Idleness, 122
Isaiah, 121–22, 195–96, 201

Jackman, Levi, 217–18, 226
Jackson County, 121, 190–91, 217, 221, 223–24
John the Baptist, 90, 93
John the Beloved, 90, 95–96; mission of, 91, 95, 97–98, 100–104; debate over death of, 91–93, 96–98; appears to men, 102–3
Joseph Smith Papers Project, 23, 39
Joseph Smith Translation, 40, 98, 125

Keller, Helen, 145
Kimball, Heber C., 103
Kingdom of God, 16, 116, 215
Kirtland, Ohio, 116
Knight, Joseph, Jr., 121
Knight, Joseph, Sr., 4, 176–77

Lamanites, 38
Lang, Bernhard, 143–44
Law of consecration, 117, 121, 124, 195, 212, 223; wording changes in, 111, 113–14, 120, 125–26, 128; and property, 118–19, 216–17, 222; and stewardship, 120, 124, 215–20; and "Family" organization, 124, 130; and supporting families, 126–27; breakers of, 132, 134; Lazarus, parable of, 220–21
Lee, Ann, 144
Lord: acceptance of, 3–4, 6–7, 12, 14–15, 19, 21–22; condemnation of, 3–4; qualities for obtaining acceptance of, 8–10; expectations of, 15; guidance from, 16, 18; conditional acceptance of, 17–18

Mack, Solomon, 174
Matthews, Robert J., 51, 92
Maxwell, Neal A., 42, 212, 215, 226
McConkie, Bruce R., 20–21
McDannell, Colleen, 143–44
McLellin, William E., 117
Melchizedek Priesthood, 103–4

INDEX

Methodism, 29, 72
Millennium, 33–34
Missionary, 13–15, 116; accepted by the Lord, 11–13
Missionary Training Center, 14
Missionary work, 11, 104, 114, 128, 200, 205
Missourian grievances against Church, 69–71, 75
Morley "Family," 124
Mormon, 101–2
Moses, 41; book of, 43–45, 48
Mount Olivet discourse, 32–34, 197–98
Murray, John, 172–73, 178, 185

Nauvoo, 147, 182, 226
New Jerusalem, 52–54, 58, 60, 126, 226
Nibley, Hugh, 69, 213, 219, 224

Obedience, 5, 8, 13–14, 22
Ohio, 33; gathering in, 56, 58, 61, 108, 118, 213; early Saints in, 66–67, 117, 126
Opposition, 51

Page, Hiram, 49, 55
Parkin, Max, 95
Partridge, Edward, 6, 118, 121, 217, 221; instructions for law of consecration, 119, 124, 216–17, 223
Peace, 1, 13–14
Peter, 94, 97, 101, 103
Pettigrew, David, 75–76
Phelps, 219
Praise, 2
Pratt, Parley P., 66–67, 74, 184
Printing process, 26
Prophet, 48–49; sustaining, 16; as mouth of the Lord, 18; as revelator, 48–49. *See* Smith, Joseph, Jr.

Quakers, 117
Quinn, Michael, 147, 152–54, 156

Redemption, 189, 193–96, 201–2, 205; repentance and, 19; physical, 196–98, 200, 203–4, 209; spiritual, 199–202, 209; of dead, 206–8
Restoration, 168
Revelation, 35

Revelations, 85; variations in, 25–26; unpublished, 37; copying and sharing, 41–42; determining dates for, 44, 95–96, 112; on spirituality, 69
Rigdon, Sidney, 17, 34, 36; receives revelation, 35, 115, 148, 169; scribe for Joseph Smith, 45–46, 98, 149; and Zion, 53, 192; congregation of, 67, 74; exposure to Swedenborg, 148
Ryder manuscript, Symonds, 111–12, 130

Sacrifice, law of, 11
Satan, 5, 49–51, 57
Savior, 4–5, 34, 204, 221; covenant relationship with, 4, 189, 191–92, 195–98, 201–7; as Judge, 5, 13, 198; oneness with, 6; talks to disciples, 94–95, 97, 100, 115–16, 168; ministry of, 96; punishes, 178–80; as Redeemer, 192, 196–98, 203–4, 206–10
Second Coming, 97, 204–5, 209
Self-worth, 3–4
Sermon on the Mount, 133
Shakers, 72, 76, 118, 144
Sherman, Lyman, 16
Shipps, Jan, 158
Signs of the times, 60
Skousen, Royal, 25–26
Slavery, 70
Smith, Asael, 172–74, 177, 181–82, 185
Smith, Emma, 53
Smith, Jesse, 173–74, 176
Smith, Joseph F., 9–10, 14, 205–6
Smith, Joseph, Jr., 39, 42, 147, 185; translates Book of Mormon, 4, 96, 99; on Christ's will, 10; accepted by the Lord, 16–17; receives revelations, 17, 35, 38, 62; translates Bible, 17, 40, 45, 149–50, 157; calling and election of, 20; scribes for, 24, 44–45; on receiving revelation, 40; command to study the scriptures, 43, 49; receives book of Moses, 48; as revelator, 49, 222; builds Zion, 56, 59, 226; gifts of, 77, 92, 97; on the Spirit, 84; receives the Law, 108–10, 115, 129, 135, 213–14, 219; on stewardship, 119–20; exposure to Swedenborg, 144, 146–48, 150, 156; sees vision of three degrees of glory,

169–70; connection to Universalism, 175–78, 181
Smith, Joseph, Sr., 37, 123, 181, 184–85; connection to Universalism, 173–74, 176–77, 185
Smith, George A., 173–74
Snow, Lorenzo, 20, 224
Sons of perdition, 154, 203
Spirit, 83, 204; gifts of, 6; peace from, 21; influence of, 83–84; teaching by, 117
Spiritual beings, 80–82, 169
Spiritual expressions: atypical manifestations, 66–67, 78; spiritual gifts, 68–69; controversy about early Saints,' 69; gift of tongues, 73–78; healing by faith, 79, 83
Success, definitions of, 1–3, 21–22
Swedenborg, Emanuel, 142, 146, 148–49; visions of, 144, 146, 155–56; *Heaven and Hell,* 149, 153, 155; *Arcana Coelestia,* 152, 157
Swedenborgianism, followers of, 145–46
Synnestvedt, Sig, 156–57

Taves, Ann, 71–72
Telestial kingdom, 151–52, 154–55
Ten Commandments, 117, 130–33
Temple work, 202, 205–8, 210
Temptation, 51
Tertullian, 99
Thayre, Ezra, 37
Thompson, Ohio, 130
Thomson, Samuel, 123
Three Nephites, 94, 100–102; appearances of, 102–3
Three Witnesses, 93
Translation, doctrine of, 91, 99–101
Truth, sources of, 9

Understanding, lack of, 1
Universal redemption, 50
Universalism, 172–73, 175–78; doctrine on punishment, 178; and Book of Mormon, 180
Urim and Thummim, 91, 96–97

Vermont, 173
Vision of three degrees of glory (D&C 76), 148–50, 154–58, 182; scriptures relating to, 150–52, 157; accepting new doctrine of, 169–72

Whitmer, John, 43–44, 49, 58, 122; on atypical spiritual expression, 67; on John the Beloved, 103; as Church historian, 103, 116, 118; on Morley "Family," 124
Whitman, Jason, 72–73
Whitney, Newel K., 38, 127
Widtsoe, John A., 8
Williams, Frederick G., 36–37, 123
Winn, Kenneth, 70
Woodruff, Wilford, 75, 123, 225

Xenoglossia. *See* Gift of tongues

Young, Brigham, 170–71, 183–85, 219–20, 222, 226

Zion, 52–53, 55–56, 58; establishing, 4, 53, 56, 59–60, 224–25; Enoch's, 52, 57, 58; early Saints' conception of, 52, 54–55; in Book of Mormon, 52–53; as geographical location, 53–55, 61; understanding of, 61, 121; redemption of, 189–95
Zion's Camp, 191–93, 224